# WOMEN
## IN A CHANGING GLOBAL ECONOMY

 **1994 WORLD SURVEY ON THE
ROLE OF WOMEN IN DEVELOPMENT**

Department for Policy Coordination
and Sustainable Development

# WOMEN
## IN A CHANGING GLOBAL ECONOMY

## 1994 WORLD SURVEY ON THE
## ROLE OF WOMEN IN DEVELOPMENT

United Nations-New York, 1995

NOTE

Symbols of United Nations documents are composed of capital letters combined with figures.

The designations employed and the presentation of the material in this publication do not imply the expression of any opinion whatsoever on the part of the Secretariat of the United Nations concerning the legal status of any country, territory, city or area or of its authorities, or concerning the delimitation of its frontiers.

ST/ESA/241

UNITED NATIONS PUBLICATION

Sales No. E.95.IV.1

ISBN 92-1-130163-7

## PREFACE

The *1994 World Survey on the Role of Women in Development* is not about women; it is about development. When the role played by women is examined in relation to the role played by men, this "gender lens" can illuminate what works and what does not in development theory, policy and practice.

Unlike its predecessors, the *1994 Survey* analyses three central development issues—poverty, productive employment and economic decision-making—using a gender perspective. In so doing, it questions some basic assumptions about gender and development. The *Survey*'s investigation is not a matter of development and women's role in it. Rather, it is a matter of women in development, men in development and those aspects of development where gender does not matter. However, the *Survey* finds few aspects of development where gender does not matter.

The *Survey* does find, when examining poverty, that women are not victims of their circumstances. Like men, they live in households that suffer from poverty. More often than not it is women who cope with poverty and, if domestic tasks are shared and women are given access to resources, they increasingly provide the way out of poverty for their families.

In employment, the myth of women as a reserve labour force is shattered. Instead, the position of women as decisive parts of the workforce in the global growth sectors is demonstrated. The *Survey* contemplates whether women will continue to accept ill-paid and unsatisfactory working conditions, or if they will insist on changes in the way work is organized.

Economic decision-making reveals the greatest asymmetry between women and men. Women are still absent from top positions, and economic decisions, good and bad, are made by men. Still, the *Survey* emphasizes the growing importance of women as entrepreneurs and traders, as well as among youth trained for business, suggesting that change is under way even in this area of male dominance.

The *Survey*, like its predecessors, has been a team effort of staff of the United Nations Secretariat and colleagues from the specialized agencies. From the Division for the Advancement of Women, the team consisted of Natalia Zakharova, Mathilde Vázquez, Semia Guermas, Marina Plutakhina and Mary Ann Knotts, under the direction of John Mathiason. The International Labour Organization (ILO) team included RoseMary Greve, Barbara Einhorn, María Angélica Ducci, Eugenia Date-Bah, Azita Berar-Awad, Mary Johnson and Christine Oppong. Valuable contributions were made by the Food and Agriculture Organization of the United Nations (FAO), the United Nations Educational, Scientific and Cultural Organization (UNESCO), the International Fund for Agricultural Development (IFAD), the United Nations Industrial Development Organization (UNIDO), the International Trade Centre (ITC), the International Research and Training Institute for the Advancement of Women (INSTRAW), the World Institute for Development Economics of the United Nations University

(UNU/WIDER), the Statistical Division of the United Nations Secretariat and the United Nations regional commissions.

The *Survey* is a basic document for the Fourth World Conference on Women: Action for Equality, Development and Peace, but it also provides background information for the work of the United Nations in implementing Agenda 21, the action programme adopted by the United Nations Conference on Environment and Development in 1992. The *Survey* constitutes an important input to the dialogue about development.

GERTRUDE MONGELLA
*Secretary-General*
*Fourth World Conference on Women:*
*Action for Equality, Development and Peace*

# CONTENTS

TABLES

# EXECUTIVE SUMMARY

The world has experienced a fundamental change in its economic relations since the 1989 World Survey on the Role of Women in Development, and women have played a major role. The 1980s ended with a slow-down in economic growth in developed and developing countries, and the 1990s started with a recession followed by a slow recovery. Progress has been uneven. Many developing countries have encountered significant difficulties in implementing structural adjustment programmes. The relative position of countries in the developing and developed world has changed, and new growth poles have emerged. Markets became further integrated through trade and global investment, and economic interdependence increased. This trend was reinforced by the conclusion of the Uruguay Round of multilateral trade negotiations, which sought to keep the world trade system open and promised its further liberalization.

These changes took place in the context of a renewed emphasis on democratization, good governance and the use of the market to direct economic development. Perceptions of the meaning, causes and conditions of development have been modified greatly. Development discourse now emphasizes sustainability and the importance of involving people in policies and programmes.

Economic development is closely related to the advancement of women. Where women have advanced, economic growth has usually been steady; where women have been restricted, there has been stagnation. The Survey is about this process, what it means and how it can be used to build a more secure future for humankind. It looks at development through a gender lens: at poverty as a failure of development, where investing in women's capacities represents a way out; at employment, where women's participation is integral to the transformation of the labour force; and at economic decision-making, where the absence of women at the top of large corporate bureaucracies and their growing presence in a dynamic middle sector affects development policies.

Despite its considerable significance for economic advancement and the sustainability of development, the evolving role of women in development has gone largely unnoticed. It is possible to see many trends in this process in the statistics contained in the Women's Indicators and Statistics Data Base (WISTAT), in a growing body of micro-studies and in the work of the United Nations and the specialized agencies. To mark these trends, the *1994 World Survey* employs gender analysis. Gender analysis views women and men in terms of the roles they play in society, roles which change as societies change. By comparing women and men rather than looking at women as an isolated group, gender analysis illuminates a key aspect of the structure of society and makes it easier to identify obstacles to improving society. Central to this analysis is the distinction between productive and reproductive roles, referring to production of goods and services and to the social reproduction of society over generations, and their relationship. Both roles are valuable and both can be performed by women and men alike. In the past, social reproductive roles were assigned mainly to women and productive roles mainly to men. This is changing, but the tension between the two remains and is a recurrent theme of the *1994 Survey*.

Two changes have occurred over the past 10 years in the enabling environment for women in the economy. One is the change in women's legal status in the direction of equality. The other is women's achievement of equal access to education and training. These developments have provided equal opportunities for an increasing number of women and allowed them to participate fully in development, contributing the particular skills and priorities that derive from their gender roles.

The gradual achievement of equality for women is reflected in the increase in the number of States that are party to the Convention on the Elimination of All Forms of Discrimination against Women. In most of these States, ratification of or accession to the Convention has required the eliomination of legal restrictions that had impeded women from obtaining access to the factors of production: land, capital and technology. While progress in exercising these rights has been less rapid where there is a gap between constitutional principle, enabling legislation and customary behaviour, progress towards equality in economic participation is evident.

In most regions of the world, considerable progress has been made towards equal access to education at all levels. By 1990 most regions had achieved, or were close to achieving, equality in primary school enrolment, a marked change from 1970. Even more rapid progress has been made in second and third levels of education. Still, there are regional differences. Progress in eliminating the gap between girls and boys has been less rapid in Africa and South Asia.

Eliminating differences in access to education does not remedy inequities in the structure of education. Curriculum materials are often gender biased, social and organizational arrangements in the schools are slow to change and few women hold decision-making positions in the school system at all levels. Girls are still channelled into typically feminine fields of study and career paths, limiting their ability to acquire the skills needed to meet informational and technological challenges. Adult illiteracy, which is far more prevalent among women than men, needs to be addressed, as does the broader issue of training. Despite these challenges, it can no longer be said that women entering the labour force have educational backgrounds inferior to those of men. The longer-term consequences of this equality remain to be seen, but its present-day effects are certain.

The economic reforms of the 1980s had different consequences for women and men in the distribution of the adjustment burden. Rapid technological innovation, changes in work organization, growing economic interdependence, and the globalization of markets and production affected women's socio-economic position in complex and multidimensional ways, bringing them into the formal labour market in unprecedented numbers. This had both positive and negative effects.

Lay-offs undertaken in developed countries to achieve cost reduction were often geared towards higher-paid workers. The workers and managers let go under these circumstances were more often men than women, since women on the whole were paid less. And higher living costs in many countries led many women to enter the labour market in circumstances that were often precarious and without social support. These developments narrowed the remuneration gap between women and men.

However, the increase in women's labour force participation was not a matter of women replacing men in their jobs. It was a consequence of structural change and greater willingness on the part of women to accept lower initial pay in the growth sectors. Also, women were more amenable to the new model of the flexible firm since their labour history often involved frequent moves in and out of the labour force in connection with pregnancy or the need to care for dependants, and a willingness to work part-time or do outwork. Moreover, the shift in the service sector to businesses requiring highly skilled staff, coupled with the increase of qualified women and the removal of barriers to employment, helped bring women into better-paid jobs.

The short-run situation has been almost the opposite in the transition economies. Women in these economies had already achieved equality in labour force participation, but the restructuring of State-owned enterprises has led to high unemployment among women. Women are at a disadvantage in the context of transition. In the sectors most affected by reform, women are laid off first. When unemployed, women face greater difficulties than men in obtaining alternative employment. Privatization has favoured those who had access to capital, information and markets in the previous system—predominately men. And evidence suggests that it is mainly men who are being employed in the new industries. However, it is not clear that these trends will persist, given the qualifications possessed by women, particularly in new growth areas. The situation is complicated by the fact that new private firms in the transition economies are unable or unwilling to maintain the social support services that were guaranteed under the former system, making it difficult for women to participate in economic activity on the same basis as before.

The effects of global restructuring varied by region in developing countries. Structural adjustment usually began with stabilization policies that were intended to promote growth by reducing inflation and achieving a sustainable balance-of-payments position. These policies inevitably increased living costs since subsidies were removed, prices for staple goods rose to market levels and government expenditures for health care and education were cut. Women bore the brunt of coping with these changes within the household. Consequently, women who had not been active in the formal economy became economically active. At the same time, several categories in which women constitute a high proportion have been among the hardest hit, including farmers who bought more food than they produced, small producers, and public and urban informal sector workers.

Changes in employment patterns that resulted from economic restructuring affected women in particular ways. In the process of intra-sectoral and inter-sectoral employment shifts, many women accepted lower-paid jobs with little security. But it was often the case that women were employed while their husbands were not. Women chose low pay over no pay, while their spouses often chose no pay. In addition, jobs for men were often not available. As a consequence, women were often better able to obtain jobs in growth sectors. This has been especially true in economies promoting export-oriented trade regimes based on labour-intensive manufacturing and international cost reduction.

In Asia, where growth has been based on outward-oriented development strategies, women constitute the larger share of those employed in export-oriented industries. Similar trends are occurring in Latin America and the Caribbean as economies move towards greater economic liberalization. In contrast, production of tradables based on primary commodities in Africa has tended to work against women, who predominate in the production of non-tradable food crops.

The short-run effects of structural adjustment have been more difficult for women than for men, and while it is difficult to evaluate the long-term effects, the major gender factor has been women's inability to benefit from the incentive structures that existed prior to the reallocation of labour. Current policies may mitigate some of the negative consequences. Similarly, where privatization benefits micro- and small-scale enterprises, into which women are moving rapidly, adjustment can have long-term benefits for women. Market deregulation, which allows firms to have high wage flexibility, has benefited women in the short run because female employment has increased. This will be a long-term benefit if women can obtain equal pay and upgrade their skills to move into high-productivity sectors.

As noted, changes in world trade patterns have increased female industrial employment in those countries where export growth has been particularly strong. In this sense, increases in trade from developing to developed countries have been determined by female workers to some extent. Whether this will translate into a long-term benefit will depend on whether women are given opportunities to refine their skills, since labour force quality is a major component in international competition. The growth in transnational corporations is also significant, since they have a clear preference for employing women in export-

processing zones. It may also be positive to the extent that these corporations implement the equal opportunity policies mandated in their headquarters countries in their subsidiaries. There is little evidence about whether a shift in international financial flows will improve the economic status of women, but if new investment reaches firms owned by or employing women, this would be positive.

Using the new data available from the Women's Indicators and Statistics Data Base (WISTAT), this *Survey* explores the relationship between economic growth and the participation of women in the labour force. The analysis shows that women generally benefit from economic growth, sometimes to a greater extent than men, but not in all places or at all times. Regional differences play a major role. Data suggest that as the economy grows and the labour market tightens, skills assume a greater role than labour cost in terms of allocating employment between women and men. Unless women are able to upgrade their skills and keep pace with the technological upgrading of the economy in developing countries, the opportunities for them to benefit from economic growth will disappear.

The relationship between the global economic environment, the enabling environment and women's role in the economy can be seen in the analysis of three central themes of the *Survey*: poverty, productive employment and women and economic decision-making.

### *Poverty*

Poverty is considered to be universally unacceptable; it represents a major failure of development. Analysing its causes and solutions from a gender perspective helps illuminate the nature of development and identify successful policies and programmes for both women and men.

There is no question that there are more poor than ever in the world, that poverty is increasing in some regions and that women and men experience poverty differently. Despite a renewal in economic growth worldwide, the number of people living in absolute poverty has increased in developing and developed regions alike. A gender perspective looks at how and why women and men experience poverty differently and become poor through different processes. While poverty can be measured at levels ranging from the individual to the national, the household is a particularly appropriate level for gender analysis. Households with shared income and consumption experience poverty together and must cope with it. Especially where sharing is unequal, poverty in the household has significant consequences for women.

Poverty at the intrahousehold level is defined in terms of consumption. Consumption within the household is determined less by the income brought in by a member than by cultural and social factors determining who can bring in income and how the goods available for consumption are shared, factors which often favour men.

One approach to understanding poverty from a gender perspective is based on concepts of entitlement and endowment. An entitlement is a right to commend resources. An endowment consists of the skills, access and other resources that make it possible to exercise an entitlement. In this sense, poverty is a failure to ensure entitlements because of inadequate endowments. In gender terms this can be seen in terms of asymmetries between women and men in their entitlements and endowments. Taken together these asymmetries perpetuate the cycle of poverty and explain why women and men experience it differently.

In the household, asymmetries can mean that women have fewer entitlements to household goods, coupled with additional responsibilities. They have less command over labour, whether their own or that of others. The division of labour is unfavourable to women, who work longer hours at largely unremunerated tasks. Similarly, women receive less return for their labour than men, though they are more likely to use their incomes for household purposes. Moreover, most women have fewer entitlements to officially distributed resources, whether in the form of land, extension services or credit, especially in rural areas. This prevents women from building up their skills and resources.

The strongest link between gender and poverty is found in female-headed households, which are a significant source of female poverty. While female headship should mean that a woman is the person most financially responsible for the household, that definition is not always used in census counts, which usually assume an adult male to be the head. Thus when the head of a household is counted as a woman, this usually means that there is no adult male present and the woman is the only support. There are major differences in the share of female-headed households in developing regions, with the highest percentage found

in sub-Saharan Africa. Globally the percentage of female-headed households is highest in Europe and North America, where they constitute the poorest segment of otherwise wealthy societies. Female headship can be the result of migration, family dissolution, male mortality or single parenthood.

Female-headed households often have a large number of dependants coupled with few adult income earners. Unlike households with two or more adult income earners, female-headed households force women to take on both productive and reproductive activities, with an inevitable trade-off between the two. Female-headed households are consequently poorer and the welfare of children in them is often lacking, though this varies by region.

Education mitigates poverty. Progress in reducing the education gap between girls and boys has been less rapid in some regions, such as Africa, and in rural areas generally. For poor households, sending children to school involves difficult choices, however positive the long-term results may be. A number of programmes have demonstrated that illiteracy and low school attendance for girls can be addressed successfully. Similarly, training women in economic sectors where their role is particularly important, such as agriculture, forestry and fishing, can lead to important economic returns. Education and training for members of refugee households, which are predominately female-headed, has also grown in importance.

Poverty is particularly acute in rural areas, where it has particular consequences for women. A number of factors combine to feminize rural poverty, including environmental degradation, female illiteracy, cutbacks in services as part of restructuring, and male migration leading to female-headed households, all coupled with women's limited access to factors of production. The least developed countries are themselves predominantly rural. Moreover, export-oriented growth in agriculture has directed resources towards export crops, which are usually controlled by men, rather than food production, which is largely undertaken by women.

Much of what is known about gender aspects of rural poverty is derived from micro-studies; there is a general absence of data disaggregated by sex, a prerequisite for recognition of women's role in agriculture. On the whole, evidence suggests that while women's economic activity in rural areas is increasing, their participation in decision-making is not.

Strengthened grass-roots organizations of women,

especially at the community level, are becoming ever more important. These organizations effectively increase participation but suffer from a lack of support and resources. National women's organizations can help remedy this situation by encouraging women's participation. A variety of programmes to establish and strengthen these organizations can be envisaged in the context of democratization, including various information and promotional campaigns.

Rural poverty has to be addressed in terms of access to and control of productive resources. Access to land is of particular concern since land is traditionally passed from father to son and reform measures have tended to perpetuate this pattern. Improving women's access to land is an important factor in the success of rural development policies. Similarly, removing obstacles to women's access to paid labour and providing access to modern technology can help address gender asymmetry.

Improved access to credit releases women's productive abilities and is an important means of reducing poverty. While many credit programmes do not take women into account, especially poor women, women on the whole are better credit risks than men, particularly when credit is accompanied by extension, training and marketing assistance. Effective credit programmes identify the particular needs of women and balance the many roles played by women and men.

Provision of extension services to women has been a problem. Not only are most extension agents men, but the programmes have been designed for male-dominated activities. As a result, many extension programmes do not meet current needs. Programmes designed with a gender approach are more likely to be effective; they require research, recruitment of female extension agents and gender-sensitive training of male extension workers.

Addressing rural poverty also requires recognizing the importance of non-agricultural work in rural areas. Many non-farm activities are particularly well suited to women, including handicrafts, petty trading and small-scale enterprises in food and beverage processing. Support for these activities requires providing access to the factors of production, including credit, marketing and technological information.

Health services, including family planning, need to be part of any poverty eradication programme in rural areas. Many of these services have been reduced as a result of restructuring. There have been gender-

effects in some cases—for example, when the introduction of fees has led to less immunization for girls than for boys.

Migration to urban areas has been one consequence of continued rural poverty. While this migration has been predominately male in some countries, in others, women have migrated in larger numbers particularly where economic opportunities are greater in urban areas. There have been reciprocal benefits from this migration: remittances from urban migrants can alleviate rural poverty, and care for the children of migrants by relatives in the rural areas relieves some of the burden on urban dwellers.

Urban poverty is an increasingly important issue, not only because urban populations are growing dramatically in the developing world, but also because the nature of and solutions to urban poverty are different. Urban life is based on a cash economy, which sharpens the effects of poverty by making households more vulnerable to price changes. Public services are more critical to well-being in urban areas; when access to them is lacking, poverty can be particularly acute. For recent migrants, there is a need to learn to deal with a new environment. Urban populations are typically young, with high proportions under 15 years of age and consequent implications for providing health and education facilities. The highest rates of urban growth are expected in Africa and Asia.

There are gender dimensions to the organization of urban space and housing, particularly as women become more likely to work outside the home. The location of workplace relative to household is important in terms of women's ability to balance productive and reproductive tasks that are not fully shared. Also important is the provision of infrastructure, especially potable water, since water provision tends to be a female responsibility even in urban areas.

Health in urban areas has gender dimensions in terms of the effects of environmental degradation and often violent living conditions, the spread of human immunodeficiency virus/acquired immunodeficiency syndrome (HIV/AIDS) and other infectious diseases, and occupational health issues that are gender-specific. The strains of urban life can be more acute for women, given their multiple tasks. Of particular concern is an increasing trend towards early pregnancies among urban adolescent girls, since their long-term consequences can significantly reduce opportunities. Because of the complexity of the services that need to be provided, the delivery of urban health programmes to women should be seen in a holistic manner.

In dealing with poverty, whether urban or rural, there are different roles for different actors in the process. Although the role of the State in the economy has been de-emphasized as privatization and other measures have been implemented, the State still plays an important role. Its function is to raise, allocate and reorganize public resources for the good of society and create the legal and regulatory environment to enable development. The role of the State depends on its priorities; in many countries State activities have not included the type of public investment and incentives that might address poverty. However, the State can provide the normative basis for change, as reflected in laws and programmes, and can increase women's access to productive resources and equal opportunities. This can be reinforced by community and other non-governmental organizations.

Women have considerably less influence than men on the priorities set for public action. The market, in contrast, responds to a multiplicity of individual choices—influence is a function of resources. Women have less influence in the market because they do not have control over their labour and have limited access to other means of production.

The State and other organizations should extend entitlements to the poor and increase their endowments so that they can improve their own situations. When entitlements are extended to women the poverty-reduction effect is considerable. This requires women to take advantage of their rights and responsibilities to make use of the State.

*Productive employment*

One of the greatest economic changes over the past decade has been the rapid influx of women into the paid labour force and the resulting employment patterns. Productive employment of women is critical in eradicating poverty at both the household and national levels. Women's employment and qualifications are increasing, but many of the jobs open to women are underpaid, poorly regulated and short term.

More than one third of all women aged 15 years and older are in the formal labour force, though there are conspicuous regional differences. Female economic activity has increased over the past two decades in almost all regions and, were activity in the informal sector counted, the increase would be even

greater. The largest growth in employment has been in manufacturing and services. There has also been growth in the share of women working in technical and professional positions. Still, despite an upward trend in the share of women in managerial and administrative categories, few women have reached the top ranks of corporate management.

Data on the exact extent of women's economic participation are uneven, partly because of the way participation is defined and partly because of under-counting of unpaid work and work in the informal sector. Women's economic participation is probably much higher than official statistics show.

Women's entry into the labour force is a function of both economic necessity and a desire to work. Entry has been abetted by a trend towards more flexible working patterns in response to competitive pressures. Atypical modes of work—part-time, temporary, outwork and home work—have been more accepted by women because of their family responsibilities. To some extent these non-standard modes reflect a proliferation of low-income jobs and a decline of higher-paid employment, which had been the domain of men. Consequently, the rise in female employment has been accompanied by a decline in male employment and a shift for men towards part-time and other atypical forms of employment. However, women continue to earn less than men, a situation that is only partially attributable to job differences.

Evidence from the economies in transition suggests that women's entry into the labour force is now a permanent feature and that, rather than considering themselves a reserve labour force, women prefer to work. This has made the transition to market economies in those countries particularly difficult for women, who experience higher unemployment than men. In Asia and the Pacific women have been the bulk of growth in the labour force in countries with export-oriented industrialization.

Technological change is a major factor in women's employment. In the past women workers tended to be displaced when cheap labour was replaced by technology. Whether this will continue is unknown. When the purpose of technology is to replace labour-intensive work, female industrial workers can be the group most affected. But when productivity improvements are the motive, women often benefit. When accompanied by skill upgrading, technology can provide a positive qualitative change in the nature of work. Some information technologies create employment in developing countries, such as remote data entry. Technology can also lead to atypical patterns of employment, including home work, and divide the labour force between a highly skilled core staff and peripheral workers who can be taken on or let go quickly. The group women fall into will depend on whether they are able to acquire the requisite skills.

The introduction of new technologies to agriculture can likewise have either positive or negative effects. Introducing high-yield varieties of grain in Asia, for example, generated employment for women because tasks like seeding, weeding and harvesting had traditionally been performed by women. Over the longer term other technologies replaced women's labour. Evidence suggests that developing appropriate technology for tasks now performed by women is a means to their empowerment.

A recent study of women in manufacturing by the United Nations Industrial Development Organization (UNIDO) indicates that women's participation in the sector has increased faster than for men. However, the study found many patterns across countries. Moreover, women are concentrated in the lower end of the spectrum; few are involved in administrative and management functions. Countries with export-oriented industries appear to prefer hiring women workers, at least partly because of their lower cost or willingness to work on a subcontracting or outwork basis. When there is stagnation in the large enterprises in the modern sector, new job opportunities often are found in labour-intensive micro- or small-scale industries. As is the case with employment generally, female employment in manufacturing is conditioned by sociocultural norms about their public participation and whether their employment is given the same value as that of men. In each of 12 country groups identified by the UNIDO study, ranging from developed countries with a high concentration of women in the tertiary sector through least developed countries with a traditional socio-economic role for women, there are specific challenges and policies to meet them.

One consequence of massive unemployment and underemployment in developing countries has been an increasing internal and international migration of women to obtain employment. The remittances of women workers can be significant for sending countries. For receiving countries, the migrant workers provide labour where national supply is inadequate. The conditions under which migration occurs are not always favourable to women, and such strategies as training and orientation to national conditions have been identified to improve the situation of female migrants.

The increase in women's employment often has been accompanied by a decrease in the quality of working conditions. One factor that affects the quality of the working environment is whether work takes place in the public, the formal private or the informal sector. Work in the public sector, where rules are generally non-discriminatory, provides better protection for women. This sector has been shrinking as a result of restructuring. Work in developing countries is typically in agriculture or the informal sector, where conditions are unregulated and often precarious.

In developed countries much of the growth in women's labour force participation has been accounted for by part-time work. As noted, this atypical form of employment is also becoming common in developing countries. The issue here is how to provide social protection, career development and employment security to these part-time workers.

There is also evidence of continued occupational segregation, which leads to lower pay and limited occupational mobility. This, however, is offset by the growing economic importance of some of the fields in which women traditionally have been represented. Even here, wage differentials cannot be explained solely by occupation, regardless of sector.

While there has been increased understanding that social protection needs to be accorded to workers, particularly in terms of such services as child care, which enable women and men to reconcile their productive and reproductive roles, global restructuring has reduced the likelihood that such facilities are provided by either the State or private enterprises, reducing the incentives for men to share in this role.

The number of women in trade unions has increased but still lags behind women's numbers in the labour force, and women are not well represented in trade union leadership or in employers' associations. Organizing in associations and unions strengthens women's bargaining power and protects their interests.

### Women and economic decision-making

The increased role of women in the formal economy, the recognition of their role in eradicating poverty and the changes that have already occurred in women's access to education and other development assets have not been reflected in their participation in economic decision-making. Changes in the underlying structure of the economy do not automatically lead to changes in decision-making processes or structures.

Economic decision makers are persons in a variety of positions who determine the short- and long-term direction of economic policy. Decision makers include entrepreneurs, executives of public bodies dealing with economic matters, managers of public and private enterprises at national and international levels, managers of international and regional financial institutions, and members of the boards of trade unions and professional and business organizations.

While data exist on women in management positions, there are no global statistics on the share of women among economic decision makers. There are many reasons why there should be more women in decision-making positions, including women's right to such positions, the growing share of women in the labour force, the increasing share of women in technical, professional, administrative and management occupations and the economic advantages of drawing on women's skills and abilities.

Women hold 10 to 30 per cent of what the International Labour Organization (ILO) classifies as management positions, but less than 5 per cent of top management. In the 1,000 largest non–United States corporations only 1 per cent of top management positions are filled by women, and in the 1,000 largest United States corporations only 8 per cent, mainly in second-level top management. These corporations constitute the bulk of transnational business. A similar situation is found in the boards of trade unions and the boards of professional and employers organizations.

In government, where only 6 per cent of ministerial positions in 1993 were held by women, women held an even lower share of posts dealing with the economy. While there was a larger percentage of women in subministerial decision-making posts, again the proportion was lower in those dealing with the economy. The situation is no different for international economic decision-making. Neither the United Nations, the specialized agencies, the Bretton Woods institutions or the regional development banks have many women in decision-making positions either in government delegations or in the secretariats themselves. Changes in the composition of classes of law, business, science and technology, where women are achieving parity in most regions, should mean that the

pool from which the next generation of economic decision makers is drawn will contain as many women as men.

Overall, the rate of increase in the share of women in top decision-making is very slow regardless of a country's level of development. This contrasts with the growth of women in the workforce and the significant increase of women among entrepreneurs. Coupled with the increase in young women with appropriate training, this growth could increase the number of women in economic decision-making positions at a rate far faster than heretofore if gender-based obstacles can be surmounted.

One basic obstacle is the lack of assured upward career paths for women in corporate structures, whether public or private, starting with recruitment and extending through career development. Corporate recruitment of women has been slow because women were considered less desirable owing to their presumed reproductive role and because many women chose education in fields that were not applicable to economic management positions.

Once recruited, women have had to deal with corporate cultures that were male-oriented. Corporate cultures tended to create obstacles to women's promotions, ranging from work-hour norms to established male networks and achievement criteria based on perceptions and stereotyped expectations, reinforced by administrative procedures. Taken together, the factors form a "glass ceiling", an invisible but impassable barrier that prevents women from rising professionally regardless of their education and experience. Even if women manage to reach higher levels of management, their minority status can produce stresses that make mobility difficult and, occasionally, undesirable.

Rather than seeking careers in large corporations, many women are choosing to become entrepreneurs, owning or running small and medium-size modern enterprises. While statistics on the number of entrepreneurs are not always comparable, data show that the gap between female and male entrepreneurs has diminished in the past 20 years. Enterprises created by women are different from those owned by men and centre on delivery of modern services and other growth sectors.

The development of female entrepreneurialism has been facilitated by the increase in educational access and the growth in sectors where women's skills in communication, multi-tasking and non-hierarchical decision-making are particularly important. At the same time, these enterprises face special obstacles in terms of obtaining financing, management training and technical assistance, and building networks and social support facilities.

Many of these factors come together as women seek to take advantage of trade-driven growth. Female entrepreneurialism finds expression at all levels of trade, but must work against the constraints already noted. A number of steps are being taken to create an environment that will permit women to compete fully in trade development. The Women in Trade Development Programme of the International Trade Centre (ITC) involves a series of interventions designed to help create that environment.

### Promoting women's participation in development

The current role of women in development is the result of trends unleashed by changes in the enabling environment coupled with the nature of global economic change. Market forces and the policy choices underlying them have propelled women into a decisive position in much of the global and national economy. However, the changes have not been fast enough, are not sufficiently secure and are not occurring everywhere. To equalize and accelerate the process, policies should be adopted by Governments, by enterprises and by women themselves to address the main obstacles.

It is increasingly clear that gender should be taken into account in global and national policy-making. Developments over the past decade, especially global economic restructuring, have proven that economic change is not gender-neutral. Yet there is little evidence that economic policy makers have considered gender as a key variable in their policy-making. Gender could be taken into account by such means as:

- Examining the gender-related employment effects of such policies as export promotion or technological change.
- Ensuring that the transition to a flexible market does not merely lead to low wages as a proxy for productivity but rather develops the skills of workers to provide a transition to industries built on skilled workforces with productivity based on output.
- Creating economic policies that consider the types of employment that women and men are able to

undertake, giving appropriate value to the sharing of reproductive roles between women and men.

Since poverty reflects a failure of development, it undermines future development and has significant gender dimensions; these gender dimensions should be addressed. Women and men experience poverty differently at the household level and therefore, by aggregation, in the economy as a whole. It follows that women constitute the most significant entry point for poverty alleviation strategies. Not having benefited from programmes that would have built up their endowments, yet charged with the responsibility for coping with lack of necessities, women have been denied the entitlements necessary to lift themselves and their families from poverty. This contradiction could be addressed by a range of actions to increase women's endowments and entitlements. Actions might include:

- Ensuring equal access to education by girls, especially from poor families and in rural areas, through programmes that support their enrolment and retention in schools.
- Providing adult women with training and non-formal education related to their work that can help compensate for lack of educational opportunity.
- Changing laws and regulations to give women equal access to productive resources and gainful employment, including—especially for poor rural women—land and credit.
- Ensuring that new employment opportunities meet income needs and are compatible with family responsibilities.
- Promoting community and public services that allow women and men, especially heads of single-parent households, to accommodate their need to earn income with the need to maintain the family, including child and dependent care.
- Encouraging the development of organizations of women at the community level that can help empower poor women.

Eradicating poverty means ensuring that women can be productively employed on equal terms. The growing incidence of production and finance, technological transformation, economic restructuring, the transition to market economies, the globalization of markets, and changes in work organizations, production processes and demographic trends will continue to create opportunities and risks for female workers. These developments pose new challenges to women's social protection, working conditions, labour market policies, and appropriate legislative framework and enforcement. They also pose challenges to Governments, employers, trade unions and other institutions and actors at the national, regional and international levels in the promotion of gender equality in the working world.

An integrated approach to employment could involve a number of actions, such as:

- Creating a legislative framework that enables equal participation, including reforms of labour codes so that women and men are treated equally and all appropriate economic activity is covered.

- Taking steps to enforce equality norms by establishing institutions to supervise conditions in both the public and private sectors, providing recourse to individuals and ensuring certain sanctions for violation of norms.

- Providing training to women workers to facilitate their skill acquisition and upgrade their skills, especially for workers in sectors undergoing structural change.

- Addressing occupational stereotyping through the educational and training systems in schools, enterprises, unions and the media.

- Taking steps, including appropriate legislation, to ensure that jobs are classified and remunerated according to the principle of equal pay for work of equal value.

- Establishing the norm that family responsibility should be shared by men and women alike and should be supported by public and private institutions.

- Creating public services and encouraging private provision of child care as part of the work environment.

- Studying new methods of permitting men and women to mesh careers with family commitment through flexible work schedules and locations and the possibility of part-time work with social security benefits.

- Taking steps to address women's occupational health and safety as reflected in unsafe work environments and sexual harassment.

- Providing training and access to resources for self-employment and entrepreneurship.

- Encouraging women's participation in existing trade unions and other workers and employers'

organizations and the formation of new organizations, especially for those in atypical jobs.

- Implementing affirmative action programmes in areas that suffer the consequences of past discrimination, especially in terms of access to decision-making.

- Increasing the amount of research on gender factors in employment.

A variety of actors are involved in achieving these ends. The Government has a responsibility to be a model employer, but more important it should promote laws and policies that create a more gender-responsive working world but do not inhibit market efficiency. Employers and trade unions have the responsibility, through collective bargaining, to ensure that employment practices provide an environment in which women and men can reconcile productive and reproductive roles. Non-governmental organizations and national women's organizations can support the promotion of gender equality by supporting innovative programmes and by monitoring developments.

Policies should take into account several trends that pose new challenges for women in the working world. The changing nature of the formal sector will increase demands on women to adjust to new opportunities as economies emphasize competitiveness and efficiency. In Central and Eastern Europe the shift from a public full-employment economy to a privatized economy makes particular demands on women to break into new, market-oriented occupations. The retrenchment of the public sector has left many unemployed and requires adjustment.

A second trend is the emergence of an intermediate sector between the formal sector of large enterprises and the increasingly crowded informal sector. This intermediate sector, made up of small and medium-sized enterprises, provides opportunities for women if they can obtain the skills, experience, financing and networking necessary to make them profitable.

A third trend is the growth of the informal sector, blurring the lines between the household and the enterprise with the growth of subcontracting, home work and self-employment. This will require regulation and social protection if the growth is not accompanied by exploitation.

A final trend is the growth of flexibility and deregulation in the economy, which can provide opportunities to balance productive and reproductive roles but could lead to a lack of social protection as well as a lessened quality and security of employment. The outcome depends on the policies and practices that are adopted.

Finally, unless policies and programmes increase women's participation in economic decision-making, opportunities to address poverty and improve the working world are unlikely to develop. The responsibility for creating such opportunities rests with the public sector, which should consider such actions as:

- Ensuring that appropriate third-level education opportunities are available to both women and men to equip them for managerial and entrepreneurial careers.

- Implementing and enforcing legislation on equal employment opportunities, including the prevention of sexual harassment.

- Encouraging private-sector firms to move women to executive positions through monitoring, information, dissemination and establishment of voluntary norms.

- Supporting networking among women executives, including sharing of information on developments and opportunities.

- Promoting gender-neutral recruitment and promotion policies by corporations, as well as the public sector, through sensitization and models.

- Setting up in the public sector and encouraging in the private sector the norm of dual career managerial couples, including appropriate policies for parental leave, job-sharing and flexible career patterns.

- Encouraging women to undertake entrepreneurship by developing an integrated approach to expedite financing, training, counselling and technical assistance services.

# Introduction

The *1994 World Survey on the Role of Women in Development* was requested by the General Assembly in resolutions 44/77 of 8 December 1989 and 44/171 of 19 December 1989. In accordance with Commission on the Status of Women resolution 36/8 of 20 March 1992, the *World Survey* will be one of the principal documents for the Fourth World Conference on Women. In accordance with General Assembly resolution 48/108, a preliminary summary of the *World Survey* was provided to the Economic and Social Council at its substantive session of 1994 through the Commission on the Status of Women.

This is the third *World Survey* that has been prepared. The *Survey* is now issued in the year before the periodic review and appraisal of the Nairobi Forward-looking Strategies for the Advancement of Women,[1] which occurs every five years. Each *Survey* has had its point of departure. The first, issued in 1986,[2] explored women's contribution to the economy to demonstrate that women were key participants in economic development. The second, issued in 1989,[3] explored women's participation in the global adjustment process that was then under way. The *1994 Survey* examines the results of the restructuring process and the emergence of women as decisive elements in the global economy. By examining the most recent data available, it seeks to project trends of how men and women affect and are affected by the global economy.

The first *Survey* was one of the few studies to examine women's role in the economy. Since then the question of women and development has been included in many surveys of the global economy. This *Survey* therefore concentrates on how a gender-based perspective might change the way development concepts are expressed.

Like its predecessors, the *1994 Survey* is a product of the United Nations system. The outline and approach to the *Survey* were discussed at annual inter-agency meetings on women. Many agencies have contributed to the text. The draft was circulated among the organizations of the United Nations system. The *Survey* is based on micro-studies, specialized studies by organizations of the United Nations system and previously unpublished United Nations statistics. The *Survey*'s focus goes beyond women, however, and examines development from a gender perspective. This approach bears some explanation.

## A.  DATA SOURCES ON WOMEN IN THE ECONOMY

Empirical studies generally suffer from a time lag. Between the time data are collected, analysed, written up and published, years may pass. Thus, any data analysis is backward-looking and risks drawing conclusions that have been superseded by changes in the global situation. The *Survey* draws heavily on studies that, while relatively recent in academic terms, involve data that are at least five years old. Most of the studies focus on women, but not all do so in terms of the relationship between women and men.

However, the *Survey* is able to take advantage of the Women's Indicators and Statistics Data Base (WISTAT), created by the Statistical Division of the Department of Economic and Social Information and Policy Analysis of the United Nations Secretariat. This source provides data for three time periods (1970, 1980 and 1990) and provides the possibility, for the first time, of examining trends in women's economic participation relative to men's. The *Survey* draws heavily on WISTAT for trends and supplements these findings with an exhaustive review of specialized and micro-studies to suggest what these trends might mean.

## B.  THE GENDER APPROACH

The first *World Survey* was an outcome of what has been termed the WID (women in development) policy approach. This approach emerged in the early 1970s to put the advancement of women on the agenda of national and international development agencies. In contrast to the welfare and family-oriented programmes of the 1960s, which emphasized women's reproductive role, the WID policy approach stressed the importance of women in economic and social (productive) development and the positive link between economic participation and women's emancipation. This approach evolved into different sub-approaches, one favouring the achievement of equality between women and men, another mainly concerned with the fate of poor women, and a later one, against the background of the adjustment programmes of the 1980s, stressing that maximizing female paid or unpaid contributions ensured more efficient investments and balance-of-payments equilibrium. Policy strategies have evolved from implementing small-scale, income-generating programmes to the objective of mainstreaming women in all policies.

Economic adjustment and difficulties showed that the benefits of targeted projects, and even of long-lasting policies to advance women, could be swept away by macroeconomic fluctuations and policy changes. Until the 1980s WID proponents viewed development mainly as "something done by development agencies", and something "women were in ... in so far as they were recipients of projects and programmes".[4] The WID policy approach deliberately avoided questioning the dominant concepts of development. It sought acceptance by mainstream economists in order to emerge from the social welfare category in which women's issues had been kept and to obtain more funding for the advancement of women. As a result, the movement accepted compromises about some of the goals that activists had originally pursued, such as empowering women through a process of social, economic and political change.

The WID approach emphasized how women could contribute to development strategies. Its focus on poor women in the 1970s can be seen as complementary to the dominant World Bank strategy of redistribution with growth. Echoing the structural adjustment strategy of the 1980s, the movement switched to showing how investment returns could be raised and balance of payments improved by investing in women. Structural adjustment played a key role in initiating a more ambitious approach to women and development. The WID movement started reflecting on the type of development into which women were to be integrated, making a gender perspective and the pursuit of equality part of the overall debate on the goals and means of development.

Committed activists from developing countries were among the initiators of this new approach. Some of these activists are grouped in international networks such as the Development Alternatives for Women Network (DAWN). Many of the members are researchers involved with non-governmental organizations. This approach, called "global feminism" by some and the "empowerment approach" by others, sees inequality between women and men as part of a continuum of inequalities between countries, social classes and ethnic groups. It stresses the capacity of people, poor women in particular, to promote development if proper support and a conducive environment are provided.

The diversity among women and the difficulty of seeing women as a class has long been noted. Highlighting the structural constraints on women's economic and social roles and their social and institutional framework is also hardly new. What is new, however, is formulating women's issues in terms of gender. This changes the emphasis from women as a homogeneous group that requires new targeting with each cohort or generation to an emphasis on relations between the sexes. Gender relations are the social, economic and political relations that determine gender identity. Gender relations shape women's access to resources and their work opportunities.

Gender relations frame the limits of what a woman may undertake at work, in the family or in public life. They also frame male behaviour, responsibilities and entitlements. Gender relations affect social and economic functioning at all levels. Relationships between spouses, children and parents, managers and employees and among community members are all influenced by the dominant model of gender relations. Gender relations often ensure that women are less powerful than men. Political, social or economic institutions and relations may also contain mechanisms that impede gender equality. For example, certain products or activities may be given priority in the economy to encourage activities undertaken by men.

Gender relations are influenced by class, ethnicity and other factors, including inequalities between countries, religions and political systems. The interaction between gender and such factors as ethnic origin and class is complex, influencing the opportunities and vulnerability of a given individual or group. For example, gender relations may shape the economic and social strategies of migrant groups. Women may be forced to enter the labour market to supplement insufficient male incomes, or may have to work as unpaid family workers in informal enterprises.

Gender relations are thus not static: they can evolve as a response to economic opportunities and obstacles or they can be kept in their traditional form to fit a chosen strategy, as women's traditional role in the family justifies unpaid employment. There is no way of knowing which course gender relations will take. This uncertainty makes possible intervention by public or other actors.

The complexity of gender relations must be taken into account when analysing trends and policies. Certain changes may have a universal impact, as with policies to combat violence against women. Others may impact poor women more than middle-class women.

One of the most important steps for researchers and activists working in the field of women in development has been recognizing that women's issues cannot be resolved in isolation from the relationships between women and men or social and economic structures and trends. Instead, changing the status of women requires the entire society to rethink the type of development it pursues.

Advancing women cannot be a marginal exercise of micro-level projects. Nor will gender-aware sectoral or macro-level plans be sufficient. The entire range of social and economic relations and policies needs to be reviewed from a gender perspective, and gender issues should help define development goals. Current trends, development strategies and State policies should be evaluated against a gender backdrop, particularly in the fields of education, employment, family law, population policy and national development.

One of the important contributions of WID activists and researchers has been to highlight the multiple dimensions of women's roles. However, WID activists have tended to focus exclusively on one role or another, ignoring how the roles are articulated or related. For example, women benefit from increased opportunities for remunerated employment only if the sharing of their domestic responsibilities is also addressed. Failure to do so can further increase their workloads. Similarly, making the general labour market more accessible to women would have greater transformation potential for women's position within the family than would creating women-only income-generating projects, which have a poor record of success.

Gender analysis seeks to define a rational, organized distinction between production and reproduction. Human reproduction activities include the care and nurturing provided inside a family (to children, spouses, sick or old people, or siblings) or inside the broader community (to neighbours). It includes raising children and transmitting social and other values. It also includes, especially in developing countries, a range of activities required for the care of the household, such as carrying water and wood. These activities are usually not assigned economic value and are often ignored in the design and evaluation of development strategies.

Human reproduction activities are undertaken mainly by women. Such work often is not recognized because of the priority given to production of commodities or remunerated services. It is not even recognized in the context of human resource development strategies, which focus exclusively on education and health inputs. Reproductive work generally does not include an entitlement to income. This leads to women's dependence on male partners or, in some cases, to the double burden of taking on additional activities to raise income.

The failure to recognize the value of reproduction activities is an obstacle to empowerment at both the microeconomic and societal levels. It restricts women to family duties, limits their life choices and hampers their chances of success in other areas of endeavour through the direct burden of the work, the time and energy constraints entailed and the negative attitudes of the society.

Hence, the United Nations Seminar on the Integration of Women in Development identified the integration of human reproduction activities as a key element of gender-aware development strategies. Any development strategy should be centrally concerned with production and reproduction and with the way these activities articulate with one another. Productive and reproductive activities should be integrated in the design, implementation and evaluation of policies and programmes.

Increasing the income associated with human reproduction activities is one aspect of this approach. Women in developing countries have traditionally increased their income by selling, for example, the small surplus generated by their work in subsistence agriculture. In developed countries, there have been claims for a "housewife wage". An alternative proposal for developed countries in Western Europe is that the State should provide all members of society with a basic income entitlement independent of their work and age. The impact of this measure on gender roles in human reproduction activities has been questioned.

Another approach seeks a different distribution of human reproduction activities among the State, the market and the community, as well as within the family. Public provision of the inputs required to perform human reproduction activities are especially important in developing countries as a way of reducing the burden on women. These inputs include clean water, electricity, transport and health care. Policies oriented towards the improvement of living standards in cities, for example, may improve gender relations, creating better conditions for human reproduction activities.

Integrating human reproduction activities and income earning is possible only if changes are introduced in mechanisms and rules governing employment of both women and men. Adapting work conditions to take child-care responsibilities into account is a recurrent recommendation in international forums. Other measures should ensure that time spent raising children is considered economically valuable, as well as a source of

new skills and capacities. Such attitudes are emerging in a few countries. There are also increasing aspirations among men for different rhythms of work and careers, including time off from paid employment to concentrate on family responsibilities. Integrating work and family responsibilities has operational consequences for programmes and projects in developing countries. It should lead to ensuring that all development programmes and projects include a child-care component, and possibly provide support to other human reproduction activities.

## C.  HUMAN DEVELOPMENT AND SUSTAINABILITY

The view that development can be considered exclusively in terms of capital and technological inputs, ignoring human development, has been challenged. In the *Human Development Report*,[5] the United Nations Development Programme (UNDP) defines human development as the process of enlarging people's choices, increasing their opportunities and covering the full range of human choices, from a sound political environment to economic and political freedom. UNDP believes that development should be woven around people, and should refer to women and men on equal terms. A successful development strategy requires that the role of women be recognized.

Applying a gender lens to development can show that some of the goals being pursued by societies might actually impede the achievement of other goals. Some development goals include less easily quantifiable objectives such as freedom, increased autonomy or the need "to live without shame and have self-respect".[6] Environmental sustainability and concepts such as empowerment, democratization and participation have also been increasingly integrated in the definition of development adopted in national, regional and international forums.

As stated by the United Nations Educational, Scientific and Cultural Organization (UNESCO) in a contribution to the *Survey*:

> The success of development efforts depends upon making women full partners. They must be enabled not only to contribute their efforts, but also to share equally in the benefits of development projects. What does this imply in practical terms? It means, first of all, that women must gain access to education in order that they may master knowledge and skills that will enable them to be more effective—and more heeded—both in the home and in the economy. To be certain, education, by itself, is not

a panacea, but it is a necessary, if often insufficient, condition for the advancement of women and girls. It is in schools and adult education programmes that the journey out of poverty and towards employment and decision-making power begins.

The International Development Strategy for the Fourth United Nations Development Decade[7] reflects these concerns. Adopted by the General Assembly in 1990, the Strategy contains the common view of United Nations Member States on development and on the measures needed to accelerate it. The Strategy includes equality between women and men as both a goal and a means of development. Among the goals and objectives to be pursued through the decade, the Strategy identifies "a significant improvement in the human condition in the developing countries and a reduction in the gap between poor and rich countries". [8] It also sets social and political objectives and states that "Development over the decade should enhance the participation of all men and women in economic and political life, protect cultural identities and assure to all the necessary means of survival."[8]

One of the six goals identified by the Strategy is "a development process that is responsive to social needs, seeks a significant reduction in extreme poverty, promotes the development and utilization of human resources and skills and is environmentally sound and sustainable". [9] Indeed, while the Strategy's main objective is accelerating economic growth, it recognizes that economic growth by itself does not ensure that its benefits will be equitably distributed or that the physical environment will be protected and improved. Hence, poverty alleviation, human resource development and the environment are identified as priority aspects of development. Population growth and the elimination of hunger are also identified as deserving special attention.[10]

Thus persisting inequality in opportunities and some of its manifestations, such as feminized poverty, educational and literacy gaps and high levels of maternal mortality, are incompatible with the realization of the Strategy's goals. Inequality is considered incompatible with environmentally sustainable development because of its consequences for population growth, resource depletion and decision-making processes.

During the past few years there have been significant changes in the world. The disappearance of the East-West political division has considerably improved the international climate. The trend towards participatory democracy and pluralistic systems of governance is clear across all regions. These changes have been mirrored by important shifts in the economic sphere.

## D.   CHANGES IN THE ENABLING ENVIRONMENT

Two changes have occurred over the past 10 years in the enabling environment for women in the economy. One is the change in women's legal status. The second is that women have achieved equal access to education. The long-term effects of these changes are as yet unknown. However, there is evidence that these changes will enable women to improve dramatically the conditions under which they participate in the economy.

### 1.   *Movement towards equality*

As noted in the 1990 review and appraisal of the Nairobi Forward-looking Strategies for the Advancement of Women, there has been significant progress towards achieving equality for women. The Convention on the Elimination of All Forms of Discrimination against Women, which was adopted by the General Assembly in 1979[11] and entered into force in 1981, set a universal standard for what was meant by equality between women and men. When the first *World Survey* was drafted in 1985, only 39 States were party to the Convention. As of August 1994 there were 134 States parties. All the States in Latin America and the Caribbean, most States in Europe, South-East Asia and East Asia and a majority of States in other regions are party to the Convention (see table 1).

The reports of States parties to the Convention that were submitted to the Committee on the Elimination of Discrimination against Women, the Convention's monitoring body, suggest that efforts are being made to live up to the terms of the Convention. Although many States have substantive reservations, few

Table 1
States parties to the Convention on the Elimination of All Forms of Discrimination against Women

| | | | |
|---|---|---|---|
| Albania | Cambodia | Finland | Japan |
| Angola | Canada | France | Jordan |
| Antigua and | Cape Verde | Gabon | Kenya |
| Barbuda | Central African | Gambia | Lao People's |
| Argentina | Republic | Germany | Democratic Republic |
| Armenia | Chile | Ghana | Latvia |
| Australia | China | Greece | Liberia |
| Austria | Colombia | Grenada | Libyan Arab |
| Bahamas | Congo | Guatemala | Jamahiriya |
| Bangladesh | Costa Rica | Guinea | Lithuania |
| Barbados | Croatia | Guinea-Bissau | Luxembourg |
| Belarus | Cuba | Guyana | Madagascar |
| Belgium | Cyprus | Haiti | Malawi |
| Belize | Czech Republic | Honduras | Maldives |
| Benin | Denmark | Hungary | Mali |
| Bhutan | Dominica | Iceland | Malta |
| Bolivia | Dominican Republic | India | Mauritius |
| Bosnia and | Ecuador | Indonesia | Mexico |
| Herzegovina | Egypt | Iraq | Mongolia |
| Brazil | El Salvador | Ireland | Morocco |
| Bulgaria | Equatorial Guinea | Israel | Namibia |
| Burkina Faso | Estonia | Italy | Nepal |
| Burundi | Ethiopia | Jamaica | Netherlands |

Table 1

(continued)

| | | | |
|---|---|---|---|
| New Zealand | Russian Federation | Sri Lanka | United Kingdom of |
| Nicaragua | Rwanda | Suriname | Great Britain and |
| Nigeria | Saint Kitts and Nevis | SwedenTajikistan | Northern Ireland |
| Norway | Saint Lucia | Thailand | United Republic of |
| Panama | Saint Vincent and the | The former Yugoslav | Tanzania |
| Paraguay | Grenadines | Republic of | Uruguay |
| Peru | Samoa | Macedonia | Venezuela |
| Philippines | Senegal | Togo | Viet Nam |
| Poland | Seychelles | Trinidad and Tobago | Yemen |
| Portugal | Sierra Leone | Tunisia | Yugoslavia |
| Republic of Korea | Slovakia | Turkey | Zaire |
| Republic of Moldova | Slovenia | Uganda | Zambia |
| Romania | Spain | Ukraine | Zimbabwe |

of these are related to women's economic rights. Most have to do with rights related to marriage and the family.

Ratification of or accession to the Convention does not mean that rights are exercised. Many States have not adjusted national laws, administrative practices or other public policies according to their obligations under the Convention. The fact that some countries have not adjusted their laws to ensure women equal access to land ownership or credit creates an obstacle to development. Moreover, the situation of women in countries that are not yet party to the Convention remains a matter of concern.

Nevertheless, the removal of legal barriers to women's economic participation should help accelerate growth in the next few years. Removing legal barriers to economic participation can have a powerful effect on women's status, with the greatest amount of progress observed in countries that have made an unequivocal commitment to legal equality (see table 2).[12]

## 2. *Progress towards educational equality*

Education is a prerequisite for effective economic participation, and most regions have made significant progress towards equality (see table 3). Primary education enrolment ratios approach equality nearly everywhere. Indeed, given that there are more boys than girls in these age groups, equality may already have been reached. There are significant differences within regions, however. In Asia and the Pacific there is a significant difference between South Asia, where in 1990 there were 73 girls for each 100 boys enrolled in first-level education, 60 at the second level and 37 at the third level and South-East and East Asia, where the figures were 92, 90 and 74, respectively.

Table 2

Average ratio of women to men in the economically active population in relation to the status of the Convention on the Elimination of All Forms of Discrimination against Women, 1970-1990

Number of women per 100 men

| Status | 1970 | 1980 | 1990 |
|---|---|---|---|
| Country has ratified the Convention without substantive reservations | 44 | 60 | 71 |
| Country has ratified the Convention with reservations | 35 | 43 | 55 |
| Country has taken no action on the Convention | 21 | 41 | 45 |

*Source*: Division for the Advancement of Women, United Nations Secretariat, from data contained in the Women's Indicators and Statistics Data Base (WISTAT), version 3, 1994.

There are also significant differences among regions. Globally, 57 per cent of school-age girls were enrolled in first or second levels of education in 1990. In Africa the average was only 37 per cent, while in Europe the proportion was 90 per cent. The relation between development and access to education is clearly reflected in the ratios for the least developed countries. On average, the least developed countries have 75 girls for each 100 boys in first-level education and just 37 for each 100 in the third level.

These figures do not address the issue of educational quality or gender bias that might be built into curricula, textbooks or teaching methods. Reports to the Committee on the Elimination of Discrimination against Women suggest that many countries are addressing these issues but the effect of the efforts cannot be demonstrated. The figures also do not reflect the consequences of past discrimination, the most pronounced of which is the disproportionate illiteracy

Table 3

Average ratio of girls to boys enrolled in schools by level and region, 1970-1990

Number of girls for each 100 boys

| Region | First-level education | | | Second-level education | | | Third-level education | | |
|---|---|---|---|---|---|---|---|---|---|
| | 1970 | 1980 | 1990 | 1970 | 1980 | 1990 | 1970 | 1980 | 1990 |
| Africa | 65 | 74 | 79 | 46 | 57 | 69 | 20 | 30 | 32 |
| Asia and the Pacific | 66 | 78 | 84 | 58 | 70 | 77 | 46 | 63 | 84 |
| Eastern Europe | 94 | 94 | 96 | 97 | 91 | 94 | 78 | 106 | 104 |
| Latin America and the Caribbean | 94 | 95 | 95 | 98 | 107 | 109 | 72 | 74 | 106 |
| Western Europe and other | 95 | 95 | 95 | 90 | 98 | 98 | 53 | 72 | 94 |
| World | 77 | 84 | 87 | 67 | 80 | 85 | 46 | 61 | 75 |

*Source*: Division for the Advancement of Women, United Nations Secretariat, from data contained in the Women's Indicators and Statistics Data Base (WISTAT), version 3, 1994.

among women. In Africa and in Asia and the Pacific, a large share of adult women are illiterate (see table 4). However, with the exception of Africa, significant progress is being made in eliminating adult illiteracy and the differentials between women and men. Of particular interest are the reduction of illiteracy generally and the gap between women and men in age group 15 to 24, the age cohort just entering the labour force (see table 5). The longer-term effect of this on the age group during which households are formed and maintained (25 to 44) is also evident (see table 6).

Even more encouraging is the growing equality in third-level education in such key growth areas as science and technology and law and business (see tables 7 and 8). Except for Africa, there has been significant progress everywhere since 1970.

Table 4

Illiteracy among those 15 years or older by region, 1980 and 1990

Percentage

| Region | 1980 | | 1990 | |
|---|---|---|---|---|
| | Men | Women | Men | Women |
| Africa | 51.8 | 71.8 | 44.6 | 61.1 |
| Asia and the Pacific | 31.8 | 49.3 | 21.7 | 34.3 |
| Eastern Europe | 1.5 | 4.9 | 0.9 | 2.3 |
| Latin America and the Caribbean | 18.2 | 23.3 | 14.3 | 16.0 |
| Western Europe and other | 5.7 | 11.4 | 8.7 | 9.9 |

*Source*: Division for the Advancement of Women, United Nations Secretariat, from data contained in the Women's Indicators and Statistics Data Base (WISTAT), version 3, 1994.

Table 5

Illiteracy among those 15 to 24 years of age by region, 1980 and 1990

Percentage

| Region | 1980 | | 1990 | |
|---|---|---|---|---|
| | Men | Women | Men | Women |
| Africa | 35.8 | 55.7 | 35.6 | 51.0 |
| Asia and the Pacific | 19.7 | 32.6 | 10.3 | 17.9 |
| Eastern Europe | 0.5 | 0.9 | .. | .. |
| Latin America and the Caribbean | 9.0 | 10.3 | 7.5 | 6.9 |
| Western Europe and other | 1.0 | 1.0 | 2.6 | 1.2 |

*Source*: Division for the Advancement of Women, United Nations Secretariat, from data contained in the Women's Indicators and Statistics Data Base (WISTAT), version 3, 1994.
*Note*: Two dots (..) indicate that data are not available.

Table 6

Illiteracy among those 25 to 44 years of age by region, 1980 and 1990

Percentage

| Region | 1980 | | 1990 | |
|---|---|---|---|---|
| | Men | Women | Men | Women |
| Africa | 50.7 | 74.4 | 35.3 | 58.3 |
| Asia and the Pacific | 26.7 | 44.7 | 20.2 | 35.8 |
| Eastern Europe | 0.7 | 2.4 | .. | .. |
| Latin America and the Caribbean | 14.1 | 19.4 | 5.3 | 7.3 |
| Western Europe and other | 2.5 | 4.7 | 5.5 | 3.7 |

*Source*: Division for the Advancement of Women, United Nations Secretariat, from data contained in the Women's Indicators and Statistics Data Base (WISTAT), version 3, 1994.
*Note*: Two dots (..) indicate that data are not available.

Table 7

Average ratio of girls to boys in science and technology fields in third-level education by region, 1970-1990

Number of girls per 100 boys

| Region | 1970 | 1980 | 1990 |
|---|---|---|---|
| Africa | 24 | 21 | 24 |
| Asia and the Pacific | 33 | 45 | 70 |
| Eastern Europe | 61 | 81 | 74 |
| Latin America and the Caribbean | 37 | 54 | 80 |
| Western Europe and other | 29 | 49 | 67 |
| World | 32 | 43 | 56 |

*Source*: Division for the Advancement of Women, United Nations Secretariat, from data contained in the Women's Indicators and Statistics Data Base (WISTAT), version 3, 1994.

Table 8

Average ratio of girls to boys in law and business in third-level education by region, 1970-1990

Number of girls per 100 boys

| Region | 1970 | 1980 | 1990 |
|---|---|---|---|
| Africa | 12 | 43 | 36 |
| Asia and the Pacific | 25 | 56 | 70 |
| Eastern Europe | 64 | 134 | 124 |
| Latin America and the Caribbean | 30 | 92 | 97 |
| Western Europe and other | 25 | 54 | 85 |
| World | 25 | 63 | 102 |

*Source*: Division for the Advancement of Women, United Nations Secretariat, from data contained in the Women's Indicators and Statistics Data Base (WISTAT), version 3, 1994.

## NOTES

[1] *Report of the World Conference to Review and Appraise the Achievements of the United Nations Decade for Women: Equality, Development and Peace, Nairobi, 15-26 July 1985* (United Nations publication, Sales No. E.85.IV.10), chap. I, sect. A.

[2] *World Survey on the Role of women in Development* (United Nations publication, Sales No. E.86.IV.3).

[3] *1989 World Survey on the Role of Women in Development* (United Nations publication, Sales No. E.89.IV.2).

[4] Diane Elson, "Gender issues in development strategies" (Paper prepared for United Nations Seminar on the Integration of Women in Development, Vienna, 9-11 December 1991), p. 13.

[5] United Nations Development Programme, *Human Development Report* (Oxford and New York, Oxford University Press, various years).

[6] K. Griffin, *Alternative Strategies for Economic Development* (London, Macmillan, 1989).

[7] General Assembly resolution 45/199, annex.

[8] Ibid., para. 13.

[9] Ibid., para. 13 (b).

[10] Ibid., para. 78.

[11] General Assembly resolution 34/180, annex.

[12] The analysis does not include States that have signed but not ratified the Convention, since the number is too small (7) for meaningful comparison. The countries in this category are extremely mixed.

# I

## Global economic restructuring: its impact on women and changes in the enabling environment

Global economic relations have undergone important changes since the *1989 World Survey*. Economic restructuring, accompanied by momentous changes in the global political landscape, has affected and been affected by women's role in the economy. These changes have had a profound effect on working women, and while some of the changes are encouraging, others suggest new problems. The consequences of these changes can only be estimated; it is too early to tell if the identified trends will continue. This chapter explores these changes and suggests some of the issues that need to be addressed.[1]

Technological change, the transition to market economies, the globalization of markets and production, and structural adjustment programmes and liberalization measures have significantly improved women's work and social status. But these phenomena have limited the capacity of Governments and bodies such as employers' organizations, trade unions and women's bureaus to improve women's employment opportunities and working and living conditions. Progress has been hampered by the systemic nature of gender-based inequalities. Eliminating these inequalities requires adopting an integrated and dynamic approach that takes full account of socio-political and economic conditions.

This chapter examines the macroeconomic changes that have shaped the global economy in recent years with a view to identifying their gender-specific impacts and highlighting the opportunities, challenges and setbacks they create for gender equality.

### A. WOMEN AND ECONOMIC REFORMS

The related phenomena that made up the global economic restructuring process of recent years include various responses to the global economic crises of the 1980s. This complex process, which will continue to influence the world economy, is the backdrop against which women's economic activity must be viewed. The phenomena include stabilization, structural adjustment, rapid technological innovation, growing economic interdependence and the globalization of markets and production.

Global economic restructuring is a continuous, multilevel process that is best viewed as a combination of economic changes at national and international levels. National economies restructure to adapt to a changing international economic environment, precipitating further change. This global restructuring is the outcome of both domestic policies and long-term trends in the international economy.

The past decade saw profound economic restructuring on a global scale, and the process has grown even more intense since the 1990s began. The consolidation of global markets has produced an integrated and interdependent global economy whose vulnerability has increased accordingly. Global recession in the early 1980s polarized the world economy—some economies grew at double-digit rates while other regions experienced economic decline. The debt crisis precipitated a massive economic restructuring as economies around the world struggled to adjust to the burden of external debt.

The set of restructuring tools consisted largely of stabilization and structural adjustment policies based on the neoclassical and monetarist principles of economic theory that have dominated Western economic thought for the past 30 years.

Structural adjustment, which is chiefly concerned with "getting prices right" and correcting supply inelasticities and structural rigidities, involves a combination of macroeconomic, systemic and institutional policies directed at removing excessive governmental controls, at getting factor and product prices to better reflect scarcity values and at promoting market competition. It is often undertaken in the broader context of stabilization and economic reform precipitated by internal or external shocks or, in the case of economies in transition, by changes in the economic and political system.

Structural adjustment programmes were accompanied by a global shift in economic management towards greater reliance on market forces and criticism of government intervention in the economic process. Government intervention came to be regarded as a source of market distortions and rigidities, and Governments worldwide have been encouraged by international economic policy observers to cease being direct actors in the economic process and limit themselves to enlightened monetary management and control of budget deficits. Privatization has swept developed and developing countries alike, and towards the beginning of the 1990s the economies in transition followed suit. The emerging international competition has intensified to an unprecedented level.

Global economic restructuring affected the socio-economic position of women in a number of ways. Cyclical changes in the world and in national economies, the globalization of world markets, increased global economic vulnerability and changes in the patterns and composition of international trade have all impacted women's employment, incomes and their role in society. However, before considering how these trends have impacted women, it is first necessary to describe the nature and policy approach of economic restructuring at national and international levels.

### 1. Restructuring in different economies

The world has undergone turbulent economic changes in the past decade. Developed market economies implemented economic reforms directed at greater stability and international competitiveness. Central and Eastern Europe and the former Soviet Union embarked on a transition from centralized forms of economic planning to market-oriented systems. Developing countries instituted programmes of stabilization and structural adjustment to mitigate the effects of the world recession.

Economic reforms involve a number of actions that must be taken into account when analysing the impact reforms have had on women's work and role in society. These impacts are seen most clearly in terms of employment. The positive or negative impact of reforms depends on how they are implemented, the type of economy involved and whether structures change as a result.

### Developed market economies

As international competition increased in a climate of recession and slow growth, the developed market economies reached a growing consensus on the need to pursue economic reform in order to improve the functioning of financial, product and labour markets to enhance private sector profitability and increase international competitiveness.[2] The restructuring involved policies focused on anti-inflationary objectives, labour market flexibility, deregulation and industrial restructuring.

Monetary and fiscal policies focused on anti-inflationary objectives, including the reduction of public spending and borrowing. Among other things, this had major implications for both public sector employment, where women are a sizeable part of the workforce, and for the social welfare systems that supported living standards and provided security for the most vulnerable groups, including certain categories of women and female-headed households. More recently, an emphasis on cost-effectiveness in the public sector has further reduced the role of the State, and the hiving off of some public sector enterprises and services to the private sector may again negatively impact employment and welfare considerations.

There has been little monitoring of assessment of this trend to date, making it difficult to judge whether women have been hit harder than men by privatization and contracting out of public sector services and enterprises. Some analysts believe that the transfer of blue-collar jobs to the private sector may reduce benefits and job security in areas that are important to women, such as parental leave or part-time work, where the divergence between public and private sectors is greatest. And even where enterprises and services remain within the public domain, management reforms such as performance-related pay and contracts, more flexible systems of hiring and laying-off staff, and a focus on raising productivity and cutting labour costs may affect the "good employer" signals Governments send to the private sector, particularly with respect to equal opportunity and affirmative action programmes.[3]

The loosening of legally and administratively established frameworks of rules and collective agreements reflects the trend towards labour market flexibility and deregulation in the interest of profitability and competitiveness. Inflexible rules and agreements constrain labour mobility and the responsiveness of wages to market conditions.[4] While some women may benefit from flexible work patterns that cater to their family responsibilities and reduced mobility, women are vulnerable to being used as part of a deregulatory strategy by virtue of their association with low pay and flexible forms of employment.[5] In addition, part-time work is incompatible with a regular family life for women who work atypical schedules—capacity-oriented variable working hours in the retail sector and the increasing incidence of latch-key children being cases in point. Furthermore, the positive aspects of labour flexibility must be set against its potential for undermining existing employment protection, social security provisions, minimum wage legislation, access to training, career prospects and trade union representation.

Some authors suggest that overall gains in employment by both men and women may reflect the emergence of more precarious and low-income forms of economic activity. The increase in part-time and other atypical forms of work among workers in some countries that are members of the Organisation for Economic Cooperation and Development (OECD) between 1979 and 1990 may be a case in point, particularly where it is involuntary and associated with increases in unemployment.[6] The halting or reversal of the trend towards diminishing self-employment, particularly among women, may be another indication of less desirable forms of economic activity;[7] by the end of the 1980s the growth rate of women's self-employment exceeded that of their overall employment.[8] Finally, while there may be some substitution of female for male employment, particularly in the more regulated labour markets of Europe and Oceania, this is not a process of replacing men with women in the same jobs, and it does not necessarily lead to an equalization of wage differentials.[2] Indeed, employment of women in previously male-dominated areas often leads to a decline in the status of these occupations since they come to be viewed as low-wage, feminized positions.[9]

The model of the flexible firm is a component of an enterprise's "lean production" strategies in response to the exigencies of competition. The flexible firm is predicated on the existence of a core group of highly skilled, well-trained workers and a periphery of temporary and casual workers, outworkers and subcontractors who together function as a labour reserve, permitting a rapid and more cost-effective adjustment to the peaks and troughs of production.[10] With their lower levels of skill and training, women workers are more likely to be found among the peripheral workers.

Industrial restructuring was the third major tool used by the developed market economies to respond to the crises of the 1970s and 1980s. Restructuring entails reorganizing labour within and across firms in response to competitive pressures and is predicated on phasing out non-competitive industries and "flexible specialization". Phasing out declining industries involves recruitment freezes, retrenchments and lay-offs and the transfer of resources, including workers, to more competitive areas. While the bulk of such activity has been in heavy industry, such as shipbuilding and steel, and was therefore less likely to affect women workers, major losses have also occurred in labour-intensive industries where women were traditionally present, including clothing, textiles, footwear, leather and other consumer goods.[11]

There is a move in some countries and localities to foster competitiveness through "flexible specialization" based on the constructive use of technology, work organization and a skilled workforce, often backed up by a periphery of subcontractors and home workers. While the periphery of these firms create employment for women workers, as in industrial districts of Italy[12] and the clothing industry in Australia,[13] there may again be a trade-off between the availability of employment and its quality in terms of wages, hours and legislative coverage and social protection. While it is difficult to separate the effects of secular trends in the labour market from those of industrial restructuring, the ILO *World Labour Report, 1992* suggests that the closing of declining industries, the introduction of more flexible production strategies and the growth of the service sector have fragmented working life, a development which is reflected in the expansion of precarious and atypical employment.

Restructuring has not been confined to the industrial sector. Most services are now restructuring in ways similar to those adopted by manufacturers in the 1980s, with recruitment freezes, early retirement and lay-offs as well as consolidations and takeovers.[14] While each of the branches that comprises the service sector is evolving differently, the financial sector, retailing and the public sector, which drove expansion in the past, appear to have exhausted their ability to absorb additional labour.

Some analysts suggest that the dual trend of rationalization and disappearance of low-skilled jobs and rising demand for specialized high-skill jobs is likely to shape the service sector of the future.[15] While traditional areas of women's employment (health services, education and personal services) will continue to be the traditional areas of employment, the high-growth area of the future will be that of services to businesses—particularly should the expected boom of the small firm sector materialize.[16] This area's high-skilled, high-prestige professions (accountancy, marketing, advertising, legal services) and its lower-skilled and precarious jobs (cleaning, corporate catering) offer women opportunities at both ends of the skills spectrum. Women's ability to access the higher end of these activities may compensate for the tightening of public employment and for the privatization and subsequent rationalization of many services previously underwritten by the State.

In sum, policies of demand management, flexibility and industrial restructuring have affected women in complex and multi-directional ways. It is difficult to ascertain the complete impact of these influences because of the lack of positive analyses and data disaggregated by sex and the methodological difficulties of separating the long-term trend of rising female employment from the immediate effects of stabilization and restructuring policies.

### Economies in transition

While the formerly centrally planned economies of Central and Eastern Europe and the Soviet Union were sheltered to some extent from the global economic crises of the 1980s by their autarkic trade and production regimes, they too experienced a decline in economic performance during the period. Confounded by structural distortions, by the difficulties inherent in a transition from extensive to intensive, efficient growth and by their inability to sustain output growth through technological progress and greater micro-economic efficiency, economic performance deteriorated during the 1982-1988 period and became negative in 1989, the last year before transition.[17] The economic collapse and subsequent political disintegration of the Soviet Union triggered radical transformation in the region that went beyond the economic to encompass ideological, political and social spheres as well.[18]

Economic reforms have focused on stabilization, liberalization and structural adjustment, with attention centred on replacing centralized forms of planning with market-oriented systems progressively integrated into global market structures.[19] While the nature of reform and its speed vary according to the resource and institutional bases of these countries and their perceived economic and social priorities, a number of aspects are of particular concern to female workers in their productive and their reproductive roles.

Almost every scenario for economic reform has been predicated on the need for radical change in the ownership of public enterprises[20] and most countries of the region have embarked on privatization programmes with varying degrees of success. The emerging private economy includes activities ranging from catering to commercial law and takes a variety of forms, from limited liability and joint stock companies to microenterprises and sole proprietorship.

Where privatization programmes are under way, as in the Czech Republic and Hungary, there is a correlation between the decline in the number of State enterprises and the increase in private entrepreneurs.[21] In addition, while a larger share of workers is still found in the State-owned enterprises, growth in the private sector is picking up speed.

Nevertheless, the ILO estimates that "job creation in the private sector has not been sufficient to compensate for large-scale job losses elsewhere".[22] While privatization could create opportunities for women in entrepreneurship and self-employment, as well as in the new business sector, data indicate that women are more reluctant than men to leave the safety of State employment for the private sector, until privatization forces them to do so. For example, in the Czech Republic about two thirds of private sector employment was male in 1991 and 1992. With their high levels of education and training there is no reason why women in the transition economies should not have equal access to the opportunities in the emerging private sector, especially in such areas as banking and insurance, where women's skills are of some relevance. Some reports suggest that managers' gender preferences for various occupations have influenced recruitment.[23]

The transition to the market and to private ownership runs parallel to a restructuring process based on a shift away from heavy industry and mining to a focus on light industry, with an emphasis on technology-based industries and consumer goods production.[24] This development should favour women's employment. A recent study in the Russian Federation confirms this pattern, noting that there were very small declines in the shares of female employment in the rapidly declining metal, chemical, engineering and wood products industries and that their shares in food processing, construction materials, and textiles and garments production had increased. However, the study warns of the possibility of eventual industrial segregation and suggests that unless the trend towards sectoral concentration is addressed, women will be "crowded into a narrow range of sectors which would lead to a decline in their relative wages and benefits".[25]

Recent survey data in Eastern and Central Europe indicate that transition-related restructuring resulted in employment shifts between industries for male and female workers and notes that the decline in employment in the goods-producing sector, particularly manufacturing, affected women more than men.[23] It was also noted that industrial establishments shed female administrative and clerical jobs ahead of male jobs on the production line because women's labour force participation could no longer be sustained in a climate that stressed profitability.[26] In addition, international competitive pressures have led some countries to substantial lay-offs in light industries, such as textiles and apparel, where women predominate.[6]

By and large, women are at a disadvantage in the context of transition. With the exception of Hungary, female unemployment rates have been higher than men's since 1990. As enterprises streamline their workforces (in both the State and private sector), women are the first to be laid off, and in greater numbers than can be explained by occupational segregation. In addition, once unemployed, women are likely to remain unemployed longer than men, in part because their income is thought to be less vital to the family budget.[6]

Reports also suggest that women have been losing jobs in favour of men even in some traditionally female branches.[27] Given high previous participation rates of women and their high levels of education and skills, there is no reason why men should take over women's jobs. And since family incomes were previously predicated on two-income families and included a range of free social services which must now be paid for, economic necessity will likely render women's earnings vital to family survival. It is widely believed that firms, driven by profit motives, are unwilling to maintain the social support services that once underwrote women's labour force participation, forcing women to drop out of the labour market as child-care costs rise.[28] This area needs immediate attention if women's equality in access to employment is to be sustained, and it has been suggested that existing protective legislation "needs to be revised and harmonized with the new market economy conditions" and that improved child-care facilities need to be put in place quickly.[23]

The process of economic and political reform provides a unique opportunity to improve the status of women in Eastern and Central Europe, bringing those countries closer to true gender equality. The process does not, however, appear to be gender-neutral, and emerging trends threaten to reverse past gains.

Although international attention is focused on the transition of the former centrally planned economies of Central and Eastern Europe and the new Commonwealth of Independent States, a quiet revolution towards socialist market economies is taking place in the centrally planned economies of the Asian region. Aimed at correcting strategic and tactical miscalculations of the past, the elements of this change include a loosening of centralized administrative controls; greater emphasis on agriculture, services and light industry; and greater efforts to integrate into the regional market to attract the foreign direct investment needed to fuel export production.[29] These developments are potentially important for women's employment within these countries.

*Developing economies*

The world recession profoundly affected the developing countries, particularly in Africa, Latin America and the Caribbean, and the Middle East. Asia as a whole proved more resilient, though here too individual countries, such as the Philippines, were adversely affected by external shocks and global developments.[30] Reduced demand for primary products, falling commodity prices, high and rising interest rates, the virtual disappearance after 1982 of private bank loans, and in the case of the Middle East, the collapse of the regional oil economy in the mid-1980s all contributed to the steady worsening of the balance of payments and the external debt burden,[31] which in developing countries almost doubled during 1983-1993.[32] For the most part, these countries have responded with stabilization and structural adjustment programmes designed to bring their economies in line with the new realities of the international marketplace, undertaken, more often than not, under the auspices of international financial institutions.

Stabilization and adjustment are inseparable elements of economic restructuring; macroeconomic stability is a prerequisite for structural adjustment at any level, whether the change is a reorientation in development strategy or a reform at the institutional level. Stabilization policy in the context of economic reform in developing countries involves a set of restrictive monetary and fiscal policies directed at restoring and maintaining the viability of the balance of payments in an environment of price stability and sustainable economic growth.

Most developing countries experienced structural adjustment in the 1980s. The World Bank made 59 structural adjustment loans between 1980 and 1988[33] for the purpose of "reducing economic distortions and financial imbalances, in the face of mounting domestic and external pressures" and promoting the resumption of "sustainable rates of economic growth consonant with relative price stability and a viable external sector position".[34]

The combined inflationary impact of devaluation, cuts in food subsidies and increased prices has been particularly severe in developing countries. Where the phasing and pace of structural adjustment and stabilization programmes were not handled well, reduced public expenditure and subsidies combined with deflationary financial stabilization efforts lowered personal incomes and increased poverty. Farmers, small producers and public and urban informal sector workers, a high proportion of whom are women, were among the hardest hit. The next section examines the impact of structural adjustment programmes, particularly in developing economies.

2.   *Structural adjustment and its impact on women*

Structural adjustment programmes typically involve the following:
- Fiscal policies aimed at reducing budgets and deficits.
- Budget policies directed at tax reform, reducing public spending, cutting social services programmes and eliminating subsidies.
- Public enterprise policies directed at restructuring, commercializing and divesting government enterprises.
- Exchange rate policies aimed at correcting exchange rate misalignments in the context of demand management policies.
- Liberalizing and deregulating the factors and goods markets and correcting relative prices to reflect opportunity costs, which in financial markets would entail ending "financial repression".[35]
- Agricultural reforms directed at increasing real producer prices for agricultural exporters and reducing the role of government in marketing food crops.
- Liberalizing trade.
- Policies aimed at increasing the role of the private sector and of foreign direct investment in economic development.

These policies are featured prominently in the conditionality attached to World Bank lending for structural adjustment and International Monetary Fund (IMF) stabilization agreements. By the end of fiscal 1989 the World Bank had concluded 143 structural adjustment loan agreements with 62 countries.

Although mainstream economists generally regard structural adjustment policies as necessary to lay the groundwork for steady economic growth, these policies are often criticized for failing to accomplish economic restructuring without adversely impacting long-term growth prospects and poverty and environmental sustainability concerns and for not taking account of the country-specific circumstances of economic reform.

Adjustment programmes have focused on government expenditures by restricting money supply and bank credit, cutting social services and economic infrastructure, removing or reducing subsidies, especially on food, and reducing real wages and public sector employment. The programmes also encourage more productive resource allocation, such as by directing funds to the internationally traded sector through devaluation, price and trade liberalization and incentives for foreign investment involving wage restraints and the reduction or elimination of labour welfare and protective measures. Privatization of State enterprises and the break-up of public and private monopolies have also been stressed.

While there is insufficient evidence on the gender impact of the adjustment policies of the 1980s, it is generally accepted that women's socio-economic position worsened, at least over the short run, because pre-existing inequalities prevented them from harnessing the positive aspects of adjustment and because of the negative elements of the process itself. The impact of structural adjustment policies on women's socio-economic position reflects the success of these policies in achieving growth, stabilization and structural change. In countries where the policies succeeded, women shared in the growing prosperity and their income status improved. However, women and men have different opportunities and face different constraints, the impact of "gender-neutral" policies is far from neutral, and women in restructuring societies tend to bear disproportionately the costs of economic restructuring.[36]

An examination of the impact of structural adjustment policies on women should consider the following:

Economics undergoing structural adjustment experience a decline in real income owing, among other things, to price liberalization and delayed wage indexation. Women are significantly affected by this decline because of their high concentration in the public sector and in the urban informal sector. In the short to medium run, women's material position might worsen both relatively and absolutely because women are more likely to lose their jobs in a time of economic instability and to have greater difficulty than men in finding alternative employment.[37]

As real wages decline women are drawn into the labour force because demand for labour might be rising in some sectors of the economy (particularly in the context of trade liberalization and real devaluation), but they are mainly driven to work by the need to augment household income.

Pressure to earn income distorts the multiple roles of women by expanding the productive role at the expense of the reproductive role.[38] Worse, the imbalance between productive and reproductive roles can lead younger females to be drawn into productive and repro-

ductive activity at the expense of school attendance, thereby perpetuating a vicious circle of inequality.[39]

Restructuring changes patterns of female employment. Economic restructuring precipitates labour shedding in the formal sector and a shift in female employment from the public sector to the private and informal sectors, and this often means that women have to take lower-paid jobs with little security and for which they are overqualified.[40]

Trade liberalization and policies directed at reducing export bias and promoting an export-oriented trade regime increase female paid employment, particularly in labour-intensive manufacturing where jobs are vulnerable to fluctuations in the world market and to protectionism in developed countries. This benefit, however, segments the labour market in terms of gender-related wage differentials, turning the existing comparative advantage into the comparative advantage of women's disadvantage.[41]

Structural adjustment, particularly in less developed dual economies, often leads to a redistribution of income between sexes as a result of expenditure-switch policies. As several sources suggest, women tend to be employed in the production of non-tradables and men in the production of cash crops. And where cash drops have the status of "women's crops", efforts are made to turn cash-crop production over to men.[42]

Structural adjustment policies may increase the unpaid work done by women and reduce the services available to them because they are often accompanied by cuts in public expenditures, subsidies and social services and the introduction of user charges.[43]

Policies geared towards a greater outward orientation in development often lead to technological changes. The impact of such changes on women varies according to the overall economic situation, the pattern of female employment, the nature of the new technologies and the divergence between prices for factors of production and their opportunity costs. New technologies in agriculture have often led to the displacement of women and loss of their social roles,[44] while product innovation technologies tend to increase income-generating opportunities for women. Technological advances in industry have created jobs for women and increased the proportion of women in the industrial labour force, but this effect is limited to developed economies and has varied from one region to another. The impact of technological change on the services sector is less clear; it has varied among regions, reflecting differences in productivity growth between services and other sectors, but the overall effect has probably been job creation.[45]

Since they focus on economic efficiency and "getting prices right", structural adjustment policies change qualitative aspects of female employment. As determined by market forces, working conditions and remuneration of female employment do not reflect adequately the dual role women play in society with respect to reproduction and the maintenance of human resources. A flexible labour market, which is desirable in the context of economic efficiency and the supply of paid employment to women, often leads to the creation of jobs with a low level of security, no prospects for upward mobility and no opportunities for acquiring marketable skills for future employment. These undesirable changes in the quality of female employment to some extent cancel out the positive impact of job creation associated with a flexible labour market and the liberalization policies of structural adjustment and can hardly be equated with female advancement.[46]

The overall impact of adjustment programmes on agricultural output, prices and incomes should be positive given the improved rural-urban terms of trade engendered by devaluation and price deregulation.[2] However, a number of factors mitigate the potentially favourable impact of these developments on vulnerable segments of society, such as people of fixed income, rural small-holders, farmers who produce less food than they consume and, particularly, women. The agricultural producers most likely to benefit from adjustment are the large and medium-sized farmers who control the supply of inputs and can offset their rising costs by decreasing wages for agricultural labour, where many women are found.[47]

Large numbers of impoverished rural households emerge with structural adjustment, especially where rising food costs constitute an added hardship—one that might worsen as the terms of the Uruguay Round on agriculture come into effect in food-importing countries. This is particularly the case in Asia, and to a lesser extent in Latin America, where a large share of villagers are landless and live by wage labour. In Africa, where small-holdings are common, rising agricultural prices and government encouragement of foreign investment in agriculture appears to be diverting land and other resources away from subsistence farming (where women predominate) to cash- and food-crop production for domestic and foreign markets (where men are in control). With women's contribution to this process limited mainly to the provision of unpaid family labour on small-holdings and unskilled, casual wage labour on plantations and in agribusinesses, the benefits derived in terms of increased household income must be weighed against the loss in food for domestic consumption and the reallocation of women's time and labour.

Where women are able to involve themselves in own-account and cash-crop production, the small scale of their activities and their limited access to credit and extension services rarely permit them to weather the lag between higher input prices and the output gains from the new price regimes. In addition, rural money-lenders form a solid barrier between government policy and actual incomes for both female and male small farmers, a situation worsened by the dismantling, under adjustment, of State-run marketing services.[47]

Analyses of the impact of structural adjustment programmes on women are riddled with conceptual, methodological and empirical problems. One of the most evident problems is the difficulty of separating long-term increases in female labour force participation from the short-term impact of structural adjustment and stabilization policies, which hit women harder than men.[2] Another problem is the shortage of comparable time-series and cross-sectional data disaggregated by sex. Despite a significant body of literature on the issue, the incorporation of analyses of the impact of structural adjustment on women into the mainstream literature on economic development and policy analysis has been slow.

The most common conclusion made in this literature is that adjustment policies worsen women's economic position and increase the burden of their unpaid work. There are several problems with this conclusion. It is not based on rigorous empirical work. And since women's socio-economic situation cannot be directly observed and no satisfactory methodology exists for its estimation, any unqualified statement about the impact of structural adjustment on women is misleading. It is more appropriate to emphasize women's inability to benefit from changes in the incentive structure under structural adjustment than the overall negative impact of adjustment policies. This inability stems from the rigidity of their socially ascribed roles and limited access to productive resources. Opportunities are limited for most women and often involve a trade-off between the number and quality of jobs being created.

Still, women should benefit from the emphasis on human investment that is being written into the third generation of structural adjustment packages. This will require a conscious effort on the part of national and international policy makers to write a gender dimension into all projects and programmes, as much at the implementation as at the formulation stage.

### 3. *Privatization and its impact on the economic position of women*

The privatization of State-owned enterprises hinges on the neoclassical hypothesis that private ownership increases efficiency and growth. The economic restructuring of the 1980s saw both developing and developed economies pursuing privatization, though for different reasons. In developing economies and transition economies privatization was viewed not only as a way to increase growth and efficiency, strengthen entrepreneurial spirit and promote individual initiative, but also as a solution to internal and external public indebtedness.

Privatization impacts the economic status of women in many complex ways. In many developing countries and in the economies in transition the public sector is the major employer of women. As noted, wage and employment conditions for women are better in public enterprises and the gender-related wage gap between public sector employees is narrower than in the private sector.[46] Unlike women in the private sector, public sector female employees enjoy fringe benefits and access to social security. Therefore female wages in economies undergoing large-scale privatization decrease in both relative and absolute terms, widening the gender gap.

Consequently, large-scale privatization affects women disproportionately in comparison to men. Redundancy adjustment affect women more because women tend to be employed in marginal, less secure positions. Male redundancy may also have negative implications for female employment in the private and informal sectors, because redundant males might pose a threat in terms of better-equipped competition.

Privatization benefits women if it strengthens opportunities or encourages productivity in the small-scale and informal sector. In Africa, where men predominate in government-controlled enterprises, privatization has opened opportunities for women in sectors that were once dominated by men. For example, maize marketing in Zaire was predominantly male under government control, but female employment in this sector has grown rapidly since privatization.[48]

When privatization is undertaken in the context of stabilization and structural adjustment policies, as occurred in the former planned economies, the likelihood of increased female unemployment is greater, at least in the short term.[49] In many countries where privatization is under way women are resorting to "informal survival responses" by engaging in low-income activities, such as knitting and sewing at home, petty trade, domestic food production and the operation of small-scale enterprises.[46] Such activities can be extremely precarious and represent little more than disguised unemployment, or they can offer a viable interim solution to the problem of female unemployment, depending to some extent on sectoral policies but primarily on overall macroeconomic and industrial policies.

The impact of privatization on women's position in the economy varies among regions. Privatization generally increases women's chances of being laid off, lowering their incomes and worsening their employment conditions. The rate of decline in employment in sectors undergoing privatization and commercialization is higher than the rate of increase in employment opportunities in the fledgling private sector. Since women have a larger share of jobs in establishments that are destined to undergo restructuring and privatization, a rapid and disproportional increase in female unemployment is likely. Still, the extent and duration of female unemployment depends on the overall context of restructuring and the degree of labour market flexibility. In East Asia, where these conditions were favourable, female labour was drawn into industrial production on a massive scale. In Russian and other economies in transition, where economic and political instability is high, the gender wage gap is narrow compared with the developing economies. Since female labour is expensive because of a strong tradition of additional benefits for working mothers, female unemployment is expected to persist for some time.[50]

### 4. *Deregulation of markets*

The world-wide increase in female employment, particularly in economies pursuing an outward-oriented development strategy, occurred in an environment of labour-market deregulation. Deregulation was an outcome of the change of emphasis in the dominant development model from the regulatory and distributive roles of government to the supremacy of markets and efficient resource allocation. This new model relies on principles of efficiency and views market regulation as potentially distortive and government interventions mainly in terms of their "crowding out" effects.[51] Countries were advised by the institutions involved in the analysis and formulation of international economic policies and development strategies that if they would let the market make economic decisions and open their economies to outward orientation and export promotion, the quality of life of their people would improve dramatically.[52]

The success of the East Asian newly industrialized countries is an example of a development strategy that leads to growth while satisfying the objectives of greater equity and poverty alleviation. The logic of outward-orientation dictates flexible wages. To ensure wage flexibility, Governments eliminated distortion in the labour market; that is, they abolished the minimum wage and regulations governing employment and labour practices. Economies worldwide started dismantling import-substitution policies and engaged in market deregulation.[53] This led to dramatic increases in female participation in economic activity. As low-wage jobs spread, female employment in them increased.[46] Some analyses regard this development as evidence that women benefit greatly, even disproportionately, from development based on an export-promoting trade strategy.[54] But examples of the strong positive impact of an export-oriented development strategy on women's participation in the modern economy and on their welfare are confined almost entirely to East Asia and, to a lesser extent, to countries in South-East Asia.

The impact of outward-oriented development strategies is most visible in countries that started pursuing an export orientation in the mid-1960s and early 1970s. Latin American countries followed suit much later and missed the opportunities offered by the unprecedented expansion of trade in the 1970s. The impact of trade liberalization on female employment is much less visible in Latin America because of the inevitable time lags in the process of resource reallocation and the persistence of capital-intensive structures that were built into the economy by import-substitution policies. The experience of East Asia, however, strongly indicates that export-led growth is good for women's incomes and employment.

But there is also evidence of worsening employment conditions for women and of the fact that rising industrial employment of women was based on the systematic violation of their right to receive equal pay for equal work.[55] Data on female wages indicate that the average female wage as a percentage of that of men has fallen in non-agriculture production, particularly in the regions that experienced export-led growth and deregulation of labour markets.

Furthermore, some data suggest that while women might have benefited in terms of job creation, these benefits were confined to a few countries and were achieved in a context of rising inequality and a widening wage gap between the genders.[56] The fact that paid jobs available to women increased following deregulation reflected pre-existing gender inequalities rather than an increase in demand for factors of production.

The "flexibilization"[46] of the labour market that accompanied the shift in development strategy further widened the wage gap. The deterioration in the quality of employment that accompanied its quantitative increase makes the latter an inadequate indicator of improvement in the economic and social status of women. Deregulation of the labour market, while increasing the participation of women in the labour force, left the market almost entirely in charge of determining the price of female labour and the conditions of female employment. That being the case, it is appropriate to ask whether the market can provide solutions that are both efficient and equitable and that adequately reflect the social value of the female role in reproduction and child-rearing.

The failure of the market to reflect this value makes a case for government intervention, though in a manner causing the least possible distortion and bearing in mind that Governments fail even more often than markets. It may be that the market cannot both secure the benefits to society associated with the reproductive role of women and achieve a more efficient utilization of resources and greater equity. It is thus not the extent of government involvement and market regulation that should be addressed through economic restructuring, but rather the nature of the policies that are used to that end.

## B.  GLOBAL DIMENSIONS OF ECONOMIC RESTRUCTURING AND ITS IMPACT ON WOMEN

Parallel to restructuring within national markets, the international economic environment has undergone profound changes. Restructuring at the national level was often undertaken in response to changes in international markets, thereby impacting the evolution of those markets. Global restructuring is thus best viewed in the context of the interdependent and mutually reinforcing processes of domestic economic restructuring and the restructuring of the international economic environment. Changes in the international economic environment continue to be determined by trends that have been at work for more than 40 years. These trends include changes in the dimension and composition of world trade, the proliferation of transnational corporations and changes in the magnitude of international financial flows.

### 1.  *Changes in the dimension and composition of world trade*

The relationship between growth of international trade and rising female participation in productive employment hinges on the employment-creating potential of trade. Trade also influences national economic development as it relates to bringing domestic resource allocation in line with the comparative advantage.

Developing countries that opened their economies to international trade experienced a dramatic rise in the number of women participating in industrial employment. There are at least three reasons why this happened. First, production for the external market increased demand for labour. Second, female labour was competitive in terms of its cost. Third, there has been a significant expansion and change in the composition of trade flows. The impact of trade on women's productive employment should be viewed against the backdrop of these developments.

The globalization of markets for goods and services increased in the 1980s. The average growth of world trade has exceeded that of world output for some time, and this trend continued in the early 1990s, confirming that trade is an engine of growth.[57]

The shifting composition of trade continued, and manufactures assumed a larger share of the composition of world exports. During the 1960s exports of manufactures by developing countries grew nearly twice as fast as the incomes of developed countries.[58] In 1980 manufactures constituted 54.2 per cent of the value of world exports and by 1990 their share had reached 71.1 per cent. The composition of developing country exports followed the same trend. The share of manufactures in developing country exports grew from 24.5 per cent in 1970 to 61.5 per cent in 1980, and to 72.4 per cent in 1990. Exports of manufactures by developing countries grew by an average of 12.8 per cent during 1987-1991, while total exports from developing countries grew by 7.7 per cent. For almost three decades trade in manufactures consistently grew faster than total trade and growth of national output, and there is no reason to doubt that this trend will continue.

*Figure 1*

Growth rates of world output and trade, 1953-1993

Percentage

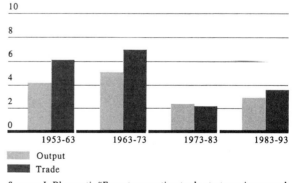

*Source*: J. Bhagwati, "Export-promoting trade strategy: issues and evidence", *Research Observer*, vol. 3, No. 1 (1988).

*Figure 2*
Composition of exports, 1980 and 1990

World 1980

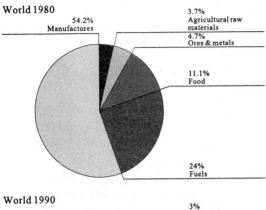

World 1990

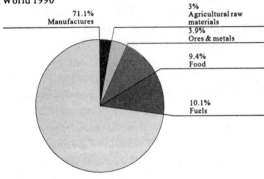

Developing countries 1980

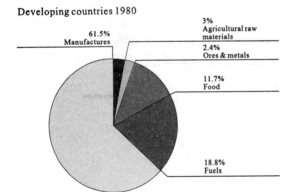

Developing countries 1990

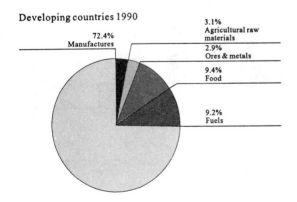

*Figure 3*
Average growth rates of total exports and manufactures, 1970-1990

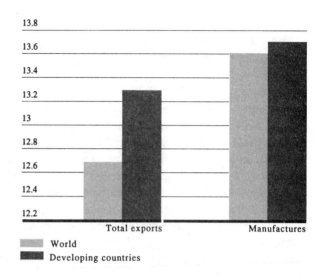

Consequently, trade flows between developed and developing countries extended beyond primary products—a development of great significance for female employment. Economic growth and export expansion are closely correlated with increases in the economically active female population. Countries where the number of female workers increased consistently between 1970 and 1990 are also those where manufactured exports grew rapidly.

However, the overall encouraging picture of world trade and its implications for female employment is somewhat less encouraging when regional differences are taken into account. Exports from a small number of developing countries accounted for most of the total expansion. In the 1987-1991 period two thirds of the growth in total exports from developing countries was due to manufactures, but eight Asian exporters (Hong Kong, Indonesia, Malaysia, Philippines, Republic of Korea, Singapore, Taiwan Province of China and Thailand) accounted for almost 80 per cent of that increase. This is also the region where expansion of the female share in the labour force was the greatest. Exports of manufactures from Latin American and Caribbean countries declined as a share of total exports of developing countries, and those of Africa increased by only 0.1 per cent in 1987-1991, with the share of manufactures in their total exports remaining low.[59] Between 1980 and 1990, the ratio of economically active female popu-

*Figure 4*
Average growth rates in GDP by region, 1970 and 1980

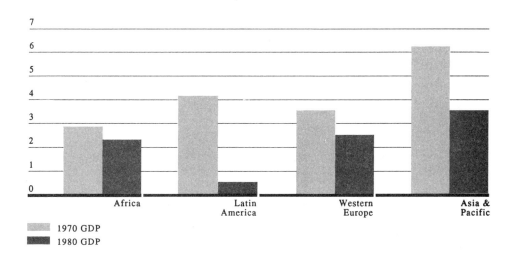

1970 GDP
1980 GDP

*Figure 5*
Average growth rates in exports by region, 1970 and 1980

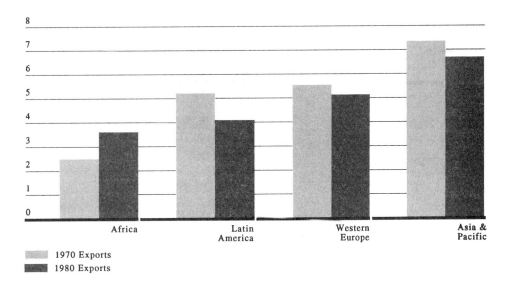

1970 Exports
1980 Exports

*Figure 6*
Ratio of the economically active female to male population, 1970, 1980 and 1990

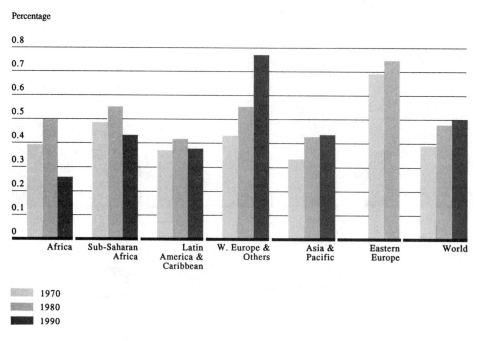

Percentage

1970
1980
1990

*Figure 7*
Changes in the ratio of the economically active female population, 1970-1980 and 1980-1990

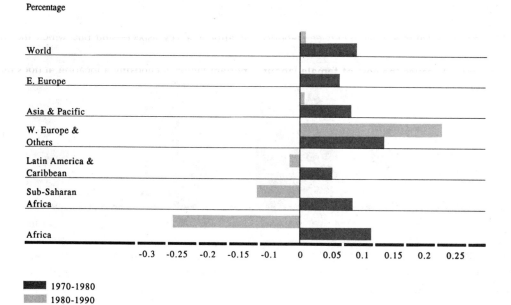

Percentage

1970-1980
1980-1990

lation declined in Latin American and African countries, where most of the decline appears to be accounted for by sub-Saharan African countries.

The growth in female industrial employment is correlated with the growth of manufactured exports from developing countries. The increase was first observed in the newly industrialized countries or areas— Hong Kong, Singapore, Taiwan Province of China and the Republic of Korea—in the 1970s, and then in Indonesia, Malaysia and Thailand, when these countries opened their economies to international trade and assumed a greater outward orientation in their economic strategies. The increase in female industrial employment can be explained in terms of relatively high price and income elasticities in the demand for manufactured exports and the sufficiently high absorptive capacity of international markets.[60] The shift towards manufactured exports allowed developing countries to free demand for their exports from the constraint of the level of expenditure in the markets of developed countries and to engage in price competition. This shift created an incentive for industrial firms to minimize their labour costs by increasing productivity or lowering wages. This increased demand for cheap female labour and increased the employment of women in manufacturing.

However, these increased shares of female labour in export-oriented industries occurred in economies with a comparative advantage in labour-intensive production. There is a causal relationship between labour-intensive exports expansion and female employment in such economies because the cost of female labour in labour-surplus developing countries is lower than the cost of male labour.[61] A reversal of this pattern may emerge in the developed economies, since the lowest level of service sector jobs are either being eliminated by technology or transferred to developing country locations. As this trend intensifies it may foster a situation in which "the unskilled worker in the developed countries ... is most vulnerable to the expansion of international trade".[62] But such a development might also present an opportunity for women in the advanced economies to upgrade their skills in ways that permit them to access the middle and higher levels of service sector activities, which are expected to boom.

The predicted negative effect of trade expansion and competition from developing countries on women's

employment in the advanced economies has not yet occurred, at least so far as aggregate employment is concerned.[61] A strong and sustained upward trend in women's employment, particularly in the non-tradable service sector, is thought to be largely responsible for this development.

Recent evidence suggests that countries pursuing an export-promotion development strategy were able to maintain their share of manufactured exports in the world market despite labour-market tightening and rising labour costs.[59] As a result of outward-oriented policies, these economies achieved macroeconomic stability and acquired enough flexibility to move swiftly into the production of more processed, complex and sophisticated products. Technological upgrading of manufactured exports in Asia and Latin America has enabled exporters from these regions to maintain their share in export markets but does not seem to be instrumental in maintaining or expanding the share of female employment in export-oriented industries. Gains in women's employment in those industries may not be sustained in the coming decade.[63]

There is also evidence of a growing concentration among developed and newly industrializing economies of flows and stocks of foreign direct investment to the detriment of much of the world's labour-surplus, low-cost locations.[62] The new determinants of comparative advantage may lie not simply in low-cost labour but in a variety of created assets, of which labour-force quality is a key aspect—and one which the State can shape. While this does not mean that cost is not an important factor in choosing a location, it does mean that the quality of the labour force will be accorded greater importance.

Since women in developing countries generally receive less education or training than their counterparts in the developed world, women in developing countries are likely to benefit less from export-oriented production than they have in the past. It is doubtful that trade expansion lays the groundwork for any long-term benefits for women in developing countries in terms of their placement in the labour market and improved access to employment. As countries become more developed they move away from reliance on unskilled, labour-intensive manufacturing, and unless women's skills acquisition keeps pace with the country's industrial and technological development, women's employment opportunities will diminish with growth.[61]

The two-way relationship between trade and women's economic activity is determined by such factors as magnitude, structure, factor intensity and direction of trade flows. The observed correlation between expansion of trade and female employment was in the context of labour-intensive manufactures. This expansion should not be expected to persist unless a significant upgrading of female labour skills takes place.

### 2.  *The proliferation of transnational corporations*

The increasing role of transnational corporations is also influencing female employment. The number of transnational corporations in the 14 major developed countries has more than tripled in the past 25 years. In the early 1990s there were some 37,000 parent transnational corporations with 170,000 foreign affiliates under their control.[64]

Transnational corporations are at the centre of global expansion, accounting for a significant volume of investment and value-added activities worldwide. These companies play an important role in employment creation by generating employment opportunities in their own operations, by stimulating employment in related enterprises, and by their catalytic effects on host-country enterprises. The direct employment of transnational corporations is estimated at over 73 million jobs, and their indirect impact, generated through links with subcontractors, suppliers and others, in both home and host countries, is thought to account for one to two indirect jobs for each direct one. Thus the total number of jobs associated with transnational corporations at the beginning of the 1990s was conservatively estimated at 150 million jobs.[65]

However, little is known about the number of jobs accounted for by female workers outside of the export processing zones (EPZs). Subcontracting in internationally traded manufacturing and services may provide entrepreneurial opportunities for women, should they be able to acquire the requisite business and marketing skills. In addition, the recent growth of the international trade-service sector offers women, particularly in the developing countries, greater employment opportunities. There has been a dramatic increase in female employment in foreign banks in India and in telecommunications in Malaysia.[66] In some of the major service-exporting developing countries such as Singapore and the Republic of Korea the intensity of female employ-

ment has increased faster in the non-manufacturing than in the manufacturing sector.[67]

Women's economic activity may be enhanced in the future by subcontracting and the growth of an intermediate sector.[68] Transnational corporations could encourage greater participation of women in high-level organizational positions by sending more of their female managerial staff abroad. A survey of 686 North American firms revealed that only 3 per cent of the 13,338 managers sent to Asia were female, and while foreign prejudice was cited as the reason such behaviour merely reinforces reservations against women in managerial positions in developing countries.[69]

The proliferation of operations by transnational corporations in developing countries was fuelled by advances in telecommunications, transportation and technology that permitted the separation of production sites and created production savings by locating labour-intensive processes in developing countries. EPZs, which were established by many Governments to promote non-traditional exports, offered transnational corporations duty-free passage for exports and imports. The combination of cheap labour and tax advantages was a lucrative incentive for transnational corporations to locate their operations in the EPZs of developing countries. Those corporations systematically preferred female labour despite the availability of cheap male labour.[70] In addition to the wage differential, women workers are regarded as more obedient, more cooperative, more diligent and easier to manage than men.[71]

For many developing countries EPZs and other special economic zones and production platforms are the most significant form of foreign direct investment in terms of jobs created. A recent report on transnational corporations and employment estimated that there are nearly 200 EPZs in some 60 developing countries, providing about 4 million direct jobs.[65] These jobs are based mainly in traditional labour-intensive manufacturing (such as textiles, clothing and electronic appliances) but also are increasingly located in such service sector activities as off-shore data-processing and office administration. As many as 250 of the Fortune 1,000 companies may be using such off-shore employment for office administration. Barbados, China, Jamaica, the Philippines and Singapore have emerged as popular locations for such "back-office" jobs.[69]

Most data-processing and keyboarding jobs in EPZs are held by women. While the jobs are important sources of income, they are isolated from the mainstream organization and carry few opportunities for advancement. This is also true of jobs in manufacturing. While the gender composition of employees in EPZ firms varies according to output, some estimates suggest that women comprise, on average, about 70 per cent of the workforce in any given enterprise. As noted, the gender composition of the workforce changes as products demand more technology and skills—to the detriment of women. For example, in the Mexican *maquiladoras* (companies established by foreign firms to process exports), the population of women workers fell from 77 per cent of the workforce in 1982 to 60 per cent in 1990. [61]

While the direct employment contribution of EPZs is large and growing rapidly, the quality and stability of employment and skills development has been less praiseworthy. In most zones transnational corporations have been observed to adopt casual labour strategies and to hire an exceptionally high share of young unskilled and semi-skilled women.[69] While these firms generally offer wages and working conditions that compare favourably with similar jobs in the domestic sector—and with the jobs that would be otherwise available to the women working in the zones—they provide little opportunity for training and skill development, and none in terms of career development. This is as true of the new service sector jobs as it is of the manufacturing jobs traditionally associated with the zones.

Two problems associated with female employment in the zones deserve emphasis. The first is the changing gender composition of the workforce with changing products and technological advancement. The second is the movement of investment away from "mature" zones as wages and working conditions improve, restrictions on union activities become less severe and capital-intensive production replaces labour-intensive activities. This movement is all the more alarming since its implications go beyond female employment to impact the national economy as a whole.

Zones already affected by such declines in foreign direct investment and employment include those in Mauritius, the Philippines and Taiwan Province of China. This development raises a serious policy issue as to whether these zones should now be phased out and the labour force absorbed elsewhere, or whether it is possible to convert them into high-technology industrial estates financed by domestic investment. In either event female workers in these zones are unlikely to benefit.

As this pattern is likely to repeat itself in the 1990s, countries can maintain their levels of growth of foreign direct investment and related employment only by investing in education and skill enhancement and encouraging transnational corporations to invest in more technology-intensive processes and products.[65] While such a strategy has been pursued successfully, as in the newly industrialized countries of Asia, its success in other developing regions requires a workforce with education and skills that many developing countries do not yet possess.

The formal links between enterprises in the EPZs and their networks of subcontractors and ancillary firms are a potential growth area for female entrepreneurs.[66] But little attention has been given to the impact the zones have on the societies and economies that surround them. The zones have the potential to create ancillary activities (such as petty trading, catering and other small-scale commercial activities) that create opportunities not for the enterprises, but for the women (and men) who work in them.

### 3.   *Changes in international financial flows*

International financial flows in the past decade were characterized by a larger volume of transactions, the growing interdependence and volatility of financial markets and the increased influence of the markets on national and international economic policies. The best example of the influence of international markets is the debt crisis. The crisis started when OPEC increased oil prices in 1974 and began "recycling" petrodollars, leading to a surge of indiscriminate lending by commercial banks to the developing countries. These developments changed the debt structure of these countries from being mostly concessional to being mostly commercial.

The consequences of the second oil shock were complicated in the early 1980s by steep interest rate increases, a drop of more than 20 per cent in primary commodity export prices and a slow-down of economic growth in the developed economies. Developing economies that had been growing buoyantly in the 1970s suddenly found themselves with depleted foreign reserves and serious balance-of-payment and foreign-debt problems. The 1980s, the decade following the onset of the debt crisis, is known as the "lost decade" in terms of the development aspirations and economic progress of many developing countries. Economic restructuring and adjustment resulted in unemployment, economic stagnation and lower per capita incomes. The crisis reversed capital flows, with capital flowing in the 1980s from the "deficit" to the "surplus" countries. In 1983 the net transfer of financial resources to developing countries became negative. Between 1987 and 1989 the transfer averaged $18 billion. Between 1990 and 1992 it became positive and averaged $43 billion. Adjustment was less successful in Africa; it was the only region that had a negative transfer of financial resources in 1992. Improvement was most notable in Latin America, where net capital inflows have increased significantly since 1990, totalling $27 billion in 1992.[72]

The outlook for developing countries is relatively bright. The revival of capital flows offers prospects for increased investment and higher growth. Countries that successfully restructured their economies in the 1980s today attract more foreign capital than ever before. The composition of the capital flowing into the developing countries has changed, and this change will help reduce the vulnerability of borrowers to sudden changes in the international economic environment. The capital flowing into developing economies and transition economies has a larger share of foreign direct investment and portfolio-financing and a smaller share of commercial bank loans than it had in the 1980s.[73]

The hope is that the increased financial flows will reinforce market reforms and that reforms will encourage the continued inflow of foreign savings, thus creating a "virtuous circle", reviving growth and security a higher standard of living. Whether this hope will materialize and whether the process will improve the economic status of women remains to be seen.

As noted, women suffer disproportionately from economic crises and the short-term constraints created by stabilization and adjustment policies. Women are more directly affected than men as labour-force participants because, for example, they are more likely to lose their employment when the economy goes into recession.[74] Women are also more likely to be affected by distribution of income within the household because consumption by women and girls tends to be reduced by more than that of men when household income declines. In Peru, for example, a decline of capital inflow and the burden of debt repayments coupled with the lack of adjustment effort made poverty worse and aggravated consumption inequalities that affected women to a greater extent.[75]

The destitution of women resulting from economic crises and the short- to medium-term effects of adjustment and stabilization policies can have far-reaching implications for the economy as a whole. This is particularly true in economies where there is a high incidence of households headed by women.[76] It is also true at the global level, given that 35 per cent of households worldwide are headed by women.[77]

## C.  A STATISTICAL ANALYSIS OF GENDER'S INFLUENCE ON ECONOMIC GROWTH

The advancement of women depends on economic growth and sound economic policies. But experience shows that policies directed towards growth resumption and stabilization are not gender-neutral. A time-series bivariate regression analysis of data for 61 countries grouped by region for the 1980-1990 period shows that there is a significant relationship between economic growth and women's participation in the labour force. The analysis also indicates that these benefits vary in relation to the level of economic development and the nature of economic growth.[78]

The largest increase in the ratio of economically active women to men was found for East and South-East Asia, where a 1 per cent growth in GDP is associated with a 0.050 per cent increase in the ratio. In other words, more women than men in that region benefited from the jobs produced by economic growth. In Africa and Latin America and the Caribbean the coefficients of the independent variable (growth rate of GDP in the 1980s) were 0.002 and 0.004, respectively. In Western Europe and North America the relationship between GDP growth and change in the ratio of economically active women to men was negative, suggesting that more men than women are gaining from the jobs produced by economic growth. A negative relationship between these two variables was also found for Western Asia, where a 1 per cent increase in GDP was associated with a 0.006 per cent decline in the ratio. This decline suggests that economic growth is led by sectors where women's labour is not competitive with that of men or that women's labour is restricted by socio-cultural factors. It thus appears that the relationship between economic growth and women's ability to benefit from it varies with the level of economic development.

As an economy grows and the labour market tightens, skills assume a greater role than price in terms of the gender-related allocation of employment. Unless women are able to upgrade their skills and keep pace with technological change, the opportunities for them to benefit from economic growth will disappear. These findings are supported by an analysis of sources of economic growth for 46 developing countries. The analysis showed that the importance of growth sources changes with the level of economic development. In more advanced economies capital formation becomes a primary source of economic expansion and the importance of labour and exports growth declines. This implies a growth in capital-intensive production and a decline in employment opportunities for unskilled labour. Thus development erodes a comparative advantage based on cheap labour and, by implication, based on female labour. Women's ability to benefit from economic growth will disappear unless they catch up with men in terms of skills and access to productive resources.

The results of this analysis are in keeping with similar studies of this issue.[79] A cross-country and time-series analysis of data for 78 countries shows that a 1 per cent rise in GNP is associated with a 0.154 per cent increase in female employment and a 0.147 per cent increase in male employment, implying that women have better access to the jobs that result from economic growth. When the share of exports in GNP was used as an explanatory variable of the increase in female non-agricultural employment the results showed that a 1 per cent increase in the share of exports is associated with a 0.2 per cent increase in female non-agricultural employment. A 1 per cent increase in the annual growth of GNP was associated with a 1.96 per cent increase in female non-agricultural employment.[80]

Non-agricultural employment has been a dynamic area of female employment growth. In the Asian economies it increased from 60 per cent to 66 per cent of total female employment in the 1980-1990 period. Most analyses of export-led growth and its impact on female employment suggest two explanations for the phenomenon. First, rapid growth increased demand for factors of production and mobilized female labour, which had been underutilized. Second, women were employed in the production of goods that had a higher degree of comparative advantage—that is, the bulk of the goods exported by outward-oriented economies was produced by women. This second explanation makes it possible to describe the growth of East Asian countries in the 1970s as having been female-led.

## D. CONCLUSION

Economic restructuring assumed global proportions in the past decade. Counties had to adjust to internal changes in their economies and to external changes in the economic environment. Restructuring policy emphasized efficiency, outward orientation, getting prices right and the role of markets in resource allocation. The move towards greater economic freedom was accompanied by the spread of democracy and broadened civil and political freedoms. Global competition intensified, and the complexity, interdependence and vulnerability of world economy increased.

Economic restructuring affected women everywhere, often to a greater extent than men. Countries that were able to stabilize their economies and achieve greater outward openness in their development efforts also experienced significant improvement in employment prospects for women. But the link between outward openness and the increase in jobs for women is based on a segment of the labour market that pays a low wage. As export promotion policies lowered the average wage in manufacturing and removed factor-price distortions, women were able to gain more jobs than men while losing in terms of equal pay and quality of employment. Women's economic position did not improve relative to men and probably deteriorated.

The success of the export-promotion development strategy in improving female labour force participation nevertheless creates a dilemma for policy makers. Export-promotion policies imply deregulation of the labour market to ensure wage flexibility. When the market is left to determine the optimal wage, the social value of the female reproductive role is not adequately accounted for. This market failure may necessitate policy intervention. But government failure to choose proper blend of pro-market regulatory policies could price female labour out of the labour market.

It is clear that economic policies and development strategies are not gender-neutral. Women bear dispro-portionately the costs of restructuring and its failure. Conversely, women benefit to a greater extent from economic growth. Although economic growth is not a sufficient condition for women's advancement, it is surely a necessary one.

## NOTES

[1] This chapter was prepared by the Division for the Advancement of Women of the United Nations Secretariat and incorporates contributions from the International Labour Organization (ILO).

[2] S. Baden, "The impact of recession and structural adjustment on women's work in developing and developed countries", Working Paper No. 19, Interdepartmental Project on Equality for Women in Employment (Geneva, International Labour Office, 1993).

[3] S. Washington, "Equal-employment opportunities in the public sector", *OECD Observer*, No. 186 (1994).

[4] J. Atkinson, "Flexibility or fragmentation? The United Kingdom labour market in the eighties" and R. Boyer, "Labour flexibilities: many forms, uncertain effects", *Labour and Society*, vol. 12, No. 1 (1987); and Baden, op. cit.

[5] J. Rubery, ed., *Women and Recession* (London, Routledge and Kegan Paul, 1988) and G. Standing, "Global feminization through flexible labour", *World Development*, vol. 17, No. 7 (1989).

[6] *World Labour Report, 1993*, (Geneva, International Labour Office, 1993).

[7] *World Labour Report, 1994*, (Geneva, International Labour Office, 1994).

[8] S. Washington, "Women at work", *OECD Observer*, No. 176 (1992).

[9] Rubery, op. cit.

[10] Atkinson, loc. cit.

[11] W. Sengenberger, "Industrial restructuring in Europe", *Labour and Society*, vol. 14, No. 2 (1989).

[12] F. Pyke, G. Becattini and W. Sengenberger, *Industrial Districts and Inter-firm Cooperation in Italy* (Geneva, International Labour Office, 1990).

[13] J. Tate, "Unions and homeworkers: organizing homeworkers in the informal sector in Australia, the Netherlands and Canada", Working Paper No. 7, Interdepartmental Project on Equality for Women in Employment (Geneva, International Labour Office, 1993).

[14] International Labour Organization, "Recent developments affecting salaried employees and professional workers" (Report for the tenth session of the Committee on Salaried Employees and Professional Workers, Geneva, 1993).

[15] F. Core, "Women and the restructuring of employment", *OECD Observer*, No. 186, (1994).

[16] G. Drilhon and M-F Estime, "Technology watch and the small firm", *OECD Observer*, No. 182, (1993).

[17] United Nations Children's Fund, "Public policy and social conditions", Regional Monitoring Report No. 1 (Florence, Italy, 1993).

[18] V. Moghadam, *Privatization and Democratization in Central and Eastern Europe and the Soviet Union: The Gender Dimension* (Helsinki, United Nations University/World Institute for Development Economics Research (UNU/WIDER), 1992).

[19] *The Impact of Economic and Political Reform on the Status of Women in Eastern Europe* (United Nations publication, Sales No. E.92.IV.4).

[20] J. Musil, "New social contracts: responses of the State and the social partners to the challenges of restructuring and privatization", *Labour and Society*, vol. 16, No. 4 (1991).

[21] L. Paukert, "Public sector adjustment through employment: retrenchment policies in the Czech and Slovak Republics" (Geneva, International Labour Office, 1994).

[22] *World Labour Report, 1994* (Geneva, International Labour Office, 1994), p. 16.

[23] L. Paukert, "Women's employment in East-Central European countries during the period of transition to a market economy system", Working Paper (Geneva, International Labour Office, 1993).

[24] B. Einhorn, "The impact of the transition from centrally planned economies on women's employment in East Central Europe", BRIDGE Paper (Brighton, England, Institute for Development Studies, 1993).

[25] G. Standing, *Labour Market Dynamics in Russian Industry in 1993* (Budpest, International Labour Office-CEET, 1994).

[26] B. Einhorn and S. Mitter, "A comparative analysis of women's industrial participation during the transition from centrally planned to market economies in East-Central Europe", in *The Impact of Economic and Political Reform on the Status of Women in Eastern Europe* (United Nations publication, Sales No. E.92.IV.4).

[27] V. Moghadam, *Gender and the Development Process in a Changing Global Environment* (Helsinki, UNU/WIDER, 1993).

[28] Z. Ferge, "Marginalization, poverty and social institutions", *Labour and Society*, vol. 16, No. 4 (1991).

[29] V. Mikheev, "The social consequences of economic reforms in the non-European planned economies" *Labour and Society*, vol. 15, No. 3 (1990).

[30] G. Andrea Cornia and others, *Adjustment with a Human Face* (Oxford, Clarendon Press, 1989).

[31] D. Ghai (ed.), *The IMF and the South: The Social Impact of Crisis and Adjustment* (Geneva, United Nations Research Institute for Social Development, 1991) and V. Moghadam, *Gender and the Development Process in a Changing Global Environment ...*

[32] The external debt of developing countries grew by 97.3 per cent, from $897 billion to $1,770 billion during the 1970-1992 period. See World Bank, *World Debt Tables, 1993-94* (Washington, D.C., 1993) and M. Todaro *Economic Development in the Third World* (London, Longman, 1989).

[33] F. Nixon, "The third world and the global economy: recent trends and future prospects", *Development Economics: An Annual Review*, vol. 6 (1990).

[34] *Finance and Development*, September 1989, p. 30.

[35] For a classic account of "financial repression", see R. McKinnon, *Money and Capital in Economic Development* (Washington, D.C., The Brookings Institution, 1973) and E. Shaw, *Finan-*

cial Deepening in Economic Development (New York and Oxford, Oxford University Press, 1973).

[36]D. Elson, "How is structural adjustment affecting women?", Development, January 1989.

[37]Uma Lele, "Women and structural transformation", Economic Development and Cultural Change, vol. 34, No. 2 (1986) and I. Blumsma, "Budushchee russkih zhenshin: tolko dom i semya?" Sosialno-politicheskiy zhurnal, No. 4 (1993).

[38]Caroline Moser, "The impact of recession and structural adjustment on women: Ecuador", Development, January 1989.

[39]In Jamaica, for example, one quarter of all primary school students were absent from school. See "UK aid groups urge World Bank and IMF reforms", IPS Daily Journal, vol. 2, No. 120.

[40]E. Gruzdeva and others, "Zhenshiny na renke truda", Nauki i sovremennost, No. 3 (1992).

[41]Jakarta Declaration for the Advancement of Women in Asia and the Pacific.

[42]Barbara Rogers, The Domestication of Women (London and New York, Tavistock Publications, 1986).

[43]In Zimbabwe, for example, government health spending fell by one third during the first three years of structural adjustment. The number of women dying in childbirth in the capital, Harare, more than doubled in the two years after adjustment, from 101 in 1989 to 242 in 1991. See IPS Daily Journal, vol. 2, No. 120.

[44]S. Joekes, Women in the World Economy (Oxford and New York, Oxford University Press, 1990). For a discussion of the loss of the "triple custodial" role by women in Africa and their functional marginalization, see A. Mazrui, "The economic role of women in Africa", Finance and Development, vol. 29, No. 3 (1992).

[45]Joekes, op. cit.

46G. Standing, "Global feminization through flexible labour", World Development, vol. 17, No. 7 (1989).

[47]Ghai, op. cit.

48"Women in development: issues for economic and sectoral analysis" (Washington, D.C., World Bank, 1989).

[49]E. Gruzdeva and others, "Zhenshiny na rynke truda", Obshestvenyie nauki soveremennost, March 1993.

[50]V. Moghadam, Gender and Restructuring: A Comparative Analysis of Third World Industrializing Countries and the Former State Socialist Societies (A Modified World-System Perspective) (Helsinki, UNU/WIDER, 1991).

[51]"Crowding out" takes place when an increase in government expenditure leads to an interest rate rise and consequently to a smaller increase in output than might otherwise have occurred in overall income and output. The reduction in private sector expenditure is said to be "crowded out" by government expenditure.

[52]World Bank, World Development Report, 1987 (Oxford and New York, Oxford University Press, 1987).

[53]Economies that actively pursued export promotion in the 1980s and established large export-processing zones were the Dominican Republic, El Salvador, Honduras, Hong Kong, Malaysia, Mexico, the Philippines, Puerto Rico, the Republic of Korea, Singapore, Sri Lanka and Thailand.

[54]Frances Perkins, "Are women benefiting from economic development?", IPA Review , vol. 46, No. 4 (1994).

[55]G. Standing, "Global feminization through flexible labour" ... and "Labour market implications of privatization in Russian industry in 1992", World Development, vol. 22, No. 2 (1994).

[56]Joekes, op. cit.

[57]World Economic Survey, 1990 (United Nations publication, Sales No. E.90.II.C.1) and Trade and Development Report, 1993 (United Nations publication, Sales No. E.93.II.D.10).

[58]J. Bhagwati, "Export-promoting trade strategy: issues and evidence", Research Observer, vol. 3, No. 1 (1988).

[59]Trade and Development Report, 1993 (United Nations publication, Sales No. E.93.II.D.10).

[60]Perkins, loc. cit. The share of manufactures from developing countries in the consumption of developed countries has always been rather low and in 1988 stood at a little over 2 per cent. Absorptive capacity therefore is not an obstacle to the increase of manufactured exports from developing countries.

[61]S. Joekes, "The influence of international trade expansion on women's work", BRIDGE Paper (Brighton, England, Institute for Development Studies, 1993).

[62]D. Campbell, "Integrated international production and labour market interdependence" (Unpublished paper, 1994).

[63]Baden (op. cit.) provides some evidence that suggests that technological upgrading, while maintaining market shares, leads to a decline in the share of female employment in export industries and EPZs. One possible explanation for this is that production of more sophisticated export products requires higher skills and formal training. Since many women lack these skills and training, they are not adequately prepared to compete with men for jobs in technologically advanced higher-productivity industries.

[64]World Investment Report, 1993: Transnational Corporations and Integrated International Production (United Nations publication, Sales No. E.93.II.A.14).

[65]"Transnational corporations and employment", Report prepared by the UNCTAD secretariat for the twentieth session of the Commission on Transnational Corporations (E/C.10/1994/3).

[66]S. Mitter, "Innovations in work organization at the enterprise level: changes in technology and women's employment", BRIDGE Paper (Brighton, England, Institute for Development Studies, 1993).

[67]Mitter, op. cit. and S. Joekes, "The influence of international trade expansion on women's work" ...

[68]Palmer defines the "intermediate sector" as lying between the modern formal sector and the informal sector and comprising modern small-scale enterprises employing between 10 and 50 workers and reputedly included in official statistics. Since modern small-scale enterprises are increasingly considered the growth area of the future, the intermediate sector is likely to assume considerable importance in the medium term. See I. Palmer, Gender and Population in the Adjustment of African Economies: Planning for Change (Geneva, International Labour Office, 1991).

[69]World Investment Report, 1992: Transnational Corporations as Engines of Growth (United Nations publication, Sales No. E.92.II.A.19).

[70]S. Joekes, Women in the World Economy ...

[71]S. Joekes, "Industrialization, trade and female employment in developing countries" (Santo Domingo, International Research and Training Institute for the Advancement of Women, 1986).

[72]World Economic Survey, 1993 (United Nations publication Sales No. E.93.II.C.1).

[73]"Survey of third-world finance", The Economist, September 1993.

[74]Elson, loc. cit.; Moser, loc. cit.; and A. Beulink, "Women and the debt crisis", Development, January 1989.

[75]The Standard of Living Survey in Peru revealed that in the

1986-1990 period per capita monthly consumption declined in female-headed households by 55 per cent, and in households headed by men by 54 per cent.

[76]S. Joekes, *Women in the World Economy* ...

[77]I. Vanore-Speer, "Women in trade development" (Statement to the Trade Policy Meeting of the United Nations Development Fund for Women (UNIFEM), 27-28 September 1993).

[78]This analysis was prepared by the Division for the Advancement of Women of the United Nations Secretariat from data in the Women's Indicators and Statistics Data Base (WISTAT), version 3, 1994. A regression equation $F/M=b_0 + b_1 ( GDP)$ was estimated for 61 countries. The dependent variable is the ratio of the percentage of economically active females to that of males. The independent variable is the mean logarithmic growth rate of GDP in constant prices.

[79]Frances Perkins, "Integration of women's concerns into development planning: market interventions", in *Integration of Women's Concerns into Development Planning in Asia and the Pacific* (Bangkok, United Nations Economic and Social Commission for Asia and the Pacific, 1992) and P. Schultz, "Women's changing participation in the labour force: a world perspective", *Economic Development and Cultural Change*, vol. 38 (March 1989), cited in Frances Perkins, "Are women benefiting from economic development?", *IPA Review*, vol. 46, No. 4 (1994).

[80]Frances Perkins, "Integration of women's concerns into development planning: market interventions" ...

# II

---

# Poverty

Although the character of poverty differs between nations, regions and communities, its intransigent nature continues to be a priority concern internationally. Having been declared a violation of human rights, poverty is a focus of the World Summit on Social Develop-ment, the United Nations Conference on Environment and Development and the International Conference on Population and Development. Its causes, effects and possible solutions have significant gender dimen-sions.[1]

## A. ECONOMIC GROWTH AND THE PERSISTENCE OF POVERTY

Although poverty declined from 1950 to 1980, the rate of decline diminished by the early 1980s and became negligible after 1985.[2] The number of people living below the poverty line, set by the World Bank at $370 a year, increased from 1 billion in 1985 to 1.2 billion in 1993, as did the number living in conditions of absolute poverty (less than $300 a year). In 1993 the world faced increasing famine and illiteracy, 800 million starving people, 34,000 children dying each day for want of food and medical care, the spread of such acquired immunodeficiency syndrome (AIDS), cholera and malaria, and high rates of unemployment and underemployment.

Strong global economic performance from 1980 to 1989 made the increased incidence of poverty paradoxical. The average annual rate of economic growth during this period was 3.2 per cent, compared with 2.4 per cent from 1965 to 1980. Economic growth in developed countries was 3 per cent a year, while in the developing countries it was 4.3 per cent a year.[3]

Despite the increase in average income in developed countries in the 1980s, a significant number of people became poorer. In the United States 33.6 million people, or 13 per cent of the population, were estimated to be living below the poverty line. In Japan 25 per cent of all households were on the verge of destitution. In the European Community at the beginning of the 1990s,

44 million people, or 18 per cent of the population, were estimated to be living in poverty, with 10 million living in extreme poverty.[3]

The number of poor in Europe was estimated at 200 million, of which 100 million were in Central and Eastern Europe.[3] The transformation from centrally planned to market economies undermined guaranteed employment, minimum wages and a range of benefits that had ensured a minimum standard of living. Economic transition in this region led to a decline of traditional industries, a transfer of certain productive activities to developing countries and a massive retrenchment in public sector institutions resulting in unemployment and a proliferation of badly paid jobs. Cutbacks in the public sector also influenced the expansion of the informal sector, which is characterized by low wages and no social security.[4] The groups most affected by these changes are women, young people and pensioners.

These factors have fostered the emergence of the "new poor", characterized by high levels of education and qualifications, and including blue- and white-collar workers and an increasing number of managers and administrators.[5] This group did not inherit poverty, but became poor because they lacked sufficient resources to meet the minimum standard of living.

## B. GENDER AND POVERTY

Examining poverty from a gender perspective involves determining how and why women and men experience poverty unequally and become impoverished through different processes. The gender dimension of poverty is manifested in the unequal burden borne by women in managing consumption under conditions of scarcity. The failure to take gender into account in policy design has contributed to the perpetuation of poverty.

The multi-dimensional nature of poverty, its causes and main attributes raise questions as to whether a universally acceptable definition of its character is possible. Still, there is a need to clarify its different meanings and to measure its incidence and magnitude. Efforts to measure poverty have been hampered by the range of complex factors associated with its occurrence in different socio-economic settings. The criteria that have been used as indices for measurement—gross domestic product, income distribution and a range of social indicators—do not provide a universal standard for comparison.

Understanding the causes of poverty requires examining the determinants of the real income of individuals and the sufficiency of that income in achieving a satisfactory level of welfare. For example, the poor have a high propensity to consume and a consequent low level of savings. This pattern affects investment and productivity at both the microeconomic and macroeconomic levels and contributes to low income levels. This vicious circle suggests that poverty is self-perpetuating unless the circle is broken by means of appropriate policies.

Policy design must first consider where to measure poverty—at the national, regional, community, household or individual level. The household is most appropriate for gender analysis. As the place where people live in common association, household is often used interchangeably with family, though its meaning is different (family members may not be part of a household and a household may include more than blood relatives). Households are where income is pooled to provide for shared consumption. And households are where gender relations are determined.

At the intrahousehold level, poverty is defined in terms of consumption. A household member's share of consumption may not be determined by that individual's contribution to household income. Rather, it may reflect cultural and social factors, which in many societies favour men over women. The level of female consumption therefore may not improve as their contributions increase or even if they succeed in gaining wage employment.

Poverty is no longer simply a matter of income distribution. Indeed, redistribution methods, based on a concept of poverty that sets those above against those below, are partly to blame for the proliferation and aggravation of poverty. Rather, the emerging concept of exclusion implies that societies in a market economy have become incapable of integrating a growing number of their members. As the new social division, exclusion sets those on the outside against those on the inside.[6] This view posits socio-economic conditions as the primary reason certain individuals or groups are excluded from society and views individual (psychological or physical) characteristics as a secondary cause. Exclusion is the direct result of the employment crisis as well as political and cultural causes. These in turn are the result of the failure of institutions, the State, the educational system, trade unions and the like.[7]

## C.  POVERTY AND FEMALE-HEADED HOUSEHOLDS

The strongest direct link between gender and poverty is found in female-headed households. Female headship emerged as an early indicator of women's poverty because it was the only gender-transparent factor in household-based approaches to poverty. An early review estimated that between 10 and 40 per cent of households fall into this category.[8] The Women's Indicators and Statistics Data Base (WISTAT) confirms this estimate.

The term "female-headed households" as used here refers to arrangements with women are financially responsible for their families and are the primary economic decision makers within them. Such households encompass quite disparate household economies and family structures. There are, for example, distinctions between female-headed households where women are the key decision makers and economic managers, those where women manage household economies on behalf of an absent male head, and female-maintained households, where women are the main economic contributors.

### 1.  Definition of the terms and measurement

There are regional and cultural differences as to who or what constitutes a household, the definition of headship, and how it is reported. The term headship has often been used in development literature to denote control in households with a patriarchal system of family governance and no internal conflicts in the allocation of resources.[9] Such usage reflects imprecisely the regional family and household dynamics that influence household arrangements. As an indicator of households that rely principally on women's resources for their support, headship is also a problematic category in censuses.[10] Still, in the absence of indicators that better reflect the relationship between family formation and poverty, it can be used for purposes of policy and programme implementation, keeping in mind that further disaggregation of the term is warranted.[11]

The validity of data yielded by population and housing censuses in identifying the economic support bases of households has been questioned repeatedly.[12] Problems include the fact that the presence of an adult male tends to mark a household as male-headed regardless of women's economic contributions.[13] During recessions households often merge as women move in with their extended families to lessen the economic burden, making it hard to identify the heads of households.[14] There is a history of lags in censuses because societies change faster than both the recording methods and the philosophy that forms the basis of these measurements. For example, United States Census indications of heads of households, constrained by an inadequate definition of headship, failed to identify trends in female economic independence and financial responsibility.[12] In regions such as the Middle East and Africa there are economic and social advantages for women who are supported by a man, which induces women who are sole providers for their families to go to great lengths to keep this fact from being recorded.[10] Smaller, more detailed household surveys and other ways of detecting female headship are needed to define power relations within households and identify the economic base of support.[14]

## 2. *Female headship incidence, implications and contributing factors*

Female headship varies by region. A comparison of census data suggests that overall female-headship rates are higher in Europe than in South-East Asia, and that rates are lower in southern than northern Europe. The Caribbean has high rates of female headship, as do several Nordic countries, while in Japan the rate is low. Female headship also varies within countries.[12] The highest proportion of female-headed households in the developing countries is in sub-Saharan Africa, at 31 per cent (see table II.1). Over time, the developing regions show little change in the incidence of female-headed households (see table II.2). In the developed regions, however, female-headed households peaked in 1990.

The determinants of female headship vary. The incidence of female headship in Africa and Latin

*Table II.1*

Female-headed households in developing countries by region, 1992

Percentage

| Region | Households |
|---|---|
| Asia | 9 |
| Asia (excluding China and India) | 14 |
| Latin America and the Caribbean | 17 |
| Near East and North Africa | 17 |
| Sub-Saharan Africa | 31 |
| All regions | 12 |
| All regions (excluding China and India) | 20 |
| Least developed countries | 23 |

Source: International Fund for Agricultural Development, *Report on Rural Women Living in Poverty* (Rome, 1992).

*Table II.2*

Female-headed households by region, 1970-1990

| Region | 1970 | 1980 | 1990 |
|---|---|---|---|
| Africa | 18.4 | 20.6 | 18.2 |
| Asia and the Pacific | 15.3 | 14.9 | 17.2 |
| Eastern Europe | .. | 23.1 | .. |
| Latin America | 24.1 | 27.6 | 20.8 |
| Western Europe | .. | 23.7 | 31.2 |

Source: Division for the Advancement of Women, United Nations Secretariat, from data contained in Women's Indicators and Statistics Data Base (WISTAT), version 3, 1994.
Note: Two dots (..) indicate that data are not available.

America, for example, stems from sociodemographic factors such as migration, divorce, desertion, political turmoil, widowhood, late marriage and unpartnered adolescent motherhood. Urbanization and migration in Latin America have resulted in a surplus of women in urban areas, raising the incidence of female-headed households. One of the most significant socio-economic factors in the rise of female-headed households is the increasingly common perception that children are a private cost to be borne primarily by women.[12]

The strong correlation between female headship and poverty results from higher dependency ratios, inadequate remittances from absent men and gender differentials in access to resources and productive employment. Overlapping productive and reproductive responsibilities affect mobility, time allocation and trade-offs between child-care arrangements and employment (or child-care arrangements and housing). Family histories of early parenthood and instability are also important and often link the intergenerational transmission of poverty.

The implications of female headship on the socio-economic status of households vary, even between countries with similar female headship rates.[12] Evidence suggests that female-headed households are increasingly concentrated in the poorest regions. A summary of research findings of 66 studies conducted between 1979 and 1989 by the International Research Center for Women[15] examined the relationship between female headship and poverty and its consequences for child welfare in the developing world. Forty-four of these studies concluded that female-headed households were poorer than their male counterparts. Studies in Brazil, Chile, Colombia, Costa Rica, India, Panama and Venezuela were inconclusive when they addressed different types of female headship or when they used different types of poverty indicators. Studies in Côte d'Ivoire, the Dominican Republic, Ghana, India, Indonesia, Jamaica and Malawi found that male-headed households were worse off than those headed by women. These studies suggest two general trends: female-headed households that result from changes in family structure (such as widowhood) are better off than those resulting from economic crises or demographic patterns and women who are left behind by migrating men who send them remittances are usually better off. Generally, however, these studies indicate that most female-headed households are at a higher risk of poverty than those that are male-headed.

### 3. *Effects of female headship on child welfare*

The International Research Center for Women also examined the correlation between female headship and child welfare. Employing such indicators as nutrition, life expectancy, labour and education they demonstrated that while poor female-headed households want to invest in their children, they may not have sufficient income to improve living standards. The results vary by region. The correlation between female headship and child welfare is negative in Latin America, positive in Africa and ambiguous in the Caribbean. Latin America reported negative consequences in terms of life expectancy, nutritional status and education. In Africa there was a lower incidence of illness among children in female-headed households, and children's education was more likely to receive priority in such households than in other households. However, the number of studies from each region was too small to draw definitive conclusions about regional trends.[15]

Of the 16 studies examining nutritional effects, seven reported negative findings, and a study in Brazil revealed that the probability of survival of children in female-headed households is lower than for children from male-headed households.[15] Studies that report positive effects of female headship on child nutrition find this to be more prevalent among poorer households. Studies on the impact of female headship on children's education reported negative effects in six of nine countries due to the fact that children in poor households are often forced to drop out of school to assist with housework or earn income.

A study in Guatemala revealed that female-headed households favoured male children, and mothers were more likely to send sons to school than daughters since they view boys as a source of support for the family. This practice has a profound impact on the intergenerational transmission of poverty. Since women's income is usually more directly channelled to collective family needs and may be used more efficiently in terms of building human capital, girls should receive the same educational opportunities as boys.

Investing in children can help stem intergenerational transmission of poverty. However, these protective effects are likely to break down as poverty worsens. Female heads of household face a conflict between their desire to provide their children with proper nutrition and education and the need to use every available resource to cope with poverty.

## D. RURAL POVERTY[16]

More than 550 million women, or 60 per cent of the world's rural population, live below the poverty line in rural areas. This is a 50 per cent increase for women since the 1970s compared with a 30 per cent increase for men for the same period.[17] Factors contributing to the feminization of rural poverty include cutbacks in essential services resulting from restructuring policies; environmental degradation, which affects the smallholder and subsistence agriculture in which women predominate; increasing male out-migration, which has contributed to the feminization of small-holder agriculture in some countries; the increased number of female-headed households, which are often the poorest and most disadvantaged of rural households; women's limited access to productive resources and services; and armed conflicts, which contribute to the growing number of refugee women forced to provide for their families under exceptionally difficult circumstances.

Rural populations are consistently underserved and difficult to reach with development resources. Their situation is affected by their remoteness from national decision-making centres, their adherence to traditional gender relations and the merging of productive and reproductive functions in the household. Institutional credit sources, for instance, may be concentrated in urban areas, and gender relations may skew credit availability in favour of men. Similarly, education facilities and services may be concentrated in urban centres, and priority access to these services is given to men and boys because of social and economic factors. Furthermore, rural women are restricted from participating in the decision-making processes that affect their lives.

Although rural women are at the end of the distribution chain for productive resources and social services, they are at the beginning of the food production chain. In developing countries rural women are responsible for more than 55 per cent of the food grown; in Africa they produce 70 per cent of the food. Moreover, women comprise 67 per cent of the agricultural labour force in developing countries.[18] Poverty alleviation strategies must take full account of rural women to ensure that productive resources and social services that flow to rural populations have a positive impact on food production for consumption by rural households and, by extension, surpluses to be consumed by the nation.

Sixty-eight per cent of developing country populations live and earn their living in rural areas; for least developed countries the figure is 80 per cent. The number of rural inhabitants in developing countries has increased, eroding gains in agricultural productivity.[17] Despite trends towards rapid urbanization, developing countries are still largely rural and will continue to be so until 2015.[19]

Factors influencing production in developing countries include post–World War II development strategies focused on industrialization and urban growth. Since the 1970s budget levels and resource allocations for agriculture have been cut even though it accounts for the livelihood of 50 to 90 per cent of the population and 30 per cent of gross national product (GNP) in developing countries. In the 1980s falling agricultural prices, the importation of products whose prices were competitive with local produce, increasingly adverse terms of trade and austere structural adjustment policies had a devastating impact on the incomes, agricultural wages and production patterns of rural families. Restructuring policies forced by the debt crisis resulted in cutbacks in health, education and services that affect rural women disproportionately.

The best land and agricultural inputs are still allocated for export crops, which tend to be controlled by men. Moreover, land tenure practices usually ensure male control of activities in the monetized sector. Although women make substantial labour contributions to agricultural production, the focus on export crops has consigned women to subsistence production, limited access to such technical knowledge or innovations as irrigation, machinery, farming techniques and extension services and restricted them to using poor infrastructure and distribution systems that do not take adequate account of rural-urban migration. Rural women's productive time is spent primarily in subsistence farming, the household and the informal sector—areas that are not well-recorded in statistics on national income.

The assessment of gender relations in rural areas is limited by insufficient data disaggregated by sex. Many of the productive and reproductive activities in which rural women are involved are not accounted for in data—reating a statistical vanishing point. Case study analysis, informed estimates and extrapolations often fill gaps in data. While the situation is improving, much needs to be done. For example, a significant volume of gender-disaggregated data from such sources as administrative records and projects should be tabulated and analysed. Other required steps include incorporating gender-sensitive approaches to data collection, processing and utilization, developing uniform concepts and classifications for statistics on women, clarifying concepts and definitions relating to the measurement of employment in the informal sector and overcoming the lack of political will by ministries of agriculture and statistical offices to collect data disaggregated by sex.[20] Sex-disaggregated data are a necessary prerequisite to the recognition of rural women as producers. Such data facilitate understanding of the support and training services needed by rural women and provide the basis for translating these needs into policy, planning and programming.

Rural women are assuming increasing responsibility for generating income and assuring the well-being of their families. Indeed, as the division of labour becomes less distinct in some developing countries, rural women are increasingly involved in activities traditionally performed by men. Rural women are making decisions about the volume and composition of agricultural output of some household food, livestock, small animals and marketing. However, the dichotomy between microeconomic and macroeconomic interests is becoming more pronounced because of rural poverty. For example, the high fertility levels associated with the economic and social value of children are contrary to efforts to reduce population growth. Rural women's increasing role in economic decision-making within the household must be translated into decision-making power in the community. This should be accomplished by increasing their participation in decision-making processes at all levels, access to and control over productive resources, opportunities for productive employment and access to education and health services.

### 1. *Increasing the participation of rural women in decision-making processes*

The establishment or strengthening of national women's machinery[21] is an essential component of rural development strategies, ensuring that women's contributions, needs and concerns are effectively assessed and incorporated into policies and programmes. This process must be coupled with sufficient human, technical and financial resources to enable national women's machinery to play a catalytic and strategic role in developing country-wide networks of rural women to facilitate the implementation of food and agricultural development programmes. The national women's machinery should coordinate with international organizations on measures to apply research on rural women's reproductive and productive roles and improve the availability and quality of data disaggregated by sex on agriculture and rural development. The machinery might, for example, lobby Governments to process the small but significant volume of sex-disaggregated data relating to agriculture and rural development.[20]

The national women's machinery should also coordinate with international organizations and national and international non-governmental organizations. Women's groups can play an important role in collecting and disseminating information about needs and activities of rural women at all levels. This role can be strengthened with technical and financial assistance by international donors that can provide assistance and establish more collaborative relationships. Such links can help facilitate the flow of resources to rural women, overcome the low status of national women's machinery among other government agencies and reduce the isola-

tion of women's units from sectoral programmes and field activities.

National women's groups can also facilitate the growth of community development organizations. Community organizations are an effective way of increasing rural women's role in decision-making and ensuring recognition of their participation in the community. Such participation increases women's visibility, enables them to learn management skills and methods for earning and saving income, and enhances their bargaining power when seeking access to land, credit, agricultural services, extension and training. Networking between national women's organizations and rural women's organizations will eventually strengthen the credibility and impact of both. Increasing the participation of rural women in local groups requires action in three main areas: establishing local organizations such as cooperatives, farmers associations, and credit and savings unions for production, political, advocacy, social and economic goals; promoting training programmes for women's associations to enhance their capacity for dialogue and negotiation; and encouraging women leaders to undertake community actions and collective initiatives, particularly in agriculture, forestry and communal fish farming.

More than other women, rural women are not represented in the decision-making positions that determine the direction, content and quality of development activities. This is caused by many factors, some of which affect all women, but many of which are related specifically to the rural situation. Poor rural women tend to be scattered over large and relatively inaccessible areas, making it hard for government services to reach them and for them to form cohesive groups. Existing farmers groups are mostly cooperative-type associations that do not address women's needs and activities, being more concerned with men's cash-crop production. Women's groups, where they do exist, often limit themselves to activities related to women's social and reproductive activities. Low levels of education and literacy, limits on their mobility outside the home and gender-biased cultural values all make it difficult for women to organize effectively.

Women's groups are lacking in technical ability, financial management skills, experience with public authorities, and capital with which to expand and invest. As a result, few women's enterprises are actually owned and managed by women's groups. A survey in six countries of forest-based small-scale enterprises, which are dominated by female labour, showed that women owned only 17 per cent of the enterprises. In Bangladesh only 3 per cent were owned by women.[22] Women's groups remain heavily dependent on external support (which may be exploitive) for administrative and technical assistance. Providers of this assistance should identify social and economic differences among members that may cause conflicts and address these differences through training in organizational and management skills.[23]

Membership in all-women's groups provides rural women with the opportunity to gain management experience, an outlet for self-expression in societies where men and women do not mix easily in political structures and the possibility of generating income and making decisions regarding group expenditures. Mixed groups, on the other hand, provide access to the infrastructure and services associated with mainstream rural development. However, rural women have often found access to these groups difficult. Women are often excluded from mixed farmers groups by membership criteria that specify land ownership, or by their illiteracy, low level of education or opposition from husbands (as, for example, in paying additional fees for a wife's membership). Women may be reluctant to join because they have no time for such activities or they can derive no benefits from membership if groups do not address women's productive activities.

The spread of democracy provides an opportunity to build awareness of gender imbalances in rural areas where education levels are lower and access to information is reduced. Women's participation in public life should be increased by strengthening rural women's associations, legal literacy training, civic and political education and information campaigns. Key to this is the legal recognition of women's groups, without which they have no power, and the subsequent creation of a women's federation, organized along professional lines if possible. Another path would be making democratization and the role of rural women therein central to legal literacy programmes. Measures should be taken to ensure that women participate in the public administration of rural development at both the national and decentralized levels. Women's organizations and external assistance agencies should lobby to place gender issues on the agenda of policy makers at all levels.

All possible routes to promoting rural women's participation in political and economic decision-making should be pursued simultaneously. Networks can provide a rapid way of exchanging information and lending support. Women's groups should learn from each other's strengths and weaknesses, and external re-

sources should be directed towards making exchanges possible. Women's groups should also be encouraged to take their experiences and agendas to political bodies, to explain their needs, to request recognition, legitimacy and assistance, and to offer their assistance and involvement in planning and decision-making.

## 2. Access to and control of productive resources

Addressing poverty among rural women implies addressing the issue of access to and control of productive resources: land, labour, capital, technology and extension services. Systems of ownership and use of land and access to water and other natural productive resources are determined by political, social and economic conditions of different countries; they are the key determinants of rural economic structures, income distribution and general conditions of rural life. Measures have been found in many countries to address these concerns.

### Access to and control of land

As noted earlier, gender asymmetries in access to land remain one of the main obstacles to the full participation of women in rural development. Inheritance practices, whereby land traditionally passes from father to son, reinforce male control of land. Although many developing countries have legally affirmed a woman's right to own land, female control of land is rare. Indeed, reform measures have not been gender-neutral and women have been excluded in varying degrees either legally or by de facto measures. For example, bestowing rights on heads of household on land that was formerly held communally has overridden a variety of land inheritance patterns in some countries and reinforced discriminatory practices against women. Moreover, many countries make no legal provision for widowed, separated or divorced women.

Women typically farm small, dispersed or remote plots of fragmented land in which they have little incentive to invest or adopt new technologies. Land titles in most countries are registered in the name of the male heads of household, and women do not have secure land tenure. Since women do not own land they cannot access agricultural support services, particularly credit and extension services where land ownership is a requirement or extension workers are reluctant to work with small, isolated plots.

The difficulties experienced by rural women in securing access to land are even greater for female heads of households. Review of land reform programmes in various countries indicates that, regardless of whether the sex of the beneficiary is specified by law, female heads of households seldom have access to land even when their productive activities call for it. Without title to land, the women lack the collateral needed to obtain credit and may face difficulties in obtaining extension services.

Improving women's access to land is a basic prerequisite for the success of rural development policies. Activities that improve women's access to and control over land include training for both women and men on women's rights, research on legislative reforms for rural areas, removing barriers to the effective implementation of existing laws, focusing on ways to improve women's participation in self-help and cooperative groups, enhancing productivity to create incentives for women to invest in the land they cultivate, and enhancing government investments in women's labour.

### Access to labour

Command over labour resources has a critical impact on the productivity of women in agriculture. The amount of land that farmers can cultivate is directly related to labour availability—their own and that of family members and hired labour. Women's larger workloads and limited financial resources for paid labour complicate the expansion of agricultural production. And increasing out-migration from countries where men migrate imply that male availability is reduced even for the limited labour inputs provided by men. The labour availability of young women is also declining as they migrate to urban areas in search of employment and improved lifestyles.

Men can mobilize the labour of wives and children in productive activities, whereas women may have access to daughters and younger sons. The need to draw upon the labour of offspring may influence children's, especially girls', rates of school attendance, and in the longer term may perpetuate poverty.

### Access to appropriate and affordable technology

New agricultural technologies should be accessible, environmentally appropriate and utilize local materials. They should also maximize efficiency without threatening jobs in the rural sector. New technologies include new crop varieties and breeds of livestock, improved tools and cultivation methods, including consistent access to draught animals, and mechanized processes. Appropriate technology is the most effective means of raising the productivity of land, labour and capital of resource-poor farmers. Technologies that save time and energy in productive and reproductive activities benefit the family, community and

society. Irrigation schemes have, for example, brought water to homes, improving sanitation and health conditions. And mechanized processes have been introduced that reduce women's workload without displacing them.[24]

A review of projects over the past decade reveals that technology, if not carefully evaluated before introduction and use, can have negative effects on women. In many parts of the developing world, mechanization (for example, the use of tractors) has resulted in the masculinization of modern agriculture and the feminization of subsistence agriculture. Another unforeseen negative impact on women results from certain types of irrigation technology. Although irrigation can increase crop production and make water more readily available to households and livestock, it can affect women negatively by increasing the time needed to transplant crops, weed and harvest. New technologies can also be too expensive for poor rural women to buy. One way to solve this problem is to minimize the use of expensive technology. The upgrading of traditional food-processing techniques can be undertaken without resorting to expensive technology.

Rural women have a rich knowledge of the production, processing, storage and nutritional characteristics of a wide range of crop and wild plants, methods of soil conservation and enrichment, and issues related to the rearing of livestock. Such knowledge can be tapped in developing appropriate technologies.

### Access to credit and financial services

Among the barriers to women's access to credit and financial markets are the assumptions that women farmers do not make cropping and input decisions even when they are heads of household, that their primary involvement in subsistence production limits the time they can devote to market-oriented activities, that they pose a high credit risk, and that they can absorb only small loans, which carry high administrative costs for financial institutions. Agricultural or seasonal credit programmes that provide group guarantees sometimes fail to extend credit to the poor because of the fear that group guarantee mechanisms will be jeopardized by including poor subsistence farmers. Moreover, women have limited access to cooperatives and other organizations that channel credit to farmers.

Credit is essential for women to obtain such agricultural inputs as seeds, fertilizers and pesticides, as well as to purchase tools, procure draught animals, hire labour, construct irrigation systems and take soil and water conservation measures. However, credit availability is not a sufficient condition for guaranteeing sustainable improvement in women's conditions. It must be accompanied by appropriate training and research in sectors in which women are involved, including traditional food crops, small livestock and home vegetable gardens.

Efforts to provide credit to rural women should begin by examining local conditions to determine the most effective mechanisms of reaching the poorest women. Provision should be made for training and for strategies that replace collateral requirements of financial institutions. Women's production activities that have seasonal components should be taken into account, including capital requirements for small investments and working capital to support market-oriented production and trading activities. The mix of infrastructure, extension, training and marketing support should be carefully targeted to meet rural women's needs in subsistence and market-oriented activities. Providers of assistance should ensure that resources are not diverted to production dominated by male members of the household.

Staff of financial institutions should be trained to understand both the productive and reproductive roles of women and identify ways to match these needs with credit availability. The special needs of women farmers should also be identified. These include, for example, the need to hire help during periods of labour shortage, appropriate food processing technologies, forestry products transformation, purchase of inputs for reforestation programmes and the organization of fish-marketing infrastructure.

Financial institutions can enhance rural women's access to financial services and technical assistance by designing action plans for increasing women's access to financial services, encouraging the exchange of experience among financial institutions on credit schemes that provide easier access to rural women, developing options for financial services, technical assistance, training and resources that pay special attention to rural women's needs and establishing closer links with women bankers in financial institutions that receive loans from international organizations. Creating and strengthening links between banks, government-sponsored seasonal credit programmes and village-based savings and credit groups also increase the availability of credit to poor rural women.

The impact of credit availability can be dramatic, both on family well-being and on the community at large. Apart from the economic advantage of increased productivity and income, the increase in women's earning power has a tremendous effect on their self-confidence. Increased self-esteem often leads women to enrol in education programmes and take on a greater role in community activities—initiatives that they would not previously have considered.

### Access to appropriate extension services and training

The needs of women farmers have generally been overlooked in the provision of extension services. Although women represent 80 per cent of the food producers in some countries, only 5 per cent of extension organizations' time and resources are allocated to women, and only 13 per cent of extension workers are women, with 7 per cent in Africa,[18] 1 per cent in Asia and the Near East and 8.5 per cent in Latin America.[25]

The effective delivery of extension services to women farmers involves gathering complete and correct information on women producers in the region, overcoming restrictions on the interaction between rural women and men, identifying ways to make extension advice available to female producers and taking extension activities to women's work sites. Extension services often do not reach women because information is geared to cash-cropping and does not apply to subsistence crops and livestock, which may be women's concerns. Modes of communication and the organization of extension information may be inappropriate for rural women of varying and usually low educational and literacy levels and scheduling of activities may fail to take into account women's fragmented schedules. Such oversights can contribute to a decline in food production and, by extension, increased malnutrition within families and communities.

Gender-sensitive research findings should be incorporated into extension programmes to ensure that rural women's production-related needs are being addressed. The provision of appropriate technology that is both labour- and energy-saving should be based on research and communication with targeted populations. Such technology should cover the range of activities in which women farmers, producers and processors are engaged. Research and data collection requirements include addressing gender concerns in baseline surveys and questionnaires and conducting gender-specific needs assessments prior to the commencement of activities. Data on agricultural activities disaggregated by sex are required for designing, implementing and monitoring extension activities, as are intrahousehold analysis and time-use studies.

Strategies should be identified to increase the number of women extension agents. Constraints to women's enrolment in agricultural educational institutions should be examined and overcome. Gender-sensitive training should be provided for male agents to enhance their understanding of the needs of women farmers. Efforts to increase the pool of women extension agents should include retraining agents in other fields in the skills required to serve women farmers, equalizing the status of female and male agents through equal training and employment conditions and increasing the involvement of local women as para-extension staff, particularly in countries where women are secluded.

### 3.    Access to off-farm employment

Off-farm employment has become an important alternative for women who have little or no access to land or live in ecologically fragile environments where farming or livestock-raising is limited. Although many of these women are employed as wage labourers on large farms or in local factories, employment is often temporary and the wages low. Many rural women are marginalized into migrant work in rural, urban and peri-urban areas as petty traders, street vendors, construction workers and domestic servants.

Seasonal agricultural employment cannot absorb the large number of rural women seeking work. And where capital-intensive technologies are introduced, employment opportunities for women may be lost. Moreover, because rural women are often uneducated and have few non-agricultural skills, they tend to be concentrated in tasks requiring limited skills and offering low wages.

Self-employment through small-scale enterprises run by women, either individually or in groups, presents a constructive option in terms of providing a reliable source of income and developing economic self-reliance. In many developing countries a high percentage of small-scale businesses that cater to local needs are controlled or owned by women. In Latin America, for example, women own between one third and one half of all small rural enterprises. Between 20 and 35 per cent of those rural households that live above the poverty line in the region are able to do so largely because of women's contributions to family welfare.[18] Women's enterprises tend to be relatively small, have informal structures, flexibility, low capital needs, modest educational requirements and high labour intensity. Most depend on local raw materials and cater to local markets.

They also are characterized by their small scale, lack of collateral (and, therefore, difficulty in obtaining credit), dependence on family labour and limited managerial and technical skills. These enterprises are not registered, maintain no business records, and do not have access to credit from formal credit institutions.

Rural women are active participants in retail trade and marketing, particularly where trade is traditional and not highly commercialized or industrialized. In much of Asia women market foods such as vegetables, in West Africa they distribute most major commodities and in the Caribbean women account for nearly all local marketing. Through their marketing efforts women provide valuable links between farms, consumer goods and buyers.

Rural women engage in such small-scale enterprises as petty trading, food and beverage processing and producing and selling handicrafts. Little, if any, technical support is provided to women pursuing these activities, and their bargaining power is limited by a lack of information about markets and pricing, particularly if they are illiterate and have to depend on intermediaries to obtain inputs and market products. The success of rural women's small-scale enterprises depends upon the establishment of links with the agricultural production cycle at all stages as well as adapting operations to their reproductive role in the household.

The features that characterize rural women's work—labour intensity, local materials and local markets—also constrain product diversification and market expansion. Other constraints include interference by men in the use of capital reserves, lack of infrastructure and transportation, lack of managerial skills, direct and indirect competition with formal enterprises and lack of access to credit and financial services. These issues require the focused attention of national Governments, donors and non-governmental organizations to improve existing activities and create new opportunities.

### 4.    Health services

Access to health care affects the productivity of rural women's labour, their physical capacity to use available resources and rates of maternal mortality. Where health services are available and not subsidized, rural women's access is influenced by their ability to generate and control income. The cost of services and limited facilities in remote areas can contribute to gender differentials in access to health care. Some studies have shown that more boys than girls are brought to clinics when fees are charged for visits. But when health visits are made to villages a higher number of ill and malnourished girls are seen. Fees have the same influence on immunization: four times as many boys as girls are brought to the clinic.

Adequate health care facilities have not yet been established in remote areas and restructuring programmes have hindered their development. In the mid-1980s, for example, 37 of the world's poorest countries cut their health budgets by half.[26] The lack of adequate health facilities increases women's vulnerability to prolonged illnesses and death. The low status of rural women in society affects their health and nutritional status. Indeed, malnutrition is a serious threat to rural women and their children, making the body less immune to disease and affecting energy levels.

Rural areas have limited health infrastructure, particularly for family planning, childbirth, prenatal and postnatal services. But in societies where motherhood still provides social security for old age and a high social status is attached to children, especially sons, there is enormous pressure on women to bear children. Women who continuously become pregnant and give birth pay a high price in terms of maternal mortality: the lifetime risk of a woman in a developing country dying in childbirth is from 1 in 25 to 1 in 40, compared with 1 in 3,000 in developed countries.

Measures should be identified to relieve women's workload and improve nutritional intake during pregnancy, provide postnatal care for mothers and children, including improved child nutrition and educating mothers in nutritional issues and sanitation, and to provide education to the general population about women's and children's health needs and women's pivotal roles in society.

## E.  URBAN POVERTY

Demographic changes in the world population are one factor explaining the persistence of poverty. The population increased by about 1 billion people in the 1980s, reducing per capita economic growth, placing additional strain on social services and making it more difficult to fight poverty.[27] More than 90 per cent of this growth took place in developing countries, which have limited resources and are less able to meet increased requirements for food, health services, housing, jobs, social services and infrastructure. Much of the growth was accompanied by urbanization.

The changing distribution of population is a significant factor in the impoverishment of urban areas. Urban populations have been growing at a rate two and a half times that of rural populations. At this rate, more than half the world's population will be urban by 2005, according to the most recent United Nations projections.[28] Most urban growth is occurring in developing countries. The magnitude of this increase is very large (see table II.3).

The projected increase from 1990 to 2025 in developing regions represents a total of 2.6 billion people—nearly twice the size of current urban populations. Growth in developed regions will be considerably lower and, consequently, more manageable. Fourteen of the 20 world megacities (those containing more than 8 million people) are located in developing countries. Such increases require a commensurate response from national and municipal authorities.

Urban trends in developing regions vary widely; most of the growth is concentrated in Africa and in Asia (see table II.4). The highest rates of growth are expected in Africa, where the urban population is expected to increase by a factor of four while in Asia it is the absolute numbers that represent the challenge, with an increase of 1.7 billion. Latin American patterns are closer to developed regions.

*Table II.3*

Urban population, 1970, 1990 and 2025

Millions

| Region | 1970 | 1990 | 2025 |
|---|---|---|---|
| Less developed regions | 654 | 1 401 | 4 011 |
| More developed regions | 698 | 881 | 1 177 |

*Source*: *World Urbanization Prospects: The 1992 Revision* (United Nations publication, Sales No. E.93.XIII.11).

*Table II.4*

Urban population in developing regions, 1990 and 2025

Millions

| Region | 1990 | | 2025 | |
|---|---|---|---|---|
| | Total | Women | Total | Women |
| Africa | 206 | 101 | 857 | 421 |
| Asia | 878 | 420 | 2 665 | 1 296 |
| Latin America | 315 | 161 | 592 | 303 |

*Source*: Population Division, United Nations Secretariat, "Urban and rural areas by sex and age: the 1992 revision" (Working paper, November 1993).

Urban population growth comes from both internal growth and from rural to urban migration, which accounts for 60 per cent of urban growth in the developing world.[28] Fertility, rural-urban and intercity migration have a major impact on the sex and age distributions of urban populations.

The urban population in developing regions is young. In Africa 41 per cent of the urban population is under 15; in Asia and Latin America 30 per cent is under 15.[29] This has a direct impact on women: domestic burdens increase, housing is overcrowded, child-care facilities are in greater demand and fewer schools are available for children. It also has an indirect impact in such areas as limiting women's flexibility for commuting to work.

Imbalances in the male to female sex ratio in urban areas are also significant. Such ratios are as high as 114 in South Asia (that is, 114 men to 100 women) and as low as 93 in Western Europe. Such imbalances are often related to different migration patterns between the sexes, and have an impact on such diverse issues as household composition, prostitution and the volume of remittances sent back to families in rural areas or in the country of origin.

Better health care is needed in urban areas. The number of family members with HIV/AIDS, alcohol or drug-abuse problems injuries or disabilities resulting from accidents or pollution is increasing. Health policies in some countries emphasize community-based care for these problems, shifting the burden of caring for these people to female members of urban households. Even in cities where there is health insurance, reproductive roles limit women's productive potential and their entitlement to health insurance. And insurance policies tend to cover institutional care more than home care.

Urban living has a major impact on women's lifestyles, and one of the major changes is in fertility. By the second half of the 1980s, contraceptive prevalence had risen to 51 per cent in urban areas (from 36 per cent (about 10 years earlier), with practically no change in the gap between urban and rural areas. These differentials could be related to the greater availability of family planning services in urban areas. But there remains an unmet need for both spacing and limiting the number of children in urban areas, even in countries with a long history of effective family planning programmes.[30]

## 1. *Migration and urbanization from a gender perspective*

Migration contributes to the increase in poverty among groups that are drawn to cities or other countries with the hope of finding better jobs and living conditions but end up with precarious employment, without social protection and vulnerable to discrimination and exploitation. The migration of women is a particularly complex and neglected issue. Although data are insufficient, female migration is believed to be as significant as that of men. Women generally migrate as part of a household or wider social network but they are also increasingly moving individually. Since local patterns vary considerably, it is difficult to generalize. Studies show a shift from rural-rural to rural-urban and then to urban-urban as development occurs. These changes are accompanied by a trend towards more balanced sex ratios.[31]

The urban poor live in an entirely monetized economy and have few buffers against contingencies. Unlike their rural counterparts, they cannot resort to subsistence agriculture, communal resources or customary patterns of reciprocity. Although informal support networks exist in urban areas, the urban poor are more susceptible to fluctuations in the cost of living and are disproportionately affected by recession, inflation and the negative impacts of economic reform policies. Families have responded by increasing the number of household members working so that income generation has become a matter of necessity for men, women and children.

The urbanization process challenges the customary gender division of labour, as evidenced by rising levels of male unemployment and the feminization of the labour force in many cities. The increase in the number of women-maintained families and families dependent on women's economic contributions is placing stress on urban gender relations.

## 2. *Housing*

When housing programmes and upgrading schemes present opportunities for improving human settlements, women are often excluded by eligibility criteria, the location of settlements, arrangements for housing and finance, lack of information about such opportunities, and methods of construction, such as self-help schemes. Projects are often designed without considering women's economic, domestic or community responsibilities and focus instead on meeting the needs of a male head of household, ignoring the large number of women who head or maintain households. Housing policy should recognize different household types and needs in housing provision and design as well as the particular constraints faced by women. Selection criteria and housing finance need to accommodate women's income streams, which are often irregular. Information that facilities access to housing schemes should take into account where women meet, their levels of literacy and their familiarity with and confidence in official procedures and documents. Attention must also be paid to the extra burdens imposed on women by urban projects that incorporate self-help schemes and loans. Such programmes should be geared towards the provision of materials and construction costs.

### 3. *Infrastructure*

The gender implications of infrastructure provision need to be clearly understood if the quality of life in urban areas is to be improved. Sufficient quantities of clean water allow women to reduce the time spent on the collection and disposal of water, increasing the time available for other productive and leisure pursuits. Adequate water supplies also reduces tensions related, for example, to competition for scare water at wells, improving social relations within households and the community. Adequate sanitation facilities are particularly important to women, who often must use communal toilets that lack privacy and expose them to harassment and danger.

Supplying electricity to households has not generally not been considered a priority when considering the gender dimension of poverty. But the lack of electricity leads to the use of such environmentally polluting fuels as charcoal, wood and kerosene. The lack of electricity also reduces the efficiency of household chores and increases the burden on women.

Community participation in the provision and maintenance of infrastructure often relies heavily on women's unpaid labour. The need for women to balance economic, domestic and community responsibilities should be borne in mind when demands are made on their time. User charges and cost recovery for infrastructure should consider the strains they put on the budgets of low-income and particularly women-supported households.

### 4. *The urban environment*

Cities and towns are growing quickly in the context of deteriorating urban environment. Environmental degradation includes industrial pollution, poor working conditions, pollution from motor vehicles, limited and con-

taminated water supplies, deficiencies in solid waste management and inadequate sanitation, sewerage and drainage. The urban poor are particularly affected, since they often establish communities on sites such as hillsides, garbage dumps and swampy areas and near sources of industrial pollution that are unsuitable for human settlement. This complicates the role that women assume as custodians of the environment, since their efforts are not usually matched by official support or encouragement, and they are frequently excluded from related decision-making processes and planning.

Overcrowding, high population density and the absence of communal spaces and recreational facilities that characterize urban life contribute to social conflict, particularly in low-income neighbourhoods. The appropriation of household space for production activities can increase stress on poor households even though it allows women to combine productive and reproductive tasks. Stressful living conditions, complicated by such factors as male unemployment and substance abuse, account for increased levels of domestic violence. Violence is not confined to the home and is exacerbated by competition for scarce resources. Tensions are manifested in neighbourhood rivalries, which often take the form of ethnic conflict.

Gender issues must be considered in relation to violence, which is becoming an increasingly important part of mortality and morbidity in many cities. Violence affects women and men in different ways, both in its nature and its location. Women are often attacked in the home, but are also vulnerable outside. Women's mobility is often restricted by fear of robbery or sexual assault in the absence of street lighting, in isolated places or overcrowded conditions. Women may avoid certain forms of transportation or destinations and try to travel at certain times or in groups. Men, particularly the young, can be victims of gang warfare, money lenders and urban mafia. Urban street children and youth face distinctive problems as targets of urban violence. Thus urban design and service provision priorities, as well as decisions about policing and public safety, need to be based on an understanding of different gender needs.

### 5. *Urban management*

Municipal governments must be strengthened in the developing world if cities are to function efficiently and deliver basic urban services. This implies decentralization and empowering local authorities to raise revenues, pass laws, hold elections and manage municipal affairs. Urban management schemes have to date emerged from the perspective of the State, concentrating on efficiency, accountability, delivery and management of urban services and finances.

One weakness of this approach is its lack of interaction with urban community groups. In the absence of effective government, local groups, community-based organizations and non-governmental organizations have been organizing to meet their own needs in terms of housing, transport, and basic infrastructure. These local actions need to be linked to improvements and reforms in urban management. Otherwise, management schemes imposed from above will not take account or advantage of local activities. Improvements in urban management result from the coordination of the activities of local government and community groups that are active in the construction, management and maintenance of housing and urban infrastructure and services.

## 6.  HIV/AIDS

A decade ago, women appeared to be on the periphery of the AIDS epidemic. Today almost half of newly affected adults are women. The World Health Organization (WHO) estimates that by 2000 more than 13 million women will be infected with HIV and 4 million will have died. More than 1 million women became infected in 1993 alone.[32] The strong association between urbanization and HIV infection is compounded by mobility. For example, a study in southern Africa found that HIV infection was three times more common among those who had changed their place of residence in the past year. Moreover, the correlation between male migration from a rural area to an urban place of employment and back to a rural area and HIV transmission to women has become an urgent problem.

The lower cultural and socio-economic status of women facilitates the heterosexual spread of HIV infection in urban areas. At the same time, the spread of HIV/AIDS threatens to erase whatever progress has been made in raising the status of women by tying them to their caring roles, thus limiting their access to education and income-generating activities. For this reason, looking at women and AIDS from a health perspective is not enough. A gender analysis of the socio-economic and cultural causes and effects of the epidemic is necessary to understand the magnitude of the problem and to develop effective strategies to combat the epidemic.[33]

Social pressures related to women's reproductive role, including expectations that women will be mothers, make it difficult for some women to consider condom use. In fulfilling reproductive expectations, women risk not only infection from unprotected vaginal intercourse, but also transmitting the virus to a foetus if they become pregnant. Modifying gender relations and changing the attitudes of men could have an important impact on reducing the spread of HIV.

## 7. Nutrition

Nutritional well-being is a prerequisite for achieving the social, mental and physical well-being of a population.[34] Access to nutritional food and safe water is often hindered by laws, discriminatory practices, natural disasters and social, economic and gender disparities. Household food supply is less secure in urban than in rural areas because there is less land on which to cultivate crops for household consumption.

Infants, children, the disabled, the elderly, alcohol and drug abusers and pregnant and nursing women are the most nutritionally vulnerable groups, particularly those within poor urban households or without home. It is particularly important to provide nutritional support for women throughout pregnancy and breast-feeding and during the early childhood period. Globally, 43 per cent of all women and 51 per cent of pregnant women suffer from iron deficiency, as do virtually all adolescent girls in developing countries.[35]

The Government and communities must give priority to protecting and promoting the nutritional well-being of these groups. Men should be taught to assume an active role in ensuring the nutritional well-being of all members of their families. Securing adequate nutrition is necessary for reduce diet-related diseases in the urban community. Governments should ensure continuous supplies of food in urban areas through proper infrastructure development, including food preservation, transportation, storage and distribution systems. Governments need to stabilize food supplies from one year to the next and during the year, ensure household access to enough food to meet nutrition needs, ensure a stable supply of fuel for cooking meals, employ production and marketing systems based on resources that protect the environment and biodiversity, and improve access to work opportunities or production factors for urban workers, especially the unemployed, underemployed, female heads of households and those employed in the informal sector.

## F.  PUBLIC RESPONSE TO POVERTY: THE ROLES OF THE STATE, MARKET AND COMMUNITY

Extreme poverty is considered unacceptable in all societies and therefore requires a public response. Determining which public responses are most effective is central to dealing with poverty, as well as to incorporating gender into national policy-making and planning.

The State plays an important role in addressing poverty. The State's functions include raising taxes, allocating and reorganizing resources and redefining priorities. Reallocating resources from, say, the military to education and health offers considerable potential for improving growth and human welfare while respecting resource constraints. In practice, there would be bureaucratic and political obstacles to rationalizing priorities along these lines. Such obstacles may limit reallocation but are unlikely to prevent it entirely. There are several views of the State's role in incorporating gender into national planning. The first holds that the State is a neutral arbiter between competing social and economic interests, and is gender-neutral. In this view, women are potentially equal competitors with men and the challenge for them is to organize and use appropriate tactics to gain power. A second view addresses the State's mode of operation, characterizing it as bureaucratic, coercive, legal and normative. This approach goes beyond the State as an organization, connecting its operational role to everyday life. The links between the State and society are considered here, with Governments making extractive and distributive decisions to achieve various goals.

During the 1980s, the preferred approach to development involved removing State interference to allow market forces to develop. While social spending was not cut proportionately more than total spending, real government spending per capita declined in about two thirds of the countries in Africa and Latin America.[36] Reduced subsidies of education, health care and housing affected the poor more than high-income groups because subsidies constituted a higher share of their income.[37]

Expanding market relations adds new economic opportunities and new ways of achieving prosperity through specialization and exchange but it also introduces vulnerability because there is no guarantee that the pattern of opportunities and prices will cover subsistence needs.[38] Particularly vulnerable are those with nothing to sell but their labour. Moreover, markets are arenas of "cooperative conflict" in which conflicts and congruence of interest coexist. Thus while it is in the interest of buyers and sellers of labour to cooperate in production, there is potential for conflict in the distribution of the benefits of production.

The kind of market opportunities that poor women should have a right to are those which recognize them as human beings with rights, capabilities and responsibilities. Even in the absence of overt discrimination, market opportunities that reduce poor women to units of capital fail to recognize their domestic responsibilities, do nothing to offset their weak bargaining position in cooperative conflicts and are inadequate and even exploitive. As noted in chapter I, the position of women in deregulated markets can be particularly disadvantaged.[39] Unprotected and treated as factors of production rather than as human beings, their incomes are in most cases too low for them to be fully self-supporting as female heads of household, free of male control and economic support.

More satisfactory opportunities are possible if markets are regulated in terms of social mechanisms, as opposed to bureaucratic and self-defeating controls. This involves government agencies that, for example, provide alternative sources of employment and credit, introduce and enforce health and safety regulations, provide such services as sanitation, electricity and child care and educate poor women workers about their rights and assist them in upholding such rights and in bargaining for higher incomes. The State can also augment the productivity of the resource base. This implies improving land quality, energy use, water availability, social support structures and transportation and construction capacity. Most such resources are either unutilized or poorly utilized.

There are several links between gender and the State. The most complex and powerful is the collection of norms, laws and ideologies that shapes the meaning of politics and the nature of political discourse.[40] These range from birth control in one country to efforts to increase the number of women in paid employment in another. The State intervenes in the sexual division of labour by promoting or not promoting equal opportunity policies. And the State has a role in forming and reforming social patterns. For example, ideological support of a distinction between public and private spheres as a reflection of natural biological differences—as a physical rather than a social construction—will have grave consequences for women, excluding them from all public activities on an equal basis with men.

Achieving gender equality is more difficult in the context of decentralized social and economic decision-making. Centralized regulation should set minimum standards and conditions for a fair social environment, including rules against discrimination. State provision for poor women should support them in their own right, rather than as dependents of men, treating them as citizens rather than as targets. Social safety nets, targeted to those unable to benefit from the growth process, tend to reproduce the social dependency of women rather than challenge it. In too many poverty alleviation schemes, poor women are recipients of welfare handouts rather than claimers of rights, and the systems lack accountability. Poor women should not be simply consulted by state agencies, but should be able to appraise the performance of state officials and affect their promotion and remuneration, and the contraction or expansion of the units in which they serve. All citizens, not only the poor, benefit from greater accountability of public officials.

Public action in extending entitlements to the poor involves much more than action by the State—it includes what is done by the public for itself. These activities are not merely the directly beneficial contributions of social institutions, but also the actions of pressure groups and political activists.[38] Thus the public is not merely a patient whose well-being commands attention, but also an agent whose actions can transform society.

The issue of empowering women acquires a special meaning in this respect. Decisions that determine the shape of socio-economic policies usually lack women's input and thus tend to reflect the values, perspectives and experiences of men. Improving women's participation in decision-making means that all citizens would have a voice in social demands with regard to the allocation and use of resources, whether they be fiscal revenues, access to power, economic resources or cultural values. It would make the decision-making process more transparent and accessible, and thus more democratic.

Consensus-building and mediation mechanisms, including political parties, trade unions, employers' associations, community organizations, non-governmental organizations and local authorities, should be reinforced in such a way that potential conflict situations are transformed into negotiation processes characterized by the acceptance of common rules of the game, by a shared view of the major strategic lines of development and by respect for the demands of different social groups, including women.

## NOTES

[1]This chapter was prepared by the Division for the Advancement of the United Nations Secretariat, and includes contributions from the International Fund for Agricultural Development (IFAD), the Food and Agriculture Organization of the United Nations (FAO) and the United Nations Educational, Scientific and Cultural Organization (UNESCO).

[2]World Bank, *World Development Report, 1990* (Oxford and New York, Oxford University Press, 1990).

[3]Maryse Gaudier, "Poverty, inequality, exclusion: new approaches to theory and practice", Série bibliographique, No. 17 (Geneva, Institut international d'études sociales, 1993).

[4]"Economic and social deprivation and the structuring of the labour market in industrialized countries", *Labour and Society*, vol. 16, No. 2 (1991).

[5]Serge Milano, *La pauvreté dans les pays riches: du constant à analyse* (Paris, Nathan, 1992) and "Pauvreté et richesse dans le monde", *Le Monde*, August and September 1990 (Series of articles).

[6]Alain Touraine, "Face à l'exclusion", *Esprit*, February 1991.

[7]Jean-Baptiste Foucauld, "Inégalité, exclusion et injustice", *Problèmes économiques*, April 1992.

[8]Mayra Buvinic, N. Youseff and B. Von Elm, "Women-headed households: the ignored factor in development planning" (Washington, D.C., International Center for Research on Women, 1978).

[9]Mayra Buvinic and Geeta Rau Gupta, "The costs and benefits of targeting poor women-headed households and women-maintained families in developing countries". (Paper presented at the United Nations Seminar on Women in Extreme Poverty: Integration of Women's Concerns in National Development Planning, Vienna, 9-12 November 1992).

[10]"Family structure, female headship and poverty in developing countries: issues for the 1990s", Seminar IV of a series on the Determinants and Consequences of Women-Headed Households, sponsored jointly by The Population Council and the International Center for Research on Women, Washington, D.C., 28 November 1989.

[11]Buvinic and Gupta, op. cit. and "Family structure, female headship and poverty in developing countries ...". It is argued that the use of some division by sex in the typology of households remains necessary, and if one rejects the concept of family-headed households because of ambiguities inherent in its definition, one may be discarding a useful policy tool for identifying a special population subgroup that may be particularly disadvantaged and transmit poverty intergenerationally.

[12]"Concepts and classifications of female-headed households: implications and applications for national statistics", Seminar I of a series on the Determinants and Consequences of Women-Headed Households, sponsored jointly by The Population Coun-

cil and the International Center for Research on Women, New York, 12 and 13 December 1988.

[13] Buvinic and Gupta, op. cit. and "Concepts and classifications of female-headed households ...".

[14] Seminar II of a series on the Determinants and Consequences of Women-Headed Households, sponsored jointly by The Population Council and the International Center for Research on Women, 27 and 29 February 1989.

[15] Seminars I-IV on the Determinants and Consequences of Women-Headed Households, sponsored jointly by The Population Council and the International Center for Research on Women, 1988-1989.

[16] This section is based on contributions from FAO and IFAD.

[17] Idriss Jazairy, Mohiuddin Alamgir and Theresa Panuccio, *The State of World Rural Poverty: An Inquiry into Its Causes and Consequences* (New York, New York University Press, 1992).

[18] *Report of the Summit on the Economic Advancement of Rural Women* (Rome, International Fund for Agricultural Development, 1992).

[19] Information provided by FAO.

[20] Food and Agriculture Organization of the United Nations, "Report of the Inter-agency Consultation on Statistics and Data Bases in Agriculture and Rural Development, Rome, 24-26 September 1991".

[21] According to a report of the Secretary-General on the improvement of the situation of women in rural areas (A/48/187-E/1983/76), national machinery is defined as "any organizational structure established with particular responsibility for the advancement of women and the elimination of discrimination against women at the national level. Such structures have usually taken the following forms: (a) ministries of under-secretaries of State for women's affairs; (b) units located in or affiliated with ministries dealing with labour and social affairs; (c) units located in or affiliated with ministries dealing with agriculture and economic planning; (d) advisory bodies such as women's bureaux, national councils or national commissions; and (e) women's wings or units or units affiliated to the national ruling party."

[22] Jeffrey Campbell, "Women's role in dynamic forest-based small-scale enterprises" (Rome, Food and Agriculture Organization of the United Nations, 1991).

[23] International Labour Organization, "Gender issues in cooperatives and other self-help organizations in developing countries", Cooperative Branch Occasional Discussion Paper (Geneva, 1992).

[24] "Issues in programmes and projects for rural women" (Background Paper prepared by the Division for the Advancement of Women of the United Nations Secretariat for the International Seminar on Women and Rural Development Programmes and Projects, Vienna, 22-26 May 1989).

[25] United Nations Environment Programme, *The State of the World Environment* (Nairobi, 1987), cited in Jazairy, op. cit.

[26] World Health Organization, "Women, health and development" (Geneva, 1992).

[27] *Report on the World Social Situation, 1993* (United Nations publication, Sales No. E.93.IV.2).

[28] *World Urbanization Prospects: The 1992 Revision* (United Nations publication, Sales No. E.93.XIII.11).

[29] "Urban and rural areas by sex and age: the 1992 revision" (Working Paper prepared by the Population Division, United Nations Secretariat, November 1992).

[30] Charles F. Wasthoff and Luis Hernando Ochoa, "Unmet need and demand for family planning", *Demographic and Health Surveys*, Comparative Studies, No. 5 (July 1991).

[31] *Internal Migration of Women in Developing Countries* (United Nations publication, Sales No. E.94.XIII.3).

[32] World Health Organization, "Global Strategy on Women and AIDS" (Geneva, November 1993, draft).

[33] J. du Guerny, "Inter-relationship between gender relations and the HIV/AIDS epidemic: some possible considerations for policies and programmes", *AIDS Journal*, vol. 7, No. 8 (1993) and "A life course approach to the inter-relationship between gender relations and the spread of the HIV/AIDS epidemic: the example of the girl child", *AIDS Journal*, vol. 7, No. 10 (1993).

[34] *World Declaration on Nutrition*, adopted by the International Conference on Nutrition, Rome, December 1992.

[35] World Health Organization, "Women's health: towards a better world" (Issues Paper prepared for the Global Commission on Women's Health, Geneva, 1994).

[36] United Nations Development Programme, *Human Development Report, 1990* (Oxford and New York, Oxford University Press, 1990).

[37] *Report on the World Social Situation, 1989* (United Nations publication, Sales No. E.89.IV.2).

[38] J. Dreze and A. Sen, *Hunger and Public Action* (Oxford, Clarendon Press, 1989).

[39] G. Standing, "Global feminization through flexible labour", *World Development*, vol. 17, No. 7 (1989).

[40] Sue Ellen Charlton, Jana Everett and Kathleen Staudt, eds., *Women, the State and Development* (Albany, State University of New York Press, 1989).

# III

## Productive employment

The feminization of employment has been one of the most important economic changes of the past decade in terms of both the rapid influx of women into the paid labour force and the emerging patterns of employment. Productive employment by women also contributes to the eradication of poverty at both the household and national level. Gender analysis can broaden understanding of the global employment picture. While global restructuring has increased the employment and qualifications of women, their labour is underpaid, poorly regulated and subject to exploitation. It is not yet known whether this situation will remain so, or whether it can form the base of a new world of work that meets the needs of both women and men and generates the growth needed for development.[1]

### A. WORKING WOMEN

Women's participation in the labour market is shaped by, among other things, class structures, socio-cultural value systems and the level and direction of national economic development. Still, a number of features characterize working women everywhere. Women play a major economic role in all countries, though their contribution is still undervalued nearly everywhere and a substantial part of their work is not recognized as economically significant.[2]

While progress has been made in promoting equality, most women are still unable to exercise their rights as freely as men, and traditional attitudes and stereotyping maintain inequality by assigning low status to women and their work. Inequality is often reflected in women's access to education, training and productive resources, in the kinds of jobs available to them, in the incomes they receive, and, sometimes, in the degree of control they have over their own labour. This marginalization is exacerbated by women's extra burden of family responsibility and work.

About 854 million women were economically active in 1990, accounting for 32.1 per cent of the global labour force. Approximately one third (34.3 per cent) of women aged 15 years and older are in the labour force. The conspicuous regional differences in rates of women's economic activity clearly indicate the range of socio-economic status and women's emancipation found across countries. The highest rates of activity are found in the developed countries and in Africa; the lowest in the Arab countries. In most regions, particularly in the developing regions, female economic activity has increased over the past two decades. But in countries at an early stage of development, particularly in sub-Saharan Africa, a sharp decline in activity was mainly the result of economic crisis, structural change and traditional economic activities losing importance.

About half of all economically active women in developing countries are found in the informal sector; informal participation rates are particularly high in Africa. Women are in charge of many informal sector activities in these countries, including petty trading, personal services and various processing activities. Studies of major cities in Africa and Latin America indicate that 25 to 40 per cent of the owners and operators of enterprises in this sector are women. Women's involvement in the informal sector has increased as economic crises and structural adjustment have reduced job opportunities in the formal sector and increased the need for additional family income.

The modern sector—defined here as activities using wage labour or outside of agriculture—contains nearly 60 per cent of all economically active women. Women in the modern sector constitute about 30 per cent of the global labour force. In developed countries the figures are much higher: about 86 per cent of the female labour force is involved in non-agricultural activities, and 79.5 per cent are employees. Women in developing countries are also gaining ground in the modern sector as the role of agriculture declines and urbanization progresses.

As a result of the shift to manufacturing and services, agriculture now employs only 37 per cent of the global female labour force; even in developing countries, services are now a more important source of income for women than agriculture (42.9 compared with 40.8 per cent). Just 8.4 per cent of the female labour force in Latin America is active in agriculture. Only in Africa does agriculture remain a stronghold of female economic activity.

The tertiary sector is now the most important employer of women. This sector comprises a number of activities ranging from petty trade to banking whose common characteristic is that they provide a service rather than a physical product. Nearly half of all economically active women work in the sector, and women constitute 36.8 per cent of its labour force. The figures are higher in developed countries. In developing countries, women constitute just over one third of the labour force in this sector, and it employs 42.9 per cent of all economically active women. Latin America is an exception, with figures similar to those found in developed countries.

The definition of particular occupations as female or male varies among regions. In some parts of the world, for example, most waiters and doctors are male; in others, most are female. Women tend to be concentrated in service occupations with a low social status. Across sectors, women are well-represented in the category of professional and technical workers. Globally, 41.8 per cent of all employees in this category are women. In developing countries the share is 39.4 per cent. In Latin America women make up half this category, which slightly exceeds the figure for developed countries. The strong position of women in this category is largely the result of women's traditional prominence in teaching and nursing, even in countries with low levels of female participation in the economy. Gender barriers in such countries create a need for female teachers, nurses and doctors who can provide for the needs of women.

Recent United Nations and International Labour Organization (ILO) data indicate that women are entering the labour force in increasing numbers for reasons ranging from a desire to work to basic economic necessity. While the proportion of economically active women varies from one region to another, 41 per cent of the world's women aged 15 and over are economically active; in the OECD countries, 53 per cent of women were active in the labour force in 1980; by 1990 it was 60 per cent.[3] It is estimated that the participation rates of women will approximate those of men in many of these countries by 2000.

Surveys commissioned by ILO in Bulgaria, the Czech Republic, Hungary and Slovakia indicate that women in Central and Eastern Europe continue to demonstrate a strong labour force attachment, and the participation rates of working-aged women remain almost as high as those of working-aged men, though both have declined in the wake of reform. However, according to the *World Labour Report, 1994* the increase in female labour force participation between 1991 and 1992 in Poland and Romania was caused solely by the increase in the number of the registered unemployed.[4]

Official statistics indicate that women account for a smaller share of the labour force (31 per cent) in developing countries than they do in the developed market economies, though here too the figures are rising. However, these figures do not reflect women's participation in the informal sector or in agriculture. For example, in India the use of a wider definition of the term "economic activity" boosted the estimated 13 per cent of economically active women to 88 per cent.[5] Some of the highest participation rates for women are in Africa, where women produce 80 per cent of the food in some countries.[5] In South-East Asia industrialization has significantly increased wage employment—women make up nearly 80 per cent of the workforce in the export-processing zones. Women's participation rates are lower in Latin America (about 35 per cent) and are concentrated in the service sector. The lowest official rates in the Arab countries where there are social, cultural and sometimes legal barriers to women's employment outside the home.

One distinguishing feature of women's employment is its concentration in a small number of occupations that tend to attract lower rewards and prestige. Between 75 and 80 per cent of female workers in developed market economies are in the service sector; 15 to 20 per cent are in industry, where they are concentrated in "women's industries" such as clothing, footwear, textiles, leather and food processing; and about 5 per cent are in agriculture. The distribution of women is somewhat different in Central and Eastern Europe, with about 50 per cent in services, 30 per cent in industry and 20 per cent in agriculture, but these figures are changing in the transition to market economies. State control of job access has meant that traditionally female employment patterns were somewhat less marked in these countries, particularly in industry. Still, here too women tend to be concentrated in certain professions (such as doctors and teachers) which have consequently had a lower status. Most working women in developing countries are engaged in agriculture, sales or service jobs. The newly industrialized and industrializing countries of South-East Asia are an exception to these employment patterns in that industrialization has been led by women—a significant and growing number of women are employed in this sector. Women have also made steady progress in manufacturing in Latin America and the Caribbean.

Although most female workers continue to be concentrated in clerical, service, sales and middle-level professional occupations, over the past decade the number of women in managerial and administrative categories and in the professional and technical categories has been increasing relative to their share in total employment, particularly in the developed market economies. In addition, more women are starting their own businesses (as opposed to being self-employed) or joining the administrative and managerial ranks of large corporations. Still, few women have reached the highest ranks of these corporations or other organizations, including government bodies and teaching and research institutions, and the concept of a "glass ceiling" is now a recognized obstacle to women's success.

The growth in women's employment has not been matched by access to quality jobs. In most developed countries the increase in women's participation in the labour force has been accounted for by part-time jobs. The share of women in the total part-time labour force of countries members of the Organization for Economic Cooperation and Development (OECD) ranges from about 65 per cent in Italy, Greece and the United States to 90 per cent in Belgium and Germany.[6] Most part-time workers are women, particularly women with young children, and there is a correlation between part-time work and the availability of child-care facilities.[6] A recent survey conducted by the Commission of the European Communities covering the 1985-1991 period showed that almost 55 per cent of women working part-time were between the ages of 25 and 49—when family responsibilities are greatest.[6] Since part-time work often does not carry the same benefits, career prospects and training opportunities as full-time work, women with family responsibilities may be marginalized.

The trend towards flexible working patterns in response to global competition has resulted in the growth of other atypical forms of work, such as temporary, casual, home and out work and self-employment. Atypical workers tend to be young women with lower-than-average education and skills, and their jobs usually fall outside the protection of the law, collective agreements and social security systems.

The pursuit of flexible, low-cost labour has encouraged industrial enterprises to subcontract, with a concomitant extension of home work and other forms of out work. In addition, outsourcing in traditional manufacturing activities is being joined by service-based work using computers at home, particularly in developed countries. In both developed and developing countries women have been more affected by this trend than men and are more likely to find themselves on the periphery of a dual labour market. In most cases home workers are women—often with small children—who are forced into these activities as much by their family responsibilities as by the lack of other income-earning opportunities. Home workers, being largely invisible and difficult to organize, are particularly vulnerable to exploitation and are often excluded from the protection and benefits afforded by labour legislation. Where home workers do fall within the purview of legislation it can have important benefits with regard to social security, but enforcing laws on working conditions and remuneration remains difficult.[7]

While some advances have been made in the area of wage equity over the past 40 years, progress has not been universal or sustained. Women still earn between 50 and 80 per cent of men's wages. Women's work is undervalued in most societies and the incomes they receive are not a true measure of their economic contribution. The segregation of the labour market, the crowding of women in a narrow range of low-skilled, low status, atypical occupations, their shorter working hours and their unavailability for overtime, night work and shift work because of legal barriers or family responsibilities contribute, in part, to the gap between the earnings of men and women.

However, a residual difference in earnings that cannot be explained by job differences is probably attributable to more direct forms of discrimination. Wage discrimination is greater in the developing countries and in the newly industrialized or industrializing countries that have not ratified the ILO's Equal Remuneration Convention. Disparity in earnings also extends to piece work done at home and to agricultural wage work, where women are found mainly in the low-skilled and casual jobs; women in the informal sector generally earn less than men. The feminization of unpaid and low-paid work has contributed to a higher incidence of poverty among women, particularly among the female-headed households estimated to comprise one in five of all households.[8]

Despite efforts to promote equality between women and men in the labour field, discrimination and inequalities still persist, concentrating women in certain jobs and occupations, making their career path more difficult, denying them fair remuneration and hindering their access to training and other vital resources. While legislation has played an important role in promoting equality, a sustained effort in its implementation, combined with affirmative action, public education and cooperative action will be necessary if women are to achieve real equality in the working world.

## B.  WOMEN WORKERS IN A CHANGING GLOBAL ENVIRONMENT

Women's labour force participation is in many countries increasingly driven by economic necessity. These processes are sometimes seen as the effects of the globalization of capital and of structural adjustment policies that have led to cutbacks in the public sector, increased women's involvement in the informal sector and necessitated international migration in search of work. In other words, although quantitative progress has been made in improving female employment over the past few years, there have been few improvements in women's working conditions. Nor is it clear that new technologies necessarily improve women's working conditions.

### 1.  *Female labour force participation rates*

Women's recorded rates of economic activity have accelerated over the past few decades. This has been accompanied by a decline in men's recorded participation rates. Recent United Nations and ILO data indicate that women are entering the official labour force in increasing numbers. This increase needs to be interpreted with some caution, as it may be partly explained by improved data collection methods. Where it is actual, the cause is often economic necessity coupled with an expansion in employment opportunities.

The regional share of economically active women varies widely (see table III.1). It is estimated that women will make up half the labour force in most countries and regions by 2000. Indeed, women are expected to form the majority of the workforce in the United Kingdom by then.[7] The ratio of women to men in the economically active population has been increasing in almost all regions since 1970 (see table III.2).

These trends have been reinforced by an increasing convergence of women's and men's employment cycles. Historically, the typical employment life cycle for women was an M-shaped curve resulting from women taking time out of the workforce for childbearing and -rearing after an initial period of economic activity, followed by a late return to the workforce. Increasingly, women's time out of the labour force is being reduced to a minimum child-bearing period, while men, at least in some countries, are encouraged by parental leave provisions to take time off.

Not only are women entering the paid labour force in increasing numbers, there is also substantial evidence from the economies in transition of their continuing labour force attachment in conditions of recession, as demonstrated in ILO surveys in Bulgaria, the Czech Republic, Hungary and Slovakia.[8] In other regions women have always been economically active, but often in jobs that have not been included in labour force statistics (see sect. C.2). There appears to be a major mismatch in Central and Eastern Europe between an ideology emphasizing women's roles as mothers that is reemerging in conditions of transition and recession, and women's own aspirations as workers. Despite the difficulties of working, women in the formerly socialist countries felt they gained more from their labour force involvement than relative economic independence. Many feel that their work collective was or is their most important social network.

An ILO survey in the Czech Republic showed that only 28 per cent of married women would like to stay at home if their husbands earned enough for them to do so.[9] Surveys conducted in several other Eastern and Central European countries corroborate the notion that labour force participation has become an integral part of women's self-perception and sense of identity. A Bulgarian study in February 1991 revealed that only 20 per cent of women wanted to stay at home. A survey of East German women in autumn 1991 found that only 10 per cent of women indicated that they would definitely give up work if they no longer needed the money, and 70 per cent thought they would still want to work.[10] A survey of desired work patterns found that three quarters of all working married women, four fifths of working single mothers and even most non-working mothers would prefer full-time to part-time work.

*Table III.1*

Female economic activity rates, selected countries, 1950-1990[a]

Percentage

| Country or area | 1950 | 1960 | 1970 | 1980 | 1990 |
|---|---|---|---|---|---|
| **Industrialized countries** | | | | | |
| France | 28.30 | 28.10 | 30.10 | 33.80 | 35.15 |
| Italy | 21.00 | 21.15 | 21.90 | 23.65 | 33.70 (1991) |
| Japan | 33.00 | 36.40 | 39.15 | 36.30 | 36.85 |
| Norway | 20.10 | 17.75 | 24.15 | 38.15 | 44.80 |
| United Kingdom | 25.35 | 28.70 | 31.85 | 36.25 | 37.00 (1991) |
| United States | 24.10 | 25.45 | 30.40 | 39.15 | 44.40 (1992) |
| **Countries in transition, Central and Eastern Europe** | | | | | |
| Bulgaria | 71 (1956) | 68 (1965) | 72 (1975) | .. | 74 |
| Czechoslovakia | .. | 59 (1961) | 65 | 75 | 77 (1988) |
| Hungary | .. | 50 | 58 | 63 | 62 (1989) |
| Poland | .. | 66 | 72 | 70 (1978) | 68 (1988) |
| **Africa** | | | | | |
| Kenya | 39.45 | 38.50 | 36.90 | 35.15 | 31.30[b] |
| Nigeria | 32.80 | 31.75 | 30.30 | 28.90 | 25.45[b] |
| Senegal | 40.75 | 39.76 | 39.05 | 3.05 | 33.70[b] |
| Swaziland | 44.60 | 42.55 | 38.90 | 35.45 | 30.95[b] |
| United Republic of Tanzania | 54.95 | 55.10 | 52.70 | 49.45 | 44.20[b] |
| Zaire | 44.10 | 41.90 | 36.60 | 29.80 | 26.35[b] |
| **Latin America** | | | | | |
| Argentina | 19.85 | 16.80 | 19.50 | 19.55 | 21.00 |
| Brazil | 10.20 | 11.25 | 14.35 | 19.65 | 21.90 (1989) |
| Costa Rica | 10.25 | 9.75 | 11.15 | 14.65 | 21.90 (1992) |
| Cuba | 9.15 | 10.55 | 11.70 | 22.35 | 25.00b |
| **Asia** | | | | | |
| China | 47.10 | 43.95 | 44.25 | 48.95 | 53.90b |
| Hong Kong | 23.90 | 22.55 | 29.50 | 37.25 | 39.40 (1991) |
| India | 30.45 | 28.45 | 24.80 | 21.70 | 22.70 (1991) |
| Republic of Korea | 18.00 | 17.30 | 23.10 | 26.60 | 28.40[b] |
| Sri Lanka | 19.70 | 18.60 | 18.05 | 20.20 | 26.60 (1992) |

*Sources*: Based on *Economically Active Population: Estimates, 1950-1980; Projections, 1985-2025* (Geneva, International Labour Office, 1986), for 1950-1980; *Year Book of Labour Statistics, 1993* (Geneva, International Labour Office, 1993), for 1990, unless otherwise indicated; and *Structural Change in Central and Eastern Europe: Labour Market and Social Policy Implications* (Paris, Organisation for Economic Cooperation and Development, 1993), for the countries of Central and Eastern Europe.

*Note*: Two dots (..) indicate that data are not available or are not separately reported.

a     The activity rates are percentages of the total female population, not just the population of active age.

b     Projection.

Recent global economic trends have severely impacted both the quantity and the quality of women's labour force participation. Economic recession has led to high levels of female unemployment in most regions of the world (see tables III.3-III.6). And the quality of working conditions has been affected by globalization, structural adjustment programmes, restructuring and flexibilization (see chap. I).

Unemployment patterns are closely linked to changes in the structure of employment. Most job losses in developed market economies and in the economies in transition have been in manufacturing, which implies that men's share of overall employment has dropped. However, gains in women's employment due to the expansion of hi-tech light industries and the service sector have not substantially altered the overall pattern of women's larger share of unemployment.

In addition, women experience greater difficulties than men in finding re-employment. This is partly due to higher skill requirements in expanding economic sectors, and hence highlights the need for technical and skills upgrading for women workers. The re-employment

*Table III.2*

Ratio of women to men in the economically active population by region, 1970-1990

Number of women for each 100 men

| Region | 1970 | 1980 | 1990 |
|---|---|---|---|
| Africa | 39 | 58 | 71 |
| Asia and the Pacific | 28 | 42 | 48 |
| Eastern Europe | 79 | 81 | 85 |
| Latin America and the Caribbean | 35 | 48 | 62 |
| Western Europe and other | 45 | 60 | 72 |
| World | 37 | 52 | 62 |

*Source*: Division for the Advancement of Women of the United Nations Secretariat, from data contained in the Women's Indicators and Statistics Data Base (WISTAT), version 3, 1994.

challenge also reflects the contraction of public sector employment in favour of private sector employment in Western developed countries. In Central and Eastern European countries in transition this contraction is driving a massive programme of privatization of State enterprises. The transition from a centrally planned to a market economy has been paralleled by a process of economic restructuring, with concomitant heavy loss of employment for men, too. None the less, women form the majority of the unemployed in all these countries except for Hungary, partly because they dominated the top-heavy administrative and clerical branches of the State sector.

Another difficulty women workers experience in finding new work is discrimination. Data from the Czech Republic show that managers manifest clear preferences for male workers when undertaking new recruitment, especially in professional, technical and skilled manual work. They also rated men much more highly than women for managerial and administrative positions. In the Czech Republic, Slovakia and Hungary, up to one third of managers saw women as "expensive labour" as a result of legislation covering workers with family responsibilities.[11]

Standard concepts of employment are more difficult to apply to developing economies, where a large share of economic activity takes place in the informal and rural sectors and is characterized by irregular and seasonal employment, and where social security systems are limited or non-existent.[12] Nevertheless, consistently higher rates of female unemployment have persisted in both sub-Saharan Africa and Latin America and the Caribbean (see table III.4). Large male-female differentials in the context of high unemployment levels

have been identified in the Caribbean (Bahamas, Jamaica) and some Central American countries (Panama). In São Paulo, Brazil, for example, economically active women were three times as likely as men to be unemployed and the average period of unemployment was also longer. Female unemployment increased rapidly between 1982 and 1985: in Bogota, Colombia by five times, and in Caracas, Venezuela by two times.[13]

In Africa female unemployment rates are usually twice those for men. Female economic activity rates in the Middle East and North Africa are lower than elsewhere. Women form only 10 per cent of the labour force in Algeria, Egypt, the Islamic Republic of Iran and Jordan, 15 per cent in the Syrian Arab Republic, 20 per cent in Morocco and Tunisia and 33 per cent in Turkey. However, huge numbers of women in agriculture in Egypt, the Islamic Republic of Iran and Jordan are not counted in these figures, and the number of female self-employed, own-account and home workers in Morocco, Tunisia and Turkey is greatly underestimated.[14]

More than half (54.2 per cent in 1993) of the world's female labour force live in Asia and the Pacific.[15] Women, especially young women, have supplied the bulk of the growth in the labour force in the export-oriented industrialization in East and South-East Asia, leading to the claim that this process was as much female-led as export-led. Nevertheless, many countries in this region are experiencing severe problems of unemployment, underemployment and poverty. Data are patchy and unreliable, but it appears that in some countries of the region, notably Pakistan, the Philippines and Sri Lanka, women suffer disproportionately from unemployment (see table III.6). This has stimulated the internal and international migration discussed later in this chapter.

## 2. *Invisible women and unreliable data*

Employment and census data continue to underestimate the level of women's labour force participation, particularly in developing countries where women work in the informal sector or in subsistence production. The four areas of activity that have tended to be uncounted or underestimated are subsistence production, informal sector work, domestic labour and related production and volunteer work. This is partly a measurement problem and partly a conceptual problem about which kinds of work are productive. Since women predominate in all four areas this exclusion renders much of women's work invisible.

*Table III.3*
Unemployment rates by gender, selected developed countries, 1970-1991
Percentage

| Country | | 1970 | 1975 | 1980 | 1983 | 1988 | 1989 | 1990 | 1991 |
|---|---|---|---|---|---|---|---|---|---|
| Australia | Total | 1.6 | 4.9 | 6.1 | 10.0 | 7.2 | 6.2 | 6.9 | 9.9 |
| | Male | 1.1 | 3.8 | 5.1 | 9.7 | 6.8 | 5.7 | 6.7 | 9.9 |
| | Female | 2.8 | 7.0 | 7.9 | 10.4 | 7.9 | 6.9 | 7.2 | 9.2 |
| Austria | Total | 2.4 | 2.0 | 1.9 | 4.5 | 5.3 | 5.0 | 3.2 | 3.5 |
| | Male | 1.6 | 1.5 | 1.6 | 4.7 | 5.1 | 4.6 | 3.0 | 3.3 |
| | Female | 3.8 | 2.8 | 2.3 | 4.1 | 5.6 | 5.5 | 3.6 | 3.7 |
| Belgium | Total | .. | 5.1 | 8.9 | 14.0 | 11.1 | 10.2 | 7.2 | .. |
| | Male | .. | 3.7 | 5.4 | 10.6 | 7.7 | 6.9 | 4.5 | .. |
| | Female | .. | 7.7 | 14.7 | 19.3 | 16.0 | 14.8 | 11.5 | .. |
| Canada | Total | 5.9 | 6.9 | 7.5 | 11.8 | 7.8 | 7.5 | 8.1 | 10.3 |
| | Male | 6.5 | 6.2 | 6.9 | 12.0 | 7.4 | 7.3 | 8.1 | 10.8 |
| | Female | 4.5 | 8.1 | 8.4 | 11.6 | 8.3 | 7.9 | 8.1 | 9.7 |
| Denmark | Total | .. | 5.1 | 7.0 | 10.5 | 8.7 | 9.4 | 9.7 | 10.6 |
| | Male | .. | 5.8 | 6.5 | 9.8 | 7.2 | 8.0 | 8.4 | 9.3 |
| | Female | .. | 3.9 | 7.6 | 11.3 | 10.3 | 11.1 | 11.3 | 12.1 |
| Finland | Total | 1.9 | 2.6 | 4.7 | 5.5 | 4.5 | 3.5 | 3.4 | 7.5 |
| | Male | 2.6 | 2.7 | 4.7 | 5.7 | 5.1 | 3.6 | 4.0 | 9.2 |
| | Female | 1.0 | 2.4 | 4.7 | 5.2 | 4.0 | 3.3 | 2.8 | 5.7 |
| France | Total | 2.4 | 4.0 | 6.3 | 8.3 | 10.0 | 9.5 | 8.9 | 9.3 |
| | Male | .. | 2.8 | 4.2 | 6.3 | 7.7 | 7.0 | 6.7 | 7.2 |
| | Female | .. | 6.1 | 9.4 | 11.2 | 13.1 | 12.8 | 11.9 | 12.1 |
| Germany, Federal Republic of | Total | 0.7 | 4.7 | 3.8 | 9.1 | 8.7 | 7.9 | 7.0 | .. |
| | Male | 0.7 | 4.3 | 3.0 | 8.4 | 7.8 | 6.9 | 5.7 | .. |
| | Female | 0.8 | 5.4 | 5.2 | 10.1 | 10.0 | 9.4 | 8.8 | .. |
| Greece | Total | .. | .. | .. | 7.9 | 7.7 | .. | 7.0 | .. |
| | Male | .. | .. | .. | 5.9 | 4.9 | .. | 4.3 | .. |
| | Female | .. | .. | .. | 12.5 | 12.5 | .. | 11.7 | .. |
| Ireland | Total | .. | .. | .. | 14.7 | 18.4 | 17.9 | 17.4 | .. |
| | Male | .. | .. | .. | 15.7 | 18.4 | 17.9 | .. | .. |
| | Female | .. | .. | .. | 12.4 | 17.9 | 17.9 | .. | .. |
| Italy | Total | 5.4 | 5.9 | 7.6 | 9.9 | 12.0 | 12.0 | 11.0 | .. |
| | Male | 3.7 | 3.8 | 4.8 | 6.6 | 8.1 | 8.1 | 7.3 | .. |
| | Female | 9.6 | 9.6 | 13.1 | 16.2 | 15.4 | 18.7 | 17.1 | .. |
| Japan | Total | 1.1 | 1.9 | 2.0 | 2.6 | 2.5 | 2.3 | 2.1 | 2.1 |
| | Male | 0.2 | 2.0 | 2.0 | 2.7 | 2.5 | 2.2 | 2.0 | 2.0 |
| | Female | 1.0 | 1.7 | 2.0 | 2.6 | 2.6 | 2.3 | 2.2 | 2.2 |
| Luxembourg | Total | .. | 0.2 | 0.7 | 1.6 | 1.6 | 1.4 | 1.3 | .. |
| | Male | .. | .. | 0.5 | 1.3 | 1.5 | .. | .. | .. |
| | Female | .. | .. | 1.2 | 2.1 | 1.7 | .. | .. | .. |
| Netherlands | Total | .. | 6.0 | 7.9 | 13.4 | 9.0 | 8.0 | 7.5 | 7.0 |
| | Male | .. | 4.6 | 6.3 | 12.1 | 7.0 | 6.0 | 5.4 | 5.3 |
| | Female | .. | 9.4 | 13.4 | 16.0 | 13.0 | 12.0 | 10.7 | 9.5 |
| New Zealand | Total | .. | 0.4 | 2.9 | 5.7 | 5.6 | 7.1 | 7.8 | 10.3 |
| | Male | .. | 0.4 | 2.6 | 5.5 | 5.6 | 7.3 | 8.2 | 10.9 |
| | Female | .. | 0.4 | 3.3 | 6.2 | 5.6 | 6.9 | 7.2 | 9.5 |
| Norway (persons aged 16-74) | Total | .. | 2.3 | 1.7 | 3.4 | 3.2 | 4.9 | 5.2 | 5.5 |
| | Male | .. | 1.9 | 1.3 | 3.2 | 3.0 | 5.1 | 5.6 | 5.9 |
| | Female | .. | 2.9 | 2.3 | 3.8 | 3.4 | 4.7 | 4.8 | 5.0 |

*Table III.3*

(continued)

| Country | | 1970 | 1975 | 1980 | 1983 | 1988 | 1989 | 1990 | 1991 |
|---|---|---|---|---|---|---|---|---|---|
| Spain | Total | 1.1 | 1.9 | 9.8 | 16.5 | 19.5 | 17.2 | 16.3 | 16.4 |
| (persons aged | Male | .. | 2.1 | 9.6 | 15.0 | 14.1 | 11.2 | 12.0 | 12.3 |
| 16 and over) | Female | .. | 1.3 | 10.3 | 20.2 | 30.0 | 28.6 | 24.2 | 25.8 |
| Sweden | Total | 1.5 | 1.6 | 2.0 | 3.5 | 1.6 | 1.4 | 1.5 | 2.7 |
| | Male | 1.3 | 1.3 | 1.7 | 3.4 | 1.6 | 1.3 | 1.5 | 3.0 |
| | Female | 1.8 | 2.0 | 2.3 | 3.6 | 1.6 | 1.4 | 1.5 | 2.3 |
| Switzerland | Total | .. | 0.3 | 0.2 | 0.9 | 0.7 | 0.6 | 0.6 | 1.3 |
| | Male | .. | 0.4 | 0.2 | 0.8 | 0.6 | 0.5 | 0.5 | 1.2 |
| | Female | .. | 0.2 | 0.3 | 0.9 | 1.0 | 0.8 | 0.7 | 1.5 |
| United Kingdom | Total | .. | 4.0 | 6.8 | 11.7 | 8.4 | 6.3 | 5.9 | 8.1 |
| | Male | .. | 5.4 | 8.3 | 13.8 | 10.1 | 7.9 | 7.6 | 10.7 |
| | Female | .. | 1.9 | 4.8 | 8.4 | 6.1 | 4.2 | 3.5 | 4.6 |
| United States | Total | 4.8 | 8.3 | 7.0 | 9.5 | 5.4 | 5.2 | 5.4 | 6.6 |
| | Male | 4.2 | 7.7 | 6.8 | 9.7 | 5.3 | 5.1 | 5.4 | 6.9 |
| | Female | 5.9 | 9.3 | 7.4 | 9.2 | 5.6 | 5.3 | 5.4 | 6.3 |
| Yugoslavia | Total | 7.7 | 10.2 | 11.9 | 8.6 | 14.1 | .. | 16.4 | .. |
| | Male | 6.2 | 7.8 | 8.6 | 9.1 | 10.9 | .. | .. | .. |
| | Female | 10.8 | 14.4 | 17.4 | 18.4 | 17.7 | .. | .. | .. |

*Sources*: *Year Book of Labour Statistics* (Geneva, International Labour Office, various issues, including 1992) and ILO INFOSTA data bank, cited in S. Baden, "The impact of recession and structural adjustment on women's work in developing and developed countries", Working Paper No. 19, Interdepartmental Project on Equality for Women in Employment (Geneva, International Labour Office, 1993), table 6.

*Note*: Two dots (..) indicate that data are not available or are not separately reported

*Table III.4*

Unemployment rates by gender, selected countries, Latin America and the Caribbean, 1983-1992

Percentage

| Country | | 1983 | 1984 | 1988 | 1989 | 1990 | 1991 | 1992 |
|---|---|---|---|---|---|---|---|---|
| Argentina | Total | 4.2 | 3.8 | 5.9 | 7.3 | .. | .. | .. |
| | Male | .. | .. | 5.2 | 7.0 | .. | .. | .. |
| | Female | .. | .. | 7.2 | 7.7 | .. | .. | .. |
| Bahamas | Total | .. | .. | 11.0 | 11.7 | .. | .. | 14.8 |
| | Male | .. | .. | 8.2 | 11.0 | .. | .. | 13.8 |
| | Female | .. | .. | 14.2 | 12.5 | .. | .. | 16.0 |
| Barbados | Total | 15.0 | .. | 17.4 | 13.7 | 15.0 | 17.1 | 23.0 |
| | Male | 5.7 | .. | 12.3 | 9.1 | 10.3 | 13.3 | 20.4 |
| | Female | 8.8 | .. | 22.9 | 18.7 | 20.2 | 21.4 | 25.7 |
| Bolivia | Total | .. | .. | .. | .. | 9.4 | 7.3 | .. |
| | Male | .. | .. | .. | .. | 9.9 | 6.9 | .. |
| | Female | .. | .. | .. | .. | 8.8 | 7.8 | .. |
| Brazil | Total | 4.9 | 4.3 | 3.8 | .. | 3.7 | .. | .. |
| | Male | 4.9 | 4.1 | 3.6 | .. | 3.8 | .. | .. |
| | Female | 4.8 | 4.6 | 4.2 | .. | 3.4 | .. | .. |
| Chile | Total | 14.6 | 13.9 | 6.3 | 5.3 | 5.6 | 5.3 | 4.4 |
| | Male | 14.6 | .. | 5.6 | 5.0 | 5.7 | 5.1 | 4.1 |
| | Female | 14.7 | .. | 7.8 | 6.1 | 5.7 | 5.8 | 5.6 |
| Costa Rica | Total | 9.0 | 5.0 | 5.5 | 3.8 | 4.6 | 5.5 | 4.1 |
| | Male | 8.8 | 5.0 | 4.4 | 3.2 | 4.2 | 4.8 | 3.5 |
| | Female | 9.6 | 5.0 | 8.0 | 5.3 | 5.9 | 7.4 | 5.4 |

*Table III.4*

(continued)

| Country | | 1983 | 1984 | 1988 | 1989 | 1990 | 1991 | 1992 |
|---|---|---|---|---|---|---|---|---|
| Ecuador | Total | .. | .. | 7.0 | 7.9 | 6.1 | 5.8 | .. |
| | Male | .. | .. | 5.1 | 5.9 | 4.3 | 4.1 | .. |
| | Female | .. | .. | 10.3 | 11.1 | 9.1 | 8.5 | .. |
| El Salvador | Total | .. | .. | 9.4[a] | 8.4 | 10.0 | 7.5 | 7.9 |
| | Male | .. | .. | 11.0[a] | 10.0 | 10.1 | 8.3 | 8.4 |
| | Female | .. | .. | 7.1[a] | 6.8 | 9.8 | 6.6 | 7.2 |
| Guadeloupe | Total | 17.5 | 20.3 | 24.0 | 14.0 | 17.0 | 19.9 | .. |
| | Male | .. | .. | 16.0 | 16.0 | .. | .. | .. |
| | Female | .. | .. | 33.0 | 34.0 | .. | .. | .. |
| Jamaica | Total | 26.4 | 25.5 | 18.9 | 16.8 | 15.7 | .. | .. |
| | Male | 16.1 | 15.8 | 11.9 | 9.5 | 9.3 | .. | .. |
| | Female | 38.4 | 36.6 | 27.0 | 25.2 | 23.1 | .. | .. |
| Mexico | Total | 6.8 | 6.0 | 3.6 | 3.0 | 2.8 | 2.6 | 2.8 |
| | Male | 6.0 | 5.3 | 3.0 | 2.6 | 2.6 | 2.5 | 2.6 |
| | Female | 8.5 | 7.6 | 4.7 | 3.8 | 3.1 | 3.0 | 3.1 |
| Nicaragua | Total | .. | .. | 6.0 | 8.4 | 11.1 | 14.0 | .. |
| | Male | .. | .. | 4.9 | 6.9 | 9.0 | 11.3 | .. |
| | Female | .. | .. | 8.3 | 12.0 | 15.4 | 19.4 | .. |
| Panama | Total | 9.7 | 10.1 | 16.3 | 16.3 | .. | 16.1 | 13.6 |
| | Male | 7.7 | 8.2 | 14.0 | 13.7 | .. | 12.8 | 10.0 |
| | Female | 14.5 | 14.2 | 21.4 | 21.6 | .. | 22.6 | |
| Paraguay | Total | 8.3 | 7.3 | 4.7 | 6.1 | 6.6 | 5.1 | .. |
| | Male | 9.8 | 9.1 | 4.8 | 6.6 | 6.6 | 5.4 | .. |
| | Female | 5.9 | 4.8 | 4.6 | 5.6 | 6.5 | 4.7 | .. |
| Peru | Total | .. | .. | .. | 7.9 | .. | 5.8 | .. |
| | Male | .. | .. | .. | 6.0 | .. | 4.8 | .. |
| | Female | .. | .. | .. | 10.7 | .. | 7.3 | .. |
| Puerto Rico | Total | 23.4 | 20.7 | 15.0 | 14.6 | 14.1 | 16.0 | 16.6 |
| | Male | 26.6 | 23.7 | 17.4 | 16.9 | 16.2 | 17.9 | 19.0 |
| | Female | 17.1 | 15.1 | 10.8 | 10.8 | 10.7 | 12.8 | 12.8 |
| Trinidad and Tobago | Total | 11.0 | 13.5 | 22.0 | 22.0 | 20.0 | 18.5 | .. |
| | Male | 9.0 | 12.0 | 21.1 | 20.8 | 17.8 | 15.7 | .. |
| | Female | 15.0 | 16.0 | 23.6 | 24.5 | 24.2 | 23.4 | .. |
| Uruguay | Total | .. | .. | 8.6 | 8.0 | 8.5 | 9.0 | .. |
| | Male | .. | .. | 6.3 | 6.1 | 6.9 | 7.2 | .. |
| | Female | .. | .. | 11.9 | 10.8 | 10.9 | 11.6 | .. |
| Venezuela | Total | 10.1 | 13.0 | 7.3 | 9.2 | 10.4 | 9.5 | .. |
| | Male | .. | .. | 7.8 | 9.8 | 10.9 | 9.6 | .. |
| | Female | .. | .. | 6.1 | 7.6 | 9.3 | 9.4 | .. |

*Source*: *Year Book of Labour Statistics* (Geneva, International Labour Office, various issues).
*Note*: Two dots (..) indicate that data are not available or are not separately reported.

a     Urban areas.

*Table III.5*

Unemployment rates by gender, selected countries, Middle East and North Africa, 1983-1992

Percentage

| Country | | 1983 | 1984 | 1988 | 1989 | 1990 | 1991 | 1992 |
|---|---|---|---|---|---|---|---|---|
| Cyprus | Total | 3.3 | 3.3 | 2.8 | 2.3 | 1.8 | 3.0 | 1.8 |
| | Male | 2.9 | 2.9 | 2.2 | 1.7 | 1.4 | 2.2 | 1.3 |
| | Female | 4.1 | 4.1 | 3.8 | 3.3 | 2.5 | 4.4 | 2.6 |
| Israel | Total | 4.5 | 5.9 | 6.4 | 8.9 | 9.6 | 10.6 | 11.2 |
| | Male | 4.0 | 5.2 | 5.7 | 7.9 | 8.4 | 8.6 | 9.2 |
| | Female | 5.3 | 7.0 | 7.6 | 10.3 | 11.3 | 13.4 | 13.9 |
| Syrian Arab Republic | Total | 4.2 | 4.7 | .. | 5.8 | .. | 6.8 | .. |
| | Male | 3.8 | 4.1 | .. | 5.1 | .. | 5.2 | .. |
| | Female | 6.3 | 8.2 | .. | 9.5 | .. | 14.0 | .. |
| Turkey | Total | 12.1 | 11.9 | 8.3 | 8.5 | 7.4 | 8.3 | 7.8 |
| | Male | 10.1 | 9.0 | 7.7 | 8.4 | 7.5 | 8.8 | 8.1 |
| | Female | 24.8 | 29.1 | 9.6 | 8.8 | 7.2 | 7.1 | 7.2 |

*Source*: *Year Book of Labour Statistics, 1993* (Geneva, International Labour Office, 1993), table 9A.

*Note*: Two dots (..) indicate that data are not available or are not separately reported.

*Table III.6*

Unemployment rates by gender, selected countries, Asia, 1983-1992

Percentage

| Country or area | | 1983 | 1984 | 1988 | 1989 | 1990 | 1991 | 1992 |
|---|---|---|---|---|---|---|---|---|
| China | Total | 2.3 | 1.9 | 2.0 | 2.6 | 2.5 | 2.3 | 2.3 |
| | Male | 0.7 | 0.6 | 0.7 | 1.3 | 0.9 | 0.8 | .. |
| | Female | 1.1 | 1.0 | 1.0 | 1.3 | 1.2 | 1.1 | .. |
| Hong Kong | Total | 4.5 | 3.9 | 1.4 | 1.1 | 1.3 | 1.8 | 2.0 |
| | Male | 5.0 | 4.2 | 1.4 | 1.1 | 1.3 | 1.9 | 2.0 |
| | Female | 3.5 | 3.4 | 1.4 | 1.1 | 1.3 | 1.6 | 1.9 |
| Japan | Total | 2.6 | 2.7 | 2.5 | 2.3 | 2.1 | 2.1 | 2.2 |
| | Male | 2.7 | 2.7 | 2.5 | 2.2 | 2.0 | 2.0 | 2.1 |
| | Female | 2.6 | 2.8 | 2.6 | 2.3 | 2.2 | 2.2 | 2.2 |
| Pakistan | Total | 3.9 | 3.9 | 3.1 | 3.1 | 3.1 | 6.3[a] | 6.3[a] |
| | Male | 4.2 | 4.2 | 3.4 | 3.4 | 3.4 | 4.5[a] | 4.5[a] |
| | Female | 1.9 | 1.9 | 0.9 | 0.9 | 0.9 | 16.8[a] | 16.8[a] |
| Philippines | Total | 4.9 | 7.0 | 8.3 | 8.4 | 8.1 | 9.0 | 8.6 |
| | Male | 3.7 | 5.2 | 7.6 | 7.3 | 7.1 | 8.1 | 7.9 |
| | Female | 6.7 | 10.0 | 9.5 | 10.3 | 9.8 | 10.5 | 9.9 |
| Republic of Korea | Total | 4.1 | 3.8 | 2.5 | 2.6 | 2.4 | 2.3 | 2.4 |
| | Male | 5.2 | 4.8 | 3.0 | 3.0 | 2.9 | 2.5 | 2.6 |
| | Female | 2.2 | 2.2 | 1.7 | 1.8 | 1.8 | 2.0 | 2.1 |
| Singapore | Total | 3.2 | 2.7 | 3.3 | 2.2 | 1.7 | 1.9 | 2.7 |
| | Male | 3.2 | 2.6 | 3.8 | 2.3 | 1.7 | 2.0 | 2.7 |
| | Female | 3.2 | 2.8 | 2.6 | 1.9 | 1.6 | 1.8 | 2.6 |
| Sri Lanka | Total | .. | .. | .. | .. | 14.4 | 14.1 | 14.1 |
| | Male | .. | .. | .. | .. | 9.1 | 10.0 | 10.6 |
| | Female | .. | .. | .. | .. | 23.5 | 21.2 | 21.0 |
| Thailand | Total | 2.9 | 2.9 | 3.1 | 1.4 | 2.2 | .. | .. |
| | Male | 2.6 | 2.5 | 2.6 | 1.2 | 2.1 | .. | .. |
| | Female | 3.3 | 3.4 | 3.6 | 1.6 | 2.4 | .. | .. |

*Source*: *Year Book of Labour Statistics, 1993* (Geneva, International Labour Office, 1993), table 9A.

*Note*: Two dots (..) indicate that data are not available or are not separately reported.

a    Computed from 1990/91 survey results.

The conceptual, theoretical and methodological constraints to measuring women's labour have eased somewhat over the past two decades. Indeed, the ILO's Fifteenth International Conference of Labour Statisticians in 1993 set out guidelines for including employment data from the informal sector in official labour force statistics. Considering the number of women employed in the informal sector world wide, this inclusion is needed to both improve women's status in the labour market and to plan economic development. Methodological difficulties remain which give rise to widely varying data depending on how questionnaires are designed and questions asked.[16] Table III.7 indicates how widely data on female labour force participation can vary according to their source and the method of collection.

The problem in the informal sector is not that women's work is unpaid, but that data on this sector are patchy and unreliable. Some studies suggest that the value of unrecorded activities ranges from one third to one half of GNP.[17] United Nations estimates put the value of unpaid housework alone at between 10 and 35 per cent of GDP world wide. These estimates are based on the cost of purchasing comparable goods and services or hiring someone to do the work.[18] Women's unremunerated domestic maintenance and child-care tasks have been described as acting "as a labour levy, or tax, on women to be paid before they can join in marketed activities"; because of the distortion in the labour market that it creates, "the reproduction tax on women sends ripples of inefficiencies throughout the economy".[19] The need to devise methods of accounting for women's full role in production and the subsidy their labour contributes to the economy has been recognized by ILO and several other international agencies.

*Table III.7*
Female labour force participation rates for selected African countries, from various sources

| Country | World Fertility Survey | Official national data | ILO estimates 1985 | 1980 |
|---|---|---|---|---|
| Cameroon | 69 | 47 | 66 | 45 |
| Ghana | 89 | 62 | 63 | 53 |
| Kenya | 13 | .. | 47 | 64 |
| Lesotho | 22 | 35 | 82 | 68 |
| Senegal | 74 | 64 | 57 | 60 |
| Sudan | 34 | 21 | 11 | 20 |

Source: R. Anker, "Measuring women's participation in the African labour force", in *Gender, Work and Population in Sub-Saharan Africa*, A. Adepoju and C. Oppong, eds. (London, James Currey, 1994).
*Note*: Two dots (..) indicate that the data are not available or are not separately reported.

## 3. *Technological transformation and women's employment*

New technology is an integral part of the globalization of products and markets, creating an international division of labour based as much on skills as on considerations of cost. While new technology may benefit some women in the short and possibly in the long term, in the medium term it displaces women workers in favour of men. Women are disproportionately vulnerable to the impact of technological change because of their concentration in lower-skilled, labour-intensive jobs in both industry and services.

Natural resources, cheap labour and financial capital are being replaced by knowledge as the key factor of production affecting development and human welfare. Technology is both a component of this knowledge explosion and an adjunct in its creation, dissemination and productive use. Two technological innovations are considered here as being of direct relevance to women's employment: the range of computer- and communications-based technologies generally termed information technology and rural-based technologies, including biotechnology.

### Technologies in manufacturing and services

Information technology has the potential to reshape the organization of production (and with it corporate goals and strategies) not just within firms but also among them. One of the central issues of the technology debate has been, and will continue to be, its effect on employment. Contradictory research findings make it difficult to draw definitive conclusions in this area; this problem is compounded by difficulty in separating out the quantitative effects of technological change from those of other factors, including recession and restructuring. While an ILO report suggests early forecasts of the employment effects of microelectronics-based technologies were unduly pessimistic, the same document identifies short-term negative effects of technological change on employment structure, particularly among the lower-skilled professions many women hold.[20]

Two issues are of particular relevance to women's employment in manufacturing. First, the impact of new technology depends on the technology used, the part (or parts) of production to which it is applied and the motive behind its application. Where rationalization and the reduction of labour-intensive work are the primary goals, labour-shedding tends to occur, particularly at the lower end of the skills spectrum where female workers are found. Where productivity improvements are the motivating factor for introducing new technology, women have often benefited from the consequent regeneration of the enterprise or industry, either directly or through outsourcing. The creation of a network of small and medium-sized subcontractors and outsource workers can be of considerable benefit to women, at least in quantitative terms.[21] However, much of this employment is outside the formal sector and therefore beyond the purview of legislative and social protection. Governments and social institutions should work towards solving this trade-off between the quantity and the quality of employment.

The second technological innovation issue that impacts industrial employment is that of changing skill requirements. As technologies are implemented, assembly workers become more versatile and go from performing manual assembly line work to machine-feeding, machine-minding, routine maintenance and quality control.[21] This often displaces female workers in favour of males, although in some industries women's skills have worked to their advantage. For example, in printing women's typing skills are used for electronic data entry, displacing compositors.[22]

The quantitative impact of advanced information technology is also a major issue for women workers in service industries, where they are to a large extent still concentrated in routine occupations—clerical, book-keeping, secretarial, typing, cashiers and sales—that are most susceptible to rationalization. But in the developing world at least, women have been the main beneficiaries of employment creation in clerical and data-entry work. This trend runs counter to a trend in the advanced economies away from clerical and secretarial work towards technical, professional and managerial employment, where women are less likely to be found. And the jobs that are likely to be increasingly in demand—computer analysts and programmers, software developers, systems analysts and management analysts and consultants—are usually not associated with women. The trend towards increasing employment in clerical and data-entry work in developing countries could therefore be associated as much with the displacement of these jobs in industrialized countries (made possible by teleworking or remote working) as with a lag in the introduction of information technology in developing countries.

As in the manufacturing sector, one of the more disturbing developments associated with the wider application of information technology in the service industries is its potential to create atypical patterns of employment, which already characterize much of service sector employment. Again, while it is difficult to separate out the influence of technology from that of other developments, it does seem likely that information technology is contributing to a new dualism between a core workforce that is highly trained, multi-skilled and adaptable and a peripheral group of workers whose services can be acquired or dispensed with in response to the needs of the moment. For example, locating telework or data processing outside the mainstream of organization structures lends itself to such dualism, and there have been reports of isolation, minimal job and income security and the disintegration of the collective work ethic.[21]

The current debate on the qualitative impact of technology on women's employment should examine the extent to which women's educational backgrounds and work experience fit the occupational profiles that are emerging. As the market becomes more competitive and as enterprises seek to provide customized services, jobs in the service sector will increasingly require social skills for interpersonal communications, product knowledge for marketing, diagnostic skills for using complex computer systems and entrepreneurial skills for ensuring the commercial viability of business operations.[23]

Surveys indicate that companies value women subcontractors' social competence, communication and "people skills", especially in developing countries.[21] Thus while advanced technologies in both industry and services may have a negative impact on the jobs currently filled by women workers, they may provide women with opportunities for new and possibly more rewarding activities in the future.

### Agricultural technologies and rural development

The division of labour that prevails in most agricultural societies allocate the most laborious, manual and labour-intensive tasks to women workers. While this has often worked to their short-term advantage as agricultural technologies are introduced, it can hinder long-term employment opportunities. Introducing high-yielding crop varieties to rural areas generated immediate employment because of the corresponding increases in acreage under cultivation and land productivity and the consequent increase in demand for total labour per acre. And since the incremental tasks included a number of those traditionally associated with women agricultural labourers (such as transplanting and weeding, applying chemical fertilizers and harvesting and processing work), there was a sharper rise in the demand for female than for male labour.

However, the increased use of bio-engineered fertilizers and pesticides quickly displaced some of these incremental tasks. Tasks that remained were both casual and sensitive to the peaks and troughs of the production cycle. In India, the demand for high-yield cultivation workers has not kept pace with the increased supply of female labourers created by the eviction of long-time tenants by larger rural landowners wishing to take the fullest possible advantage of high-yield technologies.[8] Ultimately, high-yield technology and biotechnology are likely to absorb the tasks traditionally performed by landless women workers, and so displace them in the longer term.

Mechanization and agricultural modernization have reduced women's participation in the agricultural labour force in both actual production and in post-harvest processing. For example, in Indonesia the number of female workers was drastically reduced when their traditional tasks of winnowing, threshing and pounding were mechanized, and when men were hired by the mills to run the new equipment.[8] Similar events were reported in Bangladesh and India. In Africa new techniques shift economic control, employment and profit from women to men.[8]

It is also common for men to take over female tasks upon their commercialization, as in the case of food and other cash-crop production under contractual arrangements with agribusinesses. Given their reliance on wage labour, women from landless (and often female-headed) households are particularly badly affected when labour-intensive "women's jobs" are first mechanized and subsequently annexed by men. Commercialization may again negatively affect women by reducing the land devoted to subsistence agriculture and by making greater demands on their time in connection with cash-crop production.

The negative implications of technological change on women's agricultural activities, particularly in parts of Africa where women's land use rights are better established, are exacerbated by the inadequacy of extension, credit and support systems that would enable women to access available innovations.[24] Women are disadvantaged by a number of factors, including the small size of their agricultural holdings, their lack of access to credit and to technology-related training and their ignorance concerning available innovations and their potential application to their own needs. In addi-

tion, intrahousehold patterns of decision-making on income distribution and expenditure can work to the detriment of women in that acquired technology and equipment are more likely to be of relevance to men's commercial activities than to women's.

Developing appropriate technology for women is essential to their empowerment. ILO technical cooperation projects for women from three developing regions (South Asia, Western and Southern Africa) indicate that it is feasible to widen and diversify small-scale rural and informal women's income-earning opportunities by introducing improved, appropriate technologies. Such technologies could generate women's employment in non-traditional areas, while upgrading technologies in women's traditional occupations could raise their productivity and reduce the drudgery of their work.

### 4. *Women in manufacturing*

The participation rate of women in the manufacturing sector has increased faster than that of men. The global average for women's participation in the manufacturing labour force stands at about 30 per cent, which is not much below their overall share in the economically active population, and the figure for the developing countries (29.8 per cent) is hardly different from that for developed countries (31 per cent). The highest figure is found in Asia, where a large number of young women are employed in manufacturing. Despite these figures the sector accounts for only 12.7 per cent of all economically active women. Only the developed and the Asian countries show higher shares (about 18 per cent).[25]

As in other sectors, women are often found in informal enterprises. About one third of all women in the sector are informal entrepreneurs, own-account workers or unpaid family workers, a share that rises to 41.2 per cent in developing countries and to two thirds in Africa. These figures conceal a number of patterns and trends. In countries at an early stage of development, and particularly in Africa, women are involved mainly in traditional processing in rural areas. Elsewhere, particularly in urban areas in Latin America, women's informal manufacturing activities have increased more recently as a response to poverty, unemployment and structural adjustment policies. In other countries, particularly in Asia, export-led production has provided the stimulus as certain kinds of labour-intensive assembly work are subcontracted to home workers. Entrepreneurs thus reduce fixed costs and effectively shift some of their risks to home workers.

Globally, formal manufacturing accounts for more than two thirds of all women in the manufacturing sector. In developed countries virtually all working women are formally employed. A fairly high figure (74.1 per cent) was also found for the Arab countries. However, the share of female employees in the global manufacturing labour force is just 24.3 per cent, which is well below their overall share in the formal sector. This indicates the importance of informal manufacturing for women in developing regions. Still, the share of women working in formal manufacturing will continue to rise rapidly because of the demand for young female workers by export-oriented manufacturing enterprises worldwide.

Women who work in manufacturing tend to be found in a limited number of labour-intensive industries. Garment production, for example, universally employs a disproportionate number of women: more than two thirds of the global labour force in this area is female. This industry absorbs one fifth of the female manufacturing labour force. Industries that rely on female labour (or have become feminized) vary by region. Rates of female employment in light industries are high in Asia, but in Africa—where few women are employed in formal manufacturing—the figure is much lower.

Women working in manufacturing jobs generally have low occupational status. Two thirds are categorized as workers: production and related workers, transport equipment operators and labourers. Only 5 per cent are found in professional-technical positions, and only 1.9 per cent in administrative-managerial functions. Men outnumber women five to one in professional-technical positions and eight to one in administrative-managerial positions. These figures are worse than those for other sectors, indicating that the manufacturing sector has offered few career opportunities for women. Moreover, while occupational data are incomplete, women in the worker category overwhelmingly tend to be found in unskilled jobs where promotion is unlikely.

### Global development trends and their impact on women in manufacturing

In recent years, industrial production in the developed countries has become increasingly characterized by computer-based technologies, increasing capital intensity. There has been a shift from economies of scale to economies of scope: the flexibility of these technologies has significantly altered the production process, allowing the production of small batches of widely varying products or even of individual items based on customers' specifica-

tions. The colour and some of the equipment for a car, for example, are determined by the buyer.

These technological changes have been accompanied by major organizational changes. The increasing importance of the individual consumer and of adapting to changes in demand has made marketing and after-sales services a crucial part of manufacturing. Just-in-time delivery or stockless production have been introduced as part of the trend towards greater flexibility in production, helping to increase the ability of firms to adjust rapidly to the market and cutting production costs. In some sectors, modern communication and computer systems are used extensively to decentralize production. Quality has become an important sales argument. The initial organizational response was quality circles; typical elements of a manufacturing firm's organization now include, among others, multi-skilled teams and the transfer of responsibility for key aspects of production to operators under the total quality management concept.

Information-intensive technologies have reduced the need for labour, and low-skill assembly jobs have virtually disappeared in several industries, with a corresponding loss of female employment. There has been increasing demand for higher-level technical, organizational and cognitive skills as a consequence of the organizational changes in manufacturing—but women often do not have the qualifications for such jobs. Secondary education has become a basic requirement for many manufacturing jobs.

The application of information-intensive technologies has also reduced the need for relocating labour-intensive industries to developing countries (a process described below). An increasing number of developing countries—even least developed countries where wages are very low—find that they can no longer rely on foreign investment in export industries based on cheap (female) labour. Such countries will have to create conditions that facilitate the adoption of modern technologies if they want to create or retain a competitive manufacturing sector.

Still, despite structural changes in manufacturing that are affecting investment decisions worldwide, labour-intensive production for export continues to be relocated to low-wage countries. Low labour costs are still important for industries where automation has not yet made much progress such as garment and knitwear production. Computer programming is an example of a recently created labour-intensive industry, but one which requires high educational levels and thus mainly recruits men in developing countries.

Low-wage locations are shifting. As wages have increased, some of the newly industrialized countries—which not long ago were low-wage locations for industrialized-country firms—have been shifting their own industries to neighbouring Asian countries with lower living standards: export firms from Hong Kong have established production facilities in China, firms from Singapore have invested in Malaysia and Indonesia. Even countries that have not yet reached newly industrialized status, such as Thailand, find that wage levels are forcing them to look for production locations elsewhere, such as in Viet Nam. On the other hand, wages in Singapore are still low enough to attract contracts from Japanese and United States software firms. India, with its large number of academics, is another favourite location for such production.

Other factors that have started to influence relocation decisions include the possibility of evading import quotas. A least developed country like Bangladesh is exempt from these quotas and has received a considerable amount of investment in the garment industry because of the export quotas imposed on other Asian countries by the United States and the European Union.

Much of the work that women do for export-oriented industries is not reflected in official statistics because of the widespread practice of subcontracting to women working at home. Home work is often accepted by women because no other work is available to them and it allows them to stay with their families. The entrepreneur saves overhead costs and does not have to comply with regulations concerning, for example, minimum wages; moreover, the risk of fluctuations in demand can be shifted to the home worker. Of course, all of this is a disadvantage for the workers and their families, but they usually have no choice. It has been noted that this is a classic instance of "modern" production relying on what is depicted as "pre-modern" or informal labour relations.[26]

The relocation trend has affected several North African and Latin American countries. Proximity to European Union and United States markets was an important factor in the relocation decisions. Such proximity facilitates a rapid reaction to market changes. Mauritius, an otherwise isolated country, has benefited from existing high quality shipping and airport facilities which link its export-processing zone with industrialized country markets.

In most OECD countries the tertiary sector overtook the manufacturing sector as the major source of national income and employment many years ago. The developed countries are now witnessing a further shift in the shift in the structure of the economy towards an even more dominant position of the tertiary sector; this is caused partly by the increasing demand of the technology-intensive manufacturing sector for services (consulting, accounting, maintenance and export and sales promotion) that are increasingly provided by outside firms. Such services were once an integral part of manufacturing, but the need for specialization has made it uneconomical for many firms to retain them.

The growing tertiary sector has particularly benefited women in terms of overall employment and improved access to higher-level positions. But part-time employment has also become more common in service activities like retail trade and banking, allowing employers to tailor their labour-force requirements to business peaks. Part-time work has become a distinctive characteristic of the female labour force in OECD countries (see sect. III.C).

While these trends are most advanced in the developed countries, the modern tertiary sector is also expanding rapidly in the newly industrialized economies and several other Asian countries, as well as in the former centrally planned economies.

In most developing countries, micro- and small-scale industries continue to play an important role, especially in countries where the growth of modern sector activities has been constrained by structural factors, such as in the least developed countries and most sub-Saharan Africa countries. It is unlikely that the modern sector in these countries will experience strong development in the short or medium term. New job opportunities are found mainly in the labour-intensive micro- and small-scale industries. These tend to use local inputs and simple equipment, and are therefore little affected by the lack of hard currency for essential imports—a constraint which paralyses modern large-scale industries in many of these countries. The labour force often does not need formal training, and the small firms have proved capable of responding quickly to changes in local demand and technology.

Micro-scale industries have gained importance as a source of livelihood in recent years as structural adjustment policies in a number of developing countries reduced public sector employment. While they do not necessarily use traditional technologies and materials, these industries are typical of pre-modern economies, and their size and organizational structure clearly distinguishes them from modern manufacturing enterprises.

Women are intensively involved in such traditional or informal production activities. Access for women is easier than in the formal sector because formal skills are not so important and because many enterprises are based on family labour. The pattern of women's involvement differs according to the economic and industrial structure of a country and the socio-cultural position of women.

In countries or areas where the modern sector has made very little impact, women may still be heavily involved in traditional processing activities in rural areas, largely as an extension of their role in agriculture. Rural micro- or small-scale industries provide supplementary income for, on average, 50 per cent of the women in the agricultural sector. As noted, however, these industries tend to become less important as a consequence of competition by modern-industry imports. The growth of informal sector industries as a consequence of structural adjustment measures is mostly an urban phenomenon. In such cases women's informal sector work helps compensate for the family income lost by unemployment. Women in urban areas play a major role in informal production activities which rely on their traditional skills in, for example, baking and tailoring.

## Factors affecting female employment in manufacturing

Women's employment in the manufacturing sector is less a result of general industrial development than of specific industrialization patterns. The role that women play in the industrialization process of a country depends on the kinds of industries (labour-intensive, capital-intensive) and/or the stage (early/advanced) that characterize the process. In the transition from an economy based on agriculture to one based on manufacturing, the role of women tends to be weakened as traditional household-based production is superseded by factory production.

Later, economic and industrial growth increase the need for female labour and help to create a social climate that stimulates the integration of women in the modern economy as employees or—less frequently—as entrepreneurs. High shares of female labour are found in assembly-type unskilled, labour-intensive factory operations and in those not requiring great physical strength. Examples include fruit and vegetable processing, garment and leather goods production and electronics manufacturing.

Women's employment opportunities in manufacturing diminish as industry becomes more capital- and technology-intensive. Heavy industries such as steel, basic chemicals and capital-goods production are traditional examples of such industries. But in recent years automation in, for example, the textile industries (as distinguished from the garment industries) has also led to considerable employment losses for women. Relocation of low-skill assembly operations, on the other hand, tends to increase employment opportunities for women in low-wage countries.

Female participation is also closely related to the socio-cultural factors that influence women's status in society and in the economy. These factors are particularly strong barriers to women's employment in the modern sector because such employment requires a certain level of education and often cannot be combined with household tasks.

In some societies, women lead secluded lives and interaction with unrelated males is not permitted, especially in rural areas. Particularly in developing countries, the female labour force tends to be young, as women stop working after marriage or the birth of their first child. But even in modern societies, women are mainly associated with their reproductive role and the resulting household obligations. Despite the increasing number of women who support a family and of families needing the incomes of both spouses for survival, women's employment is generally considered secondary to men's.

The socio-cultural constraints on women's advancement opportunities in paid employment are even stronger, and in consequence their occupational status is usually low. One of the main obstacles is the educational gap between men and women. Women's literacy rates in many developing countries are much lower than those of men, and this excludes them from most jobs in the manufacturing sector. There is also a large gap at higher educational levels, although female enrolment levels are slowly improving. Women are seriously underrepresented in technical and vocational training and as students of science, engineering and management. As a result, few women are found in middle-level or senior positions in the manufacturing sector. In many countries, only the tertiary sector offers women significant career opportunities. This means that women earn much less than men, a tendency exacerbated by the fact that women are more likely to work in less profitable industries and to have part-time jobs.

*Challenges facing women in manufacturing in individual country groups*

The situation of women in manufacturing varies by country groups that have been identified by the United Nations Industrial Development Organization. Based on an analysis of available data 12 clusters of countries were identified.[27] Each cluster faces a specific challenge to current and long-term prospects.

In developed countries with a high concentration of women in the tertiary sector,[28] the main challenge is enhancing women's role in management and reconciling career and family life. While women's opportunities to advance professionally have much improved in most of these countries (mainly as a result of the growth of the tertiary sector and of improved access to third-level education), women continue to be underrepresented at higher management levels, especially in the manufacturing sector (see chap. IV). The term "glass ceiling" is used to describe the limits still faced by women and minorities.

A number of countries have undertaken various initiatives to enhance the access of women to higher management positions. These include affirmative action programmes in, among others, the United States and Australia and the "glass ceiling initiative" of the United States Department of Labor. Countries in this group would benefit from a study of those countries in this group that have made the most progress regarding the role of women (in particular, the Nordic and North American countries).

Major shifts in gender roles and in the division of labour within the family have led to a great expansion of part-time work, especially for women. While this type of work has advantages for both employers and workers, it tends to be insecure and badly paid, and offers few career prospects. It is essential to identify ways of achieving a better balance between career and family life. Common interests of employers and workers should be given greater recognition. Part-timers should, for example, be given the possibility of returning to full-time work after maternity or family care leave.

In Latin American countries with a well-developed economic base and a concentration of women in the tertiary sector,[29] the main challenge is securing women's position in the modern industrial and tertiary sectors. The development of both traditional and modern services in these countries has benefited women considerably. But much of the progress has been offset by the impact of structural adjustment programmes implemented in the wake of the debt crisis of the 1980s. It has already been noted that adjustment resulted in a particularly serious loss of employment in the public sector—the sector where women played a major role.

Women's access to the modern service sector and their share in key positions in the process of economic development must continue to improve in Latin America. Additional opportunities for women may arise in, among others, the area of industrial services. If women are to strengthen their position in the economy, they will increasingly need technical and business expertise. Women should therefore concentrate on third-level studies in these areas instead of on the arts and social sciences.

In East and South-East Asian economies with high female participation in modern manufacturing,[30] the main challenge is maintaining and enhancing women's position in the economy. Structural changes in the economy and in the manufacturing sector have been accompanied by changes in the sectoral employment pattern of women in these countries. Rather than having negative effects, structural change has resulted in better employment opportunities. Women have become increasingly involved in advanced industries such as electronics, and although overall manufacturing employment may have decreased this was more than offset by new jobs in the tertiary sector. The status of female employees has also risen. The greatest labour shortages in the Asian newly industrialized countries, for example, are often in the categories of unskilled and semi-skilled workers needed for dirty, demanding and dangerous jobs.

The shift to an increasingly services-oriented economy requires that women have higher skills. Women's participation in tertiary education should be enhanced in these countries, with an emphasis on technical and business studies. This will enable women to fully benefit from the growth of the tertiary sector, and particularly from the employment and career opportunities in the highly specialized industrial services.

In formerly centrally planned European economies with a high rate of female economic activity[31] the main challenge is exploiting the opportunities offered by economic restructuring. Restructuring of the manufacturing sector has resulted in the closure of many industries that are not competitive in an open market; employment in the remaining firms has often been drastically reduced. The tertiary sector is also being restructured, and a number of public services are being privatized. But, as opposed to manufacturing, employment opportunities in this sector are likely to increase with the expansion of trade and production-related, financial and consultancy services.

The introduction of a market economy is accompanied by different skill demands and demands for greater labour flexibility. Unemployment is high, and there are indications that more women have lost their jobs than men and remain unemployed for longer periods.[32] This is related to, among other things, the large share of women in the unskilled and semi-skilled industrial labour force, and in overstaffed administrations. In addition, limited job opportunities have increased male competition for jobs that were formerly a female domain. Moreover, maternity benefits and child-care facilities have been reduced as government funding has been cut, and enterprises cannot bear the costs of these facilities, which make women workers expensive.[33] Combining work and family responsibilities has thus become increasingly difficult.

On the positive side, low wages are stimulating investment by firms from the European Union in labour-intensive export industries that employ primarily women (and that make the formerly centrally planned economies competitors of the developing countries). Despite their drawbacks, part-time work and the increasingly flexible use of labour should also be interpreted positively. Opportunities for women in Central and Eastern Europe also arise from their high educational levels and their experience in technical and administrative jobs. These economies should capitalize on this stock of knowledge and skills. However, this requires that women have equal access to the labour market and to skills retraining programmes, and that provisions allow women to combine work and family obligations.

In countries with a rapidly developing manufacturing sector and a high rate of female participation in the sector,[34] the main challenge is enabling women to cope with the shift to technology-intensive production. The manufacturing sectors in these countries, with their focus on export production, have become a key element in economic development and employ a significant number of women. But assembly operations based on cheap labour will become less important as a consequence of the technological developments described above, or will move to locations that offer even better incentives for labour-intensive production. It is therefore essential that these countries keep up with trends in technological development and organizational change, and that women are equipped to deal with technological challenges. The countries of the Association of South-East Asian Nations (ASEAN), most of which are in this cluster, have already initiated a strategy to remain competitive. This strategy emphasizes diversification into high value-added goods produced by a multi-skilled labour force, reducing the role of cheap, unskilled labour.

Skills must therefore be adapted and improved. The key challenge is ensuring better access for women to all levels of education, particularly in secondary and tertiary education. The fact that a major share of the export-oriented industries is owned by foreign investors, who are in a position to look elsewhere for skilled labour, should act as a catalyst for improving educational levels.

In medium-income countries with low shares of economically active women,[35] the main challenge is improving women's access to the formal sector. Available data do not allow a clear forecast of future development common to all the countries in this group. In Mauritius and Tunisia, for example, the future role of women depends on the future role of export production. According to the United Nations Industrial Development Organization, employment in the export-processing zones in Mauritius is declining because capital-intensive technologies are being introduced by large firms in the textile and clothing industry. Women in Sri Lanka and in some of the Latin American countries in this group will also be affected by future trends in export-oriented manufacturing. In most of the Latin American countries, the rise of industrial and social services could significantly alter the participation patterns of women in the economy.

Whatever the development pattern of the individual countries it is essential for women to exploit all opportunities to strengthen their presence in the modern manufacturing and tertiary sector. This can only be achieved if women have higher skill levels. Primary education levels are high among women in these countries, but secondary education for women (including vocational training) is not yet widespread, and they are far behind with regard to tertiary education. It will therefore be essential to ensure improved access of women to education, especially at the higher levels.

In Arab countries with low female economic activity and high female education levels,[36] the main challenge is improving the balance between education and employment opportunities. Despite the high education levels enjoyed by many women (particularly at the tertiary level), their share in formal employment is low in both quantitative and qualitative terms. Where women are found at higher employment levels, it is usually in the government services.

Forecasts indicate that demand for female employees will continue to rise, especially in the oil-producing countries, but it is the highly educated women who are most likely to benefit from the increased demand. A better balance between educational achievements and employment opportunities is thus needed, improving access to jobs for women with lower educational levels while reducing the remaining constraints on women's participation in higher-level education.

In Muslim countries with low female economic activity and limited female access to education,[37] the main challenge is preparing women for the requirements of modern sector work. Despite the limited presence of women in the economies of these countries and their low education levels, there are good prospects for an expansion of female economic activity (especially in the formal sector), and the preconditions for increasing their education levels seem relatively good.

Female employment is growing in the countries of this group pursuing a liberal investment policy. But the inadequate supply of well-trained labour in the region is likely to increase the pressure on social norms which bar women from taking up employment. In the North African countries development already relies to a considerable extent on export-led industrialization, and has been accompanied by a rapid growth of the number of women employed in manufacturing.

Women should be prepared for a more important role in the modern sector of the economy—not only in quantitative terms, but also in terms of their representation at higher job levels. Women's participation in education must therefore be improved, and measures that reduce social constraints are also needed.

In countries with a low overall status of women but with high female participation in manufacturing[38] the main challenge is enhancing women's socio-cultural status. The increasing integration of women in manufacturing employment in these countries reflects relocated export production. With the exception of Guatemala, however, the segregation of women and their confinement to the home are inhibiting women from accepting employment on a larger scale unless there is a serious economic need to do so. Such social barriers to employment must be reduced, and the participation of women in education, starting at the primary level, must be increased. This need is particularly strong in Pakistan and Bangladesh.

In countries with low rates of female participation in the formal sector but with a substantial female presence in traditional sectors,[39] the main challenge is strengthening the role of women in manufacturing. Except for Turkey, women play a very limited role in modern manufacturing in these countries despite their substantial manufacturing sectors. This may change if Cameroon's attempt to boost industrial development by setting up export-processing zones is successful. (Kenya and Togo, which exhibit similar characteristics, have also set up export-processing zones.) Women's education levels have to be improved considerably, with secondary schooling receiving particular attention, to prepare women for the shift from traditional activities to modern manufacturing.

In West African countries with high female participation rates in manufacturing and commerce,[40] the main challenge is strengthening the role of women in micro- and small-scale production. The strong position of women in certain types of traditional or informal micro-scale manufacturing in these countries is being threatened by competition from cheaper, more durable imported goods. Women have been only partly able to compensate for the decline of such activities by diversifying into other manufacturing activities, such as tailoring in Ghana and Togo. These activities will also be affected by cheap imports in the future.

The question is how this erosion of women's micro-scale production can be offset by other activities, and how the role of women in the development of small-scale production can be strengthened (which can in turn provide a sounder basis for large-scale formal manufacturing). Entrepreneurial development for women involved in traditional crafts production should be a key area of attention, with a focus on marketing and business management. Women's education levels must also be improved, along with measures to lower other socio-cultural barriers (such as high fertility levels) that restrict women's participation in economic development. Economic and social developments in Botswana, for example, should be studied to identify which factors have influenced the improved status of women in that country.

In the least developed countries that have maintained a traditional socio-economic role for women,[41] the major challenge is fully integrating women in strategies that combat poverty. In many of these countries women's role in agriculture is complemented by traditional processing activities—activities that are strongly affected by economic problems. Economic crisis and restructuring have sharply reduced the economic activities of women in sub-Saharan Africa.[42] The limited development opportunities in these countries also limit women's economic possibilities.

International technical cooperation is increasing to combat poverty in the least developed countries. The role of women must be taken fully into consideration in these activities. Given the close relationship between improvements in the social and educational status of women and improvements in overall human development indicators, education and social status must be improved for women in these countries.

## 5. Labour migration

International migration is increasing considerably, and most is underdocumented.[43] For example, about 10 per cent of the labour force in Singapore is foreign workers. The Philippines exports labour, with 1.25 million nationals working abroad in 1988.[44] International migration is also being feminized. Female migrants from the Philippines to other Asian countries outnumber male migrants by 12 to 1. In Sri Lanka the figures are 3 to 2.[15]

Massive unemployment and underemployment in developing countries has forced women into unpaid family work, casual or seasonal jobs in the informal sector and to migrate to cities or other countries in search of work. Internal migration is often strongly influenced by globalization such as among the predominantly young, unmarried women from Sichuan and Guangdong provinces in China who flock to the special economic zones in Shenzhen and elsewhere on the coast.[45] International migration among Asian women primarily involves domestic workers (both west towards the Middle East and Europe and east towards the Pacific Rim countries), but recently there has been regional migration of women into small-scale enterprises, small labour-intensive industries and informal sector jobs in parts of East Asia (Hong Kong, Japan, Singapore and Taiwan Province of China).

There are several different patterns of female migration. While women were once seen as "passive" migrants, moving to join or follow family members, women are increasingly migrating individually, and they often do so for economic rather than personal or social reasons. Surveys of female migrants in South-East Asia, Latin America and the Caribbean indicate that 50 to 70 per cent migrated in search of employment. Even in South Asia and in Africa, where most women moved primarily for family reasons, the share that migrated for economic reasons often exceeds 50 per cent.[46] Women also migrate with the aid of employment agencies or other agents that profit from female workers.

Female migrants are particularly vulnerable to exploitation. Contributing factors include their tendency to work individually and in isolation, without support networks, and their illegal status in the host country. Indeed, the increase in illegal migrant workers in many economies has been facilitated by the trend towards casualization engendered by flexibility and deregulation.[47] Female migrants tend to be clustered in low-status jobs and are often exposed to violence and sexual harassment. In rural areas they are often restricted to unpaid household labour; in urban areas they perform similar duties as paid domestic servants.

In Africa, for example, female migrants are often confined to informal sector jobs, which command the lowest wages and the least security. Women who migrate to escape poverty often turn to prostitution. In a high-migration neighbourhood in Douala, Cameroon, for example, half of female migrants reported earning their money from "friends".[48] A study of prostitution among migrants estimated that as many as 10 per cent of women aged 14 to 24 in Bangkok were prostitutes.[49] The number of women resorting to prostitution is increasing dramatically in many developing countries.

Other migration issues also have specific impacts on women. Male migration contributes to the increase in female-headed households and their impoverishment. Young girls have been sold, forced or lured into internal or international migration leading them into prostitution. And female urban migrants are at high risk of sexual exploitation and harassment.

The forces driving most economic migrants are the same—escaping from unemployment and poverty and obtaining better economic opportunities elsewhere. There is reason to believe that international migration will increase in the 1990s. The negative impacts of the economic and restructuring and structural adjustment programmes of the 1980s and early 1990s may have encouraged female international migration as a family survival strategy, especially where neighbouring countries have growing economies and labour shortages.[47] Migration from Central and Eastern Europe to Western Europe and from the poor to the rich countries of the Pacific Rim will be important in the 1990s.[20]

The political, economic and social upheaval in the formerly socialist countries has raised the respect of a stream of migration ranging between 2 and 20 million people in search of a better standard of living.[20] Data are limited but labour shortages in some service sector jobs (such as hotels and catering, nursing and cleaning personnel) suggest that women are among those migrating west in search of employment. And many young women are going west to work in what is called the "entertainment industry"—prostitution.

The upsurge of migration in East Asia has led many receiving countries to review their immigration laws. While this move is viewed favourably by trade unions concerned about existing wage levels and working conditions as well as about the possible exploitation of migrant labour, the business community, concerned with labour shortages and the reluctance of young, edu-

cated nationals to take on work that is "dirty, dangerous and difficult", is less enthusiastic. Depending on the remittances of their nationals working aborad and the migrants themselves, sending countries see changing immigration laws as the closing of an important door to both gainful employment and the long-term improvement of national living conditions.

Strategies that improve the situation of female migrants include providing relevant information to women prior to their migration and extending national labour legislation to cover migrant workers in the host country. Migrant women can also form networks to protect their interests, supported by trade unions and non-governmental organizations.

## C.  GENDER DISCRIMINATION IN THE LABOUR MARKET

The increase in women's economic activity is a quantitative phenomenon which has often been achieved at the expense of quality working conditions. Some of the gender-based inequalities persisting in the labour market include occupational segregation, wage differentials and the difficulty of harmonizing women's labour and family roles. In South Asia women's employment opportunities are often hampered by their culturally dictated inability to control their reproductive life. These phenomena are strikingly similar across the industrialized economies, the economies in transition, and the developing economies.

Macroeconomic trends also affect women's working conditions. Conditions differ according to whether women are employed in the public or private sector or the formal or informal sector and according to the strength of these sectors in different economies. Conditions also depend on whether women's work is full-time or part-time and whether it emulates male working histories (unbroken service) or female life cycles (interrupted working history).

The quality of women's working conditions is also influenced by their skill level (which depends on their access to education and training), legislation for gender equality, the level of social infrastructure such as child care, and their level of representation in trade unions and other political groups.

### 1.  *Public or private, formal or informal?*

The neo-liberal paradigm that dominates developed market economies and the countries in transition to a market economy has contracted the public or State sector in

favour of privatization.[50] In both OECD countries and the formerly centralized economies of Eastern and Central Europe the state and the public sector have been major sources of employment for women, mainly in clerical, administrative, professional and other service sector jobs. Despite mixed empirical evidence, the consensus is that the majority of jobs in the public sector provide women with better employment protection and social security than jobs in the private sector.

Thus a shrinking public sector has negative implications for working women while the neo-liberal paradigm argues that the public sector is inefficient, an OECD meeting of trade union experts suggested that the public sector may actually contribute to economic performance or that an extended welfare state is at least compatible with economic efficiency.[51] The Group further contended that a competitive public sector is possible and that public sector reform is more relevant than privatization, which of itself does not guarantee competition.

Most women in developing countries are engaged in agriculture and in the informal sector. In West Africa, for example, more than two thirds of the women in urban areas work in the informal sector, where they often earn less than the minimum wage paid in formal sector employment. Activities in this sector are often characterized by inefficient tools, time-consuming tasks, and strenuous and poor working conditions.[52] The female share of public service employment in the formal sector is highest in Latin America and the Caribbean (between 23 and 50 per cent, with most countries between 35 and 45 per cent). The figures for Asia and the Pacific (10 to 35 per cent) and Africa (11 to 41 per cent) are lower.[13]

Structural adjustment policies have reduced public sector employment in developing countries. In sub-Saharan Africa compression of the public sector has occurred in stages, beginning with a wage freeze, then by eliminating temporary workers, followed by a recruitment freeze and finally by dismissals. Although the effects of declining public sector employment on women are unclear, women are concentrated in lower-level jobs and therefore more vulnerable to retrenchment. In Africa there have been job losses for women in the professions, especially teaching. The decline in public sector employment restricts women's bargaining power in the labour market since "public sector employment is relatively free from discriminatory practices compared to the private sector".[53]

Women's participation in some types of industry is increasing, but "gender differences in labour market segmentation are extensive" and "women are recruited more extensively than men into the more casual forms of labour: short-term wage labour, disguised wage work and especially unpaid family labour."[54] With high levels of unemployment and continuing discrimination in the formal sector, women in Africa, Asia and Latin America "are increasingly forced into the informal sector as street traders, casual or seasonal labourers, domestic servants and homeworkers. They receive low pay and negligible social benefits and are usually unprotected by unions or labour legislation".[55]

Most women are concentrated in the small-scale production and personal services end of the informal sector, and in a relatively narrow ban of occupations. Women in Guayaquil, Ecuador, are mainly engaged in selling, dressmaking and personal services, while men are involved in selling, tailoring, carpentry, mechanics and personal services. Many women workers are engaged in vending, petty trading or working as maids or waitresses.[56] In Lima, Peru, more than 80 per cent of economically active women during the 1980s worked in commerce, services or domestic labour, mainly as unpaid family workers. 13 In Kenya more than 80 per cent of self-employed women work in agriculture and sales, compared with only 50 per cent of men.[57] In Ghana, 85 per cent of all trade employment was accounted for by women; in Nigeria 94 per cent of street food vendors are women.[7] The informal sector has generally been gender-blind. Still, the proportions of women relative to men in the informal sector may not have been increasing (see table III.8). Indeed, there may even have been a relative

decline in many countries. The interests of the many women working in the informal sector must be protected.

*Table III.8*

Women's share of informal sector employment, selected African countries, 1970-1990

Percentage

| Country | 1970 | 1980 | 1985 | 1990 |
|---|---|---|---|---|
| Congo | 26.7 | 26.9 | 26.8 | 24.6 |
| Ghana | 32.0 | 32.0 | 32.0 | 27.3 |
| Guinea | 31.9 | 32.0 | 32.0 | 26.8 |
| Kenya | 31.3 | 31.0 | 31.1 | 36.7 |
| Liberia | 42.8 | 43.2 | 43.0 | 39.3 |
| Madagascar | 33.3 | 33.1 | 32.8 | 29.0 |
| Nigeria | 29.8 | 30.0 | 30.0 | 25.9 |
| Somalia | 32.1 | 31.9 | 32.0 | 34.6 |
| Togo | 38.6 | 39.0 | 39.0 | 32.2 |
| United Republic of Tanzania | 30.3 | 30.0 | 30.0 | 28.4 |
| Zaire | 37.3 | 37.0 | 37.0 | 24.9 |

*Source*: S. Baden, "The impact of recession and structural adjustment on women's work in developing and developed countries", Working Paper No. 19, Interdepartmental Project on Equality for Women in Employment (Geneva, International Labour Office, 1993), table 4.

### 2. *Full time or part time?*

Much of the growth in women's labour participation in developed countries has been accounted for by part-time jobs. Between 1983 and 1987, 70 per cent of all jobs created in the European Community were part time. Part-time work is concentrated in the service sector, as are the majority of women workers. Thus the great majority of part-time workers are women. Women make up between 65 and 90 per cent of all part-time workers in OECD countries. In 1991/92, 62 per cent of all women workers were employed part time in the Netherlands, 36 per cent in New Zealand, 47 per cent in Norway and 45 per cent in the United Kingdom (see table III.9).[58]

Economic restructuring is increasing temporary and other forms of casual or non-standard employment.[26] Atypical employment patterns correlate with the feminization of the labour force. In the European Community atypical forms of employment are twice as common among women (44 per cent) as among men (23 per cent).[51] Most atypical workers are young and less educated and less skilled than average; many are migrants or minorities. 7 Although there has been some progress in extending social protection to part-time workers, especially in the public sector in developed countries, most part-time and non-standard forms of employment entail low pay, lack of rights or entitlements and no training opportunities or promotion prospects. And since the majority of part-time workers are women with young children (55 per cent of women working part-time in the European Community between 1985 and 1991 were aged between 25 and 49), there is a danger that women with family responsibilities are being marginalized.

### 3. *Occupational segregation*

A persisting feature of women's employment is its worldwide concentration in a small number of sectors and occupations. 59 At the end of the 1980s between 75 to 80 per cent of women in the OECD countries were employed in services; only 5 per cent were in agriculture and 15 to 20 per cent in industry, where they were concentrated in such female-dominated industries as clothing, footwear, textiles, leather and food processing (see table III.10). While women are entering some male-dominated occupations, clerical and service sector work is being increasingly feminized. Changes in the occupational distribution of women and men are shown in table III.11.[60]

The sectoral distribution of women in Central and Eastern Europe was somewhat different, with 50 per cent of women workers in services, about 30 per cent in industry and 20 per cent in agriculture. 7 Women's share of employment in industry was approximately 40 per cent, their share in agriculture ranged from 22 to 65 per cent and they constituted 55 to 70 per cent of service sector workers. These figures are changing in the transition to market economies (see table III.12). Unlike the developed market economies, State control of job access has

*Table III.9*

Size and composition of part-time employment, 1973-1992

Percentage

Part-time employment as a share of employment

| Country | 1973 | 1979 | 1983 | 1990 | 1991 | 1992 | Men 1993 | 1979 | 1983 | 1990 | 1991 | Women 1992 |
|---|---|---|---|---|---|---|---|---|---|---|---|---|
| Australia | 3.7 | 5.2 | 6.2 | 8.0 | 9.2 | 10.5 | 28.2 | 35.2 | 36.4 | 40.1 | 40.9 | 43.3 |
| Austria | 1.4 | 1.5 | 1.5 | 1.6 | 1.5 | .. | 15.6 | 18.0 | 20.0 | 20.2 | 20.1 | .. |
| Belgium | 1.0 | 1.0 | 2.0 | 2.0 | 2.1 | .. | 10.2 | 16.5 | 19.7 | 25.8 | 27.4 | .. |
| Canada | 4.7 | 5.7 | 7.6 | 8.1 | 8.8 | 9.3 | 19.4 | 23.3 | 26.1 | 24.4 | 25.5 | 25.9 |
| Denmark | .. | 5.2 | 6.6 | 10.4 | 10.5 | .. | .. | 46.3 | 44.7 | 38.4 | 37.8 | .. |
| Finland | .. | 3.2 | 4.5 | 4.4 | 5.1 | 5.5 | .. | 10.6 | 12.5 | 10.2 | 10.2 | 10.4 |
| France | 1.7 | 2.4 | 2.6 | 3.4 | 3.4 | 3.6 | 12.9 | 16.9 | 20.0 | 23.6 | 23.5 | 24.5 |
| Germany | 1.8 | 1.5 | 1.7 | 2.6 | 2.7 | .. | 24.4 | 27.6 | 30.0 | 33.8 | 34.3 | .. |
| Greece | .. | .. | 3.7 | 2.2 | 2.2 | .. | .. | .. | 12.1 | 7.6 | 7.2 | .. |
| Ireland | .. | 2.1 | 2.7 | 3.4 | 3.6 | .. | .. | 13.1 | 15.5 | 17.6 | 17.8 | .. |
| Italy | 3.7 | 3.0 | 2.4 | 2.4 | 2.9 | 2.7 | 14.0 | 10.6 | 9.4 | 9.6 | 10.4 | 10.5 |
| Japan | 6.8 | 7.5 | 7.3 | 9.5 | 10.1 | 10.6 | 25.1 | 27.8 | 29.8 | 3.4 | 34.3 | 34.8 |
| Luxembourg | 1.0 | 1.0 | 1.0 | 1.9 | 1.9 | .. | 18.4 | 17.1 | 17.0 | 16.7 | 17.9 | .. |
| Netherlands* | .. | 5.5 | 7.2* | 15.8 | 16.7 | .. | .. | 44.0 | 50.1* | 61.7 | 62.2 | .. |
| New Zealand | 4.6 | 4.9 | 5.0 | 8.4 | 9.7 | 10.3 | 24.6 | 29.1 | 31.4 | 35.0 | 35.7 | 35.9 |
| Norway* | 5.9 | 7.3 | 7.7* | 8.8 | 9.1 | 9.8 | 46.5 | 50.9 | 63.3* | 48.2 | 47.6 | 47.1 |
| Portugal | .. | 2.5 | ... | 3.6 | 4.0 | 4.2 | .. | 16.5 | .. | 10.1 | 10.5 | 11.0 |
| Spain | .. | .. | .. | 1.6 | 1.5 | 2.0 | .. | .. | .. | 11.8 | 11.2 | 13.7 |
| Sweden* | .. | 5.4 | 6.3* | 7.3 | 7.6 | 8.4 | .. | 46.0 | 45.9* | 40.9 | 41.0 | 41.3 |
| United Kingdom | 2.3 | 1.9 | 3.3 | 5.3 | 5.5 | 6.1 | 39.1 | 39.0 | 42.4 | 43.2 | 43.7 | 44.6 |
| United States | 8.6 | 9.0 | 10.8 | 10.0 | 10.5 | 10.8 | 26.8 | 26.7 | 28.1 | 25.2 | 25.6 | 25.4 |

*Source*: Employment Outlook, 1993 (Paris, Organisation for Economic Cooperation and Development, 1993).

*Notes*: An asterisk (*) indicates a break in series; two dots (..) indicate that data are not available or are not separately reported.

The definition of part-time work varies considerably across OECD countries. Essentially three main approaches can be distinguished: (i) a classification based on the worker's perception of his/her employment situation; (ii) a cut-off (generally 30 or 35 hours per week) based on usual working hours, with persons usually working fewer hours being considered part-timers; (iii) a comparable cut-off based on actual hours worked during the reference week.

A criterion based on actual hours will generally yield a part-time rate higher than one based on usual hours, particularly if there are temporary reductions in working-time as a result of holidays, illness, short-timing, and the like. On the other hand, it is not entirely clear whether a classification based on the worker's perception will necessarily yield estimate of part-time work that are higher or lower than one based on a fixed cut-off.

meant that the "women's job" syndrome was somewhat less marked in Central and Eastern Europe, particularly in industry. Still, women tended to be concentrated in certain jobs and professions (such as doctors and teachers) which have consequently held a lower status and lower level of remuneration.[10] The majority of working women in developing countries are engaged in agriculture, sales or clerical and service jobs.[61]

Over the past decade the number of women in managerial and administrative and professional and technical categories has increased relative to their share in total employment, particularly in the developed market economies (see table III.13). Still, few women have reached the highest ranks of large corporations or other organizations, including government bodies and teaching and research institutions, leading to the concept of a "glass ceiling".

Women working in the formal sector in developing countries are concentrated in certain occupations. They constitute a comparatively large proportion of lower and middle-level professional and technical workers and tend to concentrate in such professions as teaching and nursing. They also form the majority of clerical workers in most countries. Except in some Asian countries, few women are employed in senior administrative and managerial positions. In Africa women occupy only 13 per cent of managerial posts. Women are not found in the four highest levels of government in 21 African countries.[52]

Discrimination and inequalities persist even in countries where efforts have been made to promote equality in the labour field, concentrating women in certain jobs and occupations, making their career progression more difficult, denying them equal remuneration, and hindering their access to training and other resources essential to advancement. While legislation has promoted equality, a sustained effort in its implementation combined with affirmative action, public education and cooperative action will be necessary if women are to achieve real equality in the working world.

*Table III.10*

Employment distribution of women by sector, developed economies, 1963-1992

Percentage

| | Women's share of total employment | | | | Women's share of total employment by sector | | | Change in women's share of total employment by sector | 1973-1992 |
|---|---|---|---|---|---|---|---|---|---|
| | 1963 | 1973 | 1983 | 1992 | 1963 | 1973 | 1983 | 1992 | |
| Agriculture | | | | | | | | | |
| France | 20.2 | 11.3 | 8.0 | 5.8[a] | .. | 15[b] | 17 | .. | .. |
| Italy | 27.2 | 18.3 | 12.4 | 8.5[a] | 34 | 33 | 35 | 36[a] | 9 |
| United Kingdom | 4.4 | 2.9 | 2.7 | 2.2 | 16 | 21 | 18 | 21 | 0 |
| United States | 7.1 | 4.2 | 3.5 | 2.9 | 19 | 18 | 20 | 21 | 17 |
| Industry | | | | | | | | | |
| France | 39.6 | 39.5 | 33.8 | 29.5[a] | .. | 25[b] | 25 | 25[a] | 0 |
| Italy | 37.6 | 39.2 | 36.1 | 32.3[a] | 25 | 22 | 24 | 24[a] | 9 |
| United Kingdom | 46.4 | 42.4 | 33.6 | 26.6 | 25 | 25 | 23 | 23 | 1968 |
| United States | 35.1 | 33.2 | 28.0 | 24.6 | 21 | 23 | 26 | 26 | 13 |
| Services | | | | | | | | | |
| France | 40.2 | 49.3 | 58.2 | 64.8[a] | .. | 48[b] | 51 | 54[a] | 13 |
| Italy | 35.2 | 42.5 | 51.5 | 59.2[a] | 33 | 33 | 39 | 41[a] | 24 |
| United Kingdom | 49.2 | 54.6 | 63.8 | 71.2 | 44 | 49 | 52 | 54 | 10 |
| United States | 57.8 | 62.6 | 68.5 | 72.5 | 44 | 48 | 52 | 53 | 10 |

Source: S. Baden, "The impact of recession and structural adjustment on women's work in developing and developed countries", Working Paper No. 19, Interdepartmental Project on Equality for Women in Employment (Geneva, International Labour Office, 1993), table 3.

*Note*: Two dots (..) indicate that data are not available or are not separately reported.

a    Data for 1991.
b    Data for 1975.

*Table III.11*

Occupational category, by gender, 1970-1990

Percentage

| Occupational group | 1970 Women | Men | 1980 Women | Men | 1990 Women | Men |
|---|---|---|---|---|---|---|
| Professional and technical | 11.94 | 5.62 | 11.76 | 6.56 | 13.17 | 8.22 |
| Administrative and management | 0.78 | 2.07 | 1.25 | 2.54 | 1.80 | 3.22 |
| Clerical | 10.81 | 5.86 | 11.79 | 5.71 | 13.25 | 6.51 |
| Sales | 7.76 | 5.98 | 7.93 | 5.27 | 9.91 | 7.22 |
| Service | 18.34 | 5.87 | 13.56 | 6.20 | 14.65 | 6.83 |
| Agriculture | 27.02 | 33.54 | 29.10 | 32.72 | 24.69 | 27.97 |
| Production | 14.54 | 32.06 | 29.73 | 29.71 | 12.63 | 31.66 |
| Not classified, unemployed | 6.07 | 6.27 | 9.52 | 7.53 | 9.00 | 7.45 |

*Source*: Division for the Advancement of Women of the United Nations Secretariat, from data contained in the Women's Indicators and Statistics Data Base (WISTAT), version 3, 1994.

*Table III.12*

Change in women's share of employment by sector, economies in transition, 1990-1992

Percentage

A.   BULGARIA

|  | Women's share of employment | | | |
|---|---|---|---|---|
| Sector | 1990 | 1991 | 1992 | Change, 1990-1992 |
| Agriculture | 43.39 | 47.26 | 42.58 | −0.82 |
| Forestry | 40.08 | 38.49 | 36.30 | −3.78 |
| Industry | 49.06 | 48.95 | 48.33 | −0.73 |
| Construction | 20.93 | 20.39 | 21.51 | 0.58 |
| Transport | 21.54 | 22.90 | 23.41 | 1.86 |
| Communications | 63.05 | 62.90 | 63.32 | 0.27 |
| Trade | 64.83 | 66.10 | 67.24 | 2.42 |
| House/communal services | 46.16 | 41.69 | 41.93 | −4.23 |
| Science research and development | 53.81 | 55.08 | 53.88 | 0.07 |
| Education | 76.39 | 76.03 | 76.42 | 0.03 |
| Culture/arts | 58.70 | 61.50 | 63.30 | 4.60 |
| Health/sports | 75.16 | 77.11 | 77.97 | 2.82 |
| Finance/insurance | 83.68 | 82.35 | 79.24 | −4.43 |
| Public administration | 57.88 | 55.92 | 58.12 | 0.24 |
| Other | 55.78 | 58.06 | 59.65 | 3.88 |
| All sectors | 49.63 | 51.32 | 51.85 | 2.22 |

B.   HUNGARY

|  | Women's share of employment | | | | |
|---|---|---|---|---|---|
| Sector | 1989 | 1990 | 1991 | 1992 | Change, 1989-1992 |
| Agriculture | 41.45 | 41.35 | 39.93 | 38.58 | −2.86 |
| Water management | 25.37 | 25.47 | 26.53 | 25.57 | 0.20 |
| Industry | 45.66 | 44.80 | 43.94 | 43.49 | −2.17 |
| Construction | 21.45 | 21.68 | 21.28 | 24.07 | 2.62 |
| Transport | 25.53 | 25.83 | 27.85 | 27.43 | 1.91 |
| Communications | 55.11 | 54.70 | 56.64 | 55.89 | 0.78 |

*Table III.12*
B. HUNGARY
(continued)

|  | | | | Women's share of employment | |
| Sector | 1989 | 1990 | 1991 | 1991 | Change, 1989-1992 |
| --- | --- | --- | --- | --- | --- |
| Trade | 66.71 | 66.82 | 66.00 | 66.83 | 0.12 |
| Services | | | | | |
| Production | 46.81 | 47.97 | 47.56 | 59.17 | 12.36 |
| Non-production | 64.04 | 64.31 | 64.25 | 64.44 | 0.39 |
| All sectors | 48.56 | 48.63 | 48.48 | 49.62 | 1.06 |

C.  SLOVAKIA

|  | | | Women's share of employment | |
| Sector | 1989 | 1990 | 1991 | Change, 1989-1991 |
| --- | --- | --- | --- | --- |
| Agriculture | 38.52 | 36.95 | 36.19 | -2.33 |
| Forestry | 27.97 | 29.72 | 29.14 | 1.17 |
| Water management | 24.36 | 23.70 | 22.97 | −1.39 |
| Industry | 40.94 | 39.74 | 36.19 | −4.75 |
| Construction | 16.58 | 16.23 | 13.86 | −2.72 |
| Transport | 20.53 | 21.44 | 19.84 | −0.69 |
| Communications | 64.13 | 63.60 | 62.81 | −1.32 |
| Domestic trade | 77.02 | 72.33 | 72.66 | −4.36 |
| Foreign trade | 45.49 | 45.20 | 45.10 | −0.39 |
| Science research and development | 40.35 | 41.03 | 41.67 | 1.33 |
| Dwelling management | 38.68 | 38.15 | 36.23 | −2.45 |
| Housing services | 72.17 | 72.51 | 69.87 | −2.30 |
| Tourist services | 57.21 | 61.85 | 64.80 | 7.59 |
| Communal services | 46.71 | 35.75 | 40.00 | −6.71 |
| Education | 72.12 | 73.11 | 74.28 | 2.16 |
| Culture | 54.35 | 54.58 | 54.74 | 0.39 |
| Health | 78.16 | 78.35 | 78.40 | 0.24 |
| Social care | 88.43 | 88.09 | 88.25 | 0.18 |
| Business/technical services | 50.57 | 50.35 | 49.48 | 1.09 |
| Finance/bank services | 81.74 | 82.15 | 79.67 | −2.08 |
| Insurance | 67.20 | 69.50 | 68.08 | 0.88 |
| Legal/public services | 62.93 | 59.78 | 60.11 | −2.82 |
| Civic activities | 39.89 | 35.40 | 35.07 | −4.82 |
| All sectors | 45.45 | 44.51 | 43.26 | −2.19 |

*Source*: L. Paukert, "Women's employment in East-Central European countries during the period of transition to a market economy system", Working Paper (Geneva, International Labour Office, 1993), table 13A.

4.  *Wage differentials*

While some advances have been made in wage equity over the past 40 years, progress has not been universal or sustained—most women still earn between 50 and 80 per cent of men's wages (see table III.14). Women's work is undervalued in most societies and the incomes they receive are not a true measure of their contribution to the economy. The segregation of the labour market, the crowding of women into a narrow range of low-skilled, low status occupations and atypical working arrangements and their unavailability for overtime, night work and shift work because of legal barriers or family responsibilities contribute to the gap between the earnings of women and men.

There is also a residual difference in earnings whic h cannot be explained by job differences and "indicates

*Table III.13*
Ratio of women to men in professional and technical,
and administrative and management occupations,
by region, 1970-1990

Number of women for each 100 men

| Region | 1970 | 1980 | 1990 |
|---|---|---|---|
| Africa | 19 | 40 | 66 |
| Asia and the Pacific | 27 | 47 | 55 |
| Eastern Europe | 47 | 105 | 124 |
| Latin America and the Caribbean | 50 | 82 | 85 |
| Western Europe and other | 50 | 66 | 86 |
| World | 36 | 58 | 70 |

*Source*: Division for the Advancement of Women of the United
Nations Secretariat, from data contained in the Women's Indicators
and Statistics Data Base (WISTAT), version 3, 1994.

that even when one controls for a wide range of productivity-related characteristics that determine wages, a sizeable male-female wage gap still prevails",[62] which is probably attributable to various forms of wage discrimination. Recent data from the United Kingdom show that while the salary gap between male and female executives is narrowing, the gap remains wide and is wider at higher levels. The gap between the average base salary of male and female directors is 23 per cent, for functional heads, 10.2 per cent, and for departmental heads, 9 per cent.[63]

Wage segregation is especially marked in those developing countries pursuing export-led industrialization or which have export processing zones. According to Economic Commission for Latin America and the Caribbean data, women in Latin America earn between 44 and 77 per cent of men's wages. 64 In Asia in 1990/91, the average wage of women working in manufacturing relative to men was 88 per cent in Sri Lanka, 70 per cent in Hong Kong, 56 per cent in Singapore, 51 per cent in Korea and 43 per cent in Japan. 15 Disparity in earnings also extends to piece work done at home and to much agricultural wage work. Women in the informal sector generally earn less than men. The feminization of unpaid and low-paid work has contributed to a higher incidence of poverty among women, particularly among female-headed households.[8]

### 5. *Social security and protection*

Social security schemes have been rendered increasingly inappropriate by socio-economic and demographic change because they are still based on the idea of male breadwinners and female dependants. Only a few countries have universal social security schemes, though benefits are often limited by the costs involved. Social security

schemes that are related to employment status and earnings remain the dominant form of social protection in developed countries. Since the social protection of men varies according to their occupation or social security scheme, the problem here is defining equal treatment between women and men. The social security entitlements of women and men in the same employment situation must be compared to arrive at valid comparisons. Securing equality usually involves two elements: first, guaranteeing the same rights for women, particularly married women, with regard to the income replacement function of social security and, second, guaranteeing female workers the same entitlements for family members as male workers receive.

Employment benefits for women differ in a number of ways from those for men. During periods out of the paid labour force, such as for child-rearing, working women may not be covered by social security, or may even lose rights that they have acquired. Even when part-time workers, the majority of whom are women, are covered by social security, they accrue lower benefits. Women are more likely to be unemployed than men, and for longer periods of time. Women's earnings are lower than men's on average, resulting in lower benefits in earnings-related social security schemes. And fewer women are covered by private benefit schemes for a variety of reasons, including the concentration of women in the service sector, the exclusion of part-time workers from such schemes and provisions that restrict participation to higher-paid employees. Thus equal treatment in social security legislation should go beyond direct discrimination to include the effects of indirect discrimination which derive from such factors as employment, marital status or family situation.

While the countries of Central and Eastern Europe had highly developed social protection systems over many years, the economic crisis affecting the region raises serious questions about their capacity to sustain existing levels of protection while responding to recession and rising unemployment. The situation is particularly troublesome for women since their labour force participation has long been predicated on social security systems designed to help them combine their career with family demands.

Coverage in the developing countries is generally restricted to formal sector workers. While Governments recognize the need to develop more comprehensive forms of social protection and are generally committed to doing so, measures designed to protect living

*Table III.14*

Women's earnings as a percentage of men's earnings in non-agricultural industries,
selected countries or areas, 1980-1991

| Country or area | 1980 | 1981 | 1982 | 1983 | 1984 | 1985 | 1986 | 1987 | 1988 | 1989 | 1990 | 1991 |
|---|---|---|---|---|---|---|---|---|---|---|---|---|
| Australia (non-managerial employees) | 86.0 | 84.4 | 82.9* | 83.5 | 85.8 | 87.2 | 86.6 | 87.0 | 87.9 | .. | 90.8 | 90.9* |
| Belgium (salaried employees) | .. | .. | .. | .. | .. | 62.0 | 62.4 | 63.3 | 64.1 | .. | .. | .. |
| Belgium (wage-earners) | 69.4 | 72.5. | 73.6 | 74.5 | 74.7 | 74.6 | 74.4 | 75.1 | 75.0 | .. | .. | .. |
| Cyprus | 54.3 | 56.8 | 58.2 | 58.1 | 57.9 | 58.5 | 47.9 | 58.8 | 59.1 | 59.5 | 59.0 | 59.2* |
| Czechoslovakia | 68.4 | 68.4 | 68.4 | 64.4 | 68.4 | 68.4 | 68.4 | 69.2 | 70.1 | 70.1 | 70.6 | 70.6[a] |
| Denmark | 84.5 | 84.5 | 83.9 | 84.4 | 84.4 | 83.8 | 82.3 | 81.7 | 82.1 | 82.7 | 82.6 | 83.3 |
| France | 79.2 | 80.4 | 80.1 | 80.6 | 80.7 | 81.4* | 82.2 | 81.8 | .. | .. | 80.8 | .. |
| Germany (Federal Republic of) | 72.4 | 72.5 | 72.7 | 72.2 | 72.3 | 72.8 | 73.1 | 73.4 | 73.6 | 73.5 | 73.1 | 73.6 |
| Gibraltar | 65.9 | 67.9 | 62.0 | 62.3 | 60.0 | 74.4 | 63.5 | 62.8 | .. | .. | 67.1 | .. |
| Iceland | 85.5 | 84.7 | 85.0 | 85.6 | 94.1 | 90.4 | 89.3 | 89.6 | 90.6 | .. | 77.8 | 80.1 |
| Japan | 53.8 | 53.3 | 52.8* | 52.2 | 51.8 | 51.8* | 52.1 | 52.3 | 50.7 | 50.3 | 49.6 | 50.8 |
| Luxembourg (salaried employees) | 49.7 | 50.7 | 52.7 | 54.2 | 53.8 | 55.2 | 54.7 | 55.3 | 55.6 | .. | 54.9 | .. |
| Luxembourg (wage-earners) | 64.7 | 63.4 | 63.5 | 65.2 | 64.9 | 66.1 | 64.5 | 65.9 | 63.1 | .. | 65.1 | .. |
| Netherlands | 78.2 | 77.4 | 76.9 | 76.7 | 76.3 | 76.2 | 76.4 | 76.3 | 76.8 | .. | 77.5 | .. |
| Netherlands (wage-earners) | 77.9 | 77.0 | 76.7 | 76.8 | 77.0 | 76.4 | 76.4 | 76.1 | 76.7 | .. | 76.9 | .. |
| New Zealand | 77.2* | 77.8 | 77.6* | 78.4 | 78.4 | 77.4 | 78.8 | 79.4 | 80.4 | 80.9 | 80.6 | 80.9 |
| Switzerland | 67.6 | 67.8 | 67.3 | 67.2 | 67.2 | 67.5 | 67.3 | 67.4 | 67.4 | .. | 67.6 | .. |
| United Kingdom | 69.7 | 69.5 | 69.1 | 69.6* | 69.5 | .. | .. | .. | .. | .. | .. | .. |

*Notes*: Unless otherwise stated, the figures cover both wage-earners and salaried employees. Earnings are average hourly earnings, except for Cyprus and Gibraltar which are weekly and Belgium (salaried employees), Czechoslovakia, Japan and Luxembourg (salaried employees), which are monthly. For these series, the differences in hours worked by women and men will have an impact on the percentages. An asterisk (*) denotes a change in the series (e.g., a new sample design) so that figures may not be fully comparable; two dots (..) indicate that data are not available or are not separately reported.

a    Beginning in 1991, enterprises with fewer than 100 employees are excluded.

standards and facilitate income growth have fallen victim to the exigencies of structural adjustment programmes. Recession and restructuring of the labour market have created additional problems—the number of women in the informal sector has increased considerably and their jobs in domestic services, petty trading, small family businesses and self-employment rarely come within the purview of social protection schemes. Economic restructuring programmes have reduced social spending, therefore worsening the poor's access to social services and emphasizing the need for social safety nets.

Child-care facilities in many countries are inadequate to meet the needs of working mothers, and Governments, trade unions, employers, national women's organizations and non-governmental organizations often do not fully address this issue. Some employers have set up child-care facilities and introduced other measures to make their enterprises family-friendly, which appear to improve employee performance and morale. But there has been little change in the tradi-

tional sexual division of labour and in men's attitude towards child care and domestic responsibilities. While parental and paternal leave has been introduced in some countries, it is largely unused by men. Although maternity protection provisions exist in most areas, many women outside the formal sector, especially in the developing world, do not have access to them.

## 6.   *Women workers, trade unions and other worker associations*

The significant increase in women's memberships in trade unions during the past decade still lags behind women's numbers in the workforce despite concerted efforts by some unions to recruit more women, to introduce changes in their structure and to respond better to the needs of women workers. The increase also varies among regions, countries and industries.

In Europe, for example, women's membership in unions varies from 13 per cent in Switzerland to 51 per cent in Sweden. In Africa women make up 30 per cent of union membership.[52] Women constitute 37 per cent of union members int the United States and 39 per cent in Canada, though these figures are about twice as high in the garment and textile sectors and about half as much in the automobile and steel industry.[65]

Few women are found in union leadership despite strategies adopted to enhance women's representation at this level and in unions generally. And while collective bargaining can be used as an important vehicle for promoting gender equality, it has not yet been fully exploited for this purpose. Trade unions have also not expanded to cover the unorganized and vulnerable sectors—informal, rural, domestic, home-based and other areas—which mainly involve women.[66] These observations also apply to employers' organizations.

Mobilizing and strengthening the associations of informal sector and rural women workers can enhance their access to essential productive resources such as credit, training markets and improved technology, as well as increase their bargaining power and protect their interests.

## NOTES

[1]This chapter is largely based on input from the International Labour Organization (ILO), with a special analysis of manufacturing by the United Nations Industrial Development Organization. The contribution of ILO is based in part on the framework paper on women workers in a changing global environment, prepared by the ILO's International Institute for Labour Studies for the International Forum on Equality for Women in the World of Work: Challenges for the Future (Geneva, June 1994), as well as on the proceedings of the Forum.

[2]Unless otherwise indicated, the data in this section were taken from World Labour Report, 1992 (Geneva, International Labour Office, 1992).

[3]World Labour Report, 1994 (Geneva, International Labour Office, 1994), p. 29.

[4]Ibid., p. 16.

[5]Women: Challenges to the Year 2000 (United Nations publication, Sales No. E.91.I.21).

[6]World Labour Report, 1994 ..., chap. 2.

[7]International Confederation of Free Trade Unions, "Equality—The continuing challenge: strategies for success" (Brussels, unpublished paper, April 1991).

[8]The Report on Rural Women Living in Poverty (Rome, International Fund for Agricultural Development, 1993).

[9]L. Paukert, "Women's employment in East-Central European countries during the period of transition to a market economy system", Working Paper (Geneva, International Labour Office, 1993).

[10]B. Einhorn, "The impact of the transition from centrally planned economies on women's employment in East Central Europe", BRIDGE Paper (Brighton, England, Institute for Development Studies, 1993).

[11]M. Fong and G. Paul, "The changing role of women in employment in Eastern Europe", Report No. 8213 (Washington, D.C., World Bank, February 1992).

[12]F. Bourguignon and C. Morrisson, "Adjustment and equity in developing countries: a new approach" (Paris, Organisation for Economic Cooperation and Development, unpublished paper, 1992).

[13]S. Baden, "The impact of recession and structural adjustment on women's work in developing and developed countries", Working Paper No. 19, Interdepartmental Project on Equality for Women in Employment (Geneva, International Labour Office, 1993).

[14]V. Moghadam, "An overview of global employment and unemployment in a gender perspective" (Paper prepared for the United Nations University/World Institute for Development Economics Research (UNU/WIDER) Conference on the Politics and Economics of Global Employment, Helsinki, 17 and 18 June 1994.

[15]L. L. Lim, "Women at work in Asia and the Pacific: recent trends and future challenges" (Regional report prepared for the ILO International Forum on Equality for Women in the World of Work: Challenges for the Future, Geneva, 1-3 June 1994).

[16]Studies conducted in India and Egypt show that 16 per cent of sample rural women were reported to have performed labour force activity for more than 47 hours (India) and 130 hours (Egypt) in response to using the key words "main activity". This rate changed to 41 per cent (India) and 27 per cent (Egypt) when a question about "secondary activity" was included and rose to 48 per cent and 29 per cent, respectively, when the key word used was simply "work". Disaggregated by specific activities from a list of 13, including farming, animal care, petty trading, wage employment and the like, the rates rose dramatically, to 88 per cent and 54 per cent. As well as the impact of key words, adequate training and sensitization to gender issues need to be part of reform efforts in data collection methods (see R. Anker, "Women and work: continuing inequality", unpublished paper, 1994).

[17]L. Goldschmidt-Clermont, "Unpaid work in the household", Women, Work and Development, No. 1, 1989 (Geneva, International Labour Office).

[18]The World's Women, 1970-1990: Trends and Statistics, Social Statistics and Indicators, Series K, No. 8 (United Nations publication, Sales No. E.90.XVII.3), chap. 6.

[19]I. Palmer, Gender and Population in the Adjustment of African Economies: Planning for Change (Geneva, International Labour Office, 1991), pp. 163-164).

[20]International Labour Organization, Report of the Tripartite European Meeting on the Impact of Technological Change on Work and Training, Geneva, 28 October-2 November 1991.

[21]S. Mitter, "Innovations in work organization at the enterprise level, changes in technology and women's employment", BRIDGE Paper (Brighton, England, Institute for Development Studies, 1993).

[22]International Labour Organization, "Skills, training and retraining required to match new occupational profiles in commerce and offices" (Report prepared for the tenth session of the Committee on Salaried Employees and Professional Workers, Geneva, 1993).

[23]A. Rajan, Services: The Second Industrial Revolution? (London, Butterworth, 1990).

[24]I. Palmer, *Gender and Population in the Adjustment of African Economies: Planning for Change* (Geneva, International Labour Office, 1991).

[25]This section is based on a study entitled "Women in manufacturing: participation patterns, determinants and trends", prepared by the United Nations Industrial Development Organization (UNIDO).

[26]G. Standing, "Global feminization through flexible labour", *World Development*, vol. 17, No. 7 (1989).

[27]Details of the methodology may be obtained from UNIDO.

[28]Australia, Austria, Belgium, Canada, Denmark, Germany, Finland, France, Ireland, Israel, Italy, Netherlands, New Zealand, Norway, Spain, Sweden, United Kingdom of Great Britain and Northern Ireland and United States of America.

[29]Argentina, Brazil, Chile, Colombia, Costa Rica, Cuba, El Salvador, Panama, Suriname, Trinidad and Tobago, Uruguay and Venezuela.

[30]Hong Kong, Japan, Malaysia, Republic of Korea and Singapore.

[31]Bulgaria, Czechoslovakia, Hungary and Poland.

[32]B. Einhorn and S. Mitter, "A comparative analysis of women's industrial participation during the transition from centrally-planned to market economies in East-Central Europe", in *The Impact of Economic and Political Reform on the Status of Women in Eastern Europe* (United Nations publication, Sales No. E.92.IV.4) and V. Moghadam, *Privatization and Democratization in Central and Eastern Europe and the Soviet Union: The Gender Dimension* (Helsinki, UNU/WIDER, 1992), p. 46.

[33]Moghadam, op. cit., p. 6.

[34]Barbados, Cyprus, Greece, Haiti, Indonesia, Philippines, Portugal, Thailand and former Yugoslavia.

[35]Bolivia, Botswana, Ecuador, Fiji, Honduras, Mauritius, Mexico, Nicaragua, Paraguay, Peru, Sri Lanka and Tunisia.

[36]Bahrain, Jordan, Kuwait, Qatar and United Arab Emirates.

[37]Algeria, Egypt, Iran (Islamic Republic of), Iraq and Syrian Arab Republic.

[38]Bangladesh, Guatemala, Morocco and Pakistan.

[39]Cameroon, India, Turkey and Zambia.

[40]Ghana, Mali, Nigeria and Togo.

[41]Burundi, Gambia, Liberia, Malawi and Nepal.

[42]*The World's Women, 1970-1990: Trends and Statistics*, Social Statistics and Indicators, Series K, No. 8 (United Nations publication, Sales No. E.90.XVII.3).

[43]On the issue of migration, see *Population Distribution and Migration: Proceedings of the United Nations Expert Meeting on Population Distribution and Migration, Santa Cruz, Bolivia, 18-22 January 1993* (to be issued as a United Nations publication).

[44]International Labour Organization, *Migration* (Geneva, 1992).

[45]S. Baden and S. Joekes, "Gender issues in the development of the special economic zones and open areas in the People's Republic of China" (Paper prepared for the Fudan University Seminar on Women's Participation in Economic Development, Shanghai, 15 April 1993).

[46]United Nations Population Fund, *The State of the World Population* (New York, 1993).

[47]L. L. Lim, "Growing economic interdependence and its implications for international migration", in *Population Distribution and Migration* ....

[48]S. E. Findley and L. Williams, "Women who go and women who stay: reflections of family migration processes in a changing world", World Employment Programme Working Paper, WEP 2-21/WP.176 (Geneva, International Labour Office, 1991).

[49]P. Pasuk, "From peasant girls to Bangkok masseuses" (Geneva, International Labour Office, unpublished paper, 1982).

[50]M. Molyneux, "Women's rights in post-communist states: some reflections on the international context", *Millenium: Journal of International Studies*, vol 23, No. 2 (Summer 1994).

[51]G. Schmid, "Women and structural change in the 90s" (Report on a meeting of trade union experts, held under the OECD Labour/Management Programme, Paris 1993).

[52]E. Date-Bah, "African trade unions and the challenge of organizing women workers in the unorganized sectors", *Labour Education*, issue 92, No. 3 (1993).

[53]Baden, op. cit., p. 21; based on D. Elson, "Male bias in macroeconomics: the case of structural adjustment", in *Male Bias in the Development Process* (Manchester, England, Manchester University Press, 1991).

[54]I. Baud and G. A. de Bruijne, eds., *Gender, Small-Scale Industry and Development Policy* (London, IT Publications, 1993).

[55]International Confederation of Free Trade Unions, "Equality—The continuing challenge: strategies for success" (Brussels, unpublished paper, April 1991); see also *1989 World Survey on the Role of Women in Development* (United Nations publication, Sales No. E.89.IV.2).

[56]C. Moser, "Adjustment from below: low-income women, time and the triple role in Guayaquil, Ecuador", in *Women and Adjustment Policies in the Third World*, H. Afshar and C. Dennis (eds.) (London, Macmillan, 1992).

[57]S. Joekes, "Kenya: report of an ILO exploratory mission on women's employment, with recommendations for follow-up" (Geneva, International Labour Office, 1991).

[58]International Labour Organization, "Part-time work" (Report prepared for the eightieth session of the International Labour Conference, Geneva, 2-22 June 1993).

[59]D. Barbezat, "Occupational segmentation by sex in the world", Working Paper No. 13, Interdepartmental Project on Equality for Women in Employment (Geneva, International Labour Office, 1994).

[60]J. Rubery and J. Fagan, "Occupational segregation of women and men in the European Community" (Report of the Network of Experts on the Situation of Women in the Labour Market, Manchester School of Management, University of Manchester, England, 1993).

[61]*Year Book of Labour Statistics* (Geneva, International Labour Office, various issues).

[62]M. Gunderson, "Comparable worth and gender discrimination: an international perspective" (Geneva, International Labour Office, 1994).

[63]*Financial Times*, 25 July 1994.

[64]P. Ulshoefer, "Comments on women's labour and employment in Latin America in the nineties: present situation and future outlook" (Regional report prepared for the ILO International Forum on Equality for Women in the World of Work: Challenges for the Future, Geneva, 1-3 June 1994).

[65]S. Eaton, "Women workers, unions and industrial sectors in North America", Working Paper No. 1, Interdepartmental Project on Equality for Women in Employment (Geneva, International Labour Office, 1992).

[66]M. Martens and S. Mitter, eds., *Women in Trade Unions: Organizing the Unorganized* (Geneva, International Labour Office, forthcoming).

# IV

## Women and economic decision-making

Economic decisions made by the State or by corporate actors in the market determine present and future economic performance. The level of participation by women and men influences the content of these decisions as well as the processes that shape them. Despite the increased importance of women in the formal economy, the recognition of their role in reducing poverty and the changes in their access to education and other human development assets, their participation in economic decision-making remains limited. Over the past 20 years the proportion and growth rate of female employment have increased in most of the world and in all sectors. Women are entering the third level of education, nearly closing the gap between men and women, and diversifying their fields of study. Despite these trends, women are still largely absent from economic decision-making positions. Equal participation in economic decision-making is essential if women are to be involved in exercising power.

Economic decision makers are the persons, groups and institutions whose power derives from possessing the knowledge, organization and means of production which affect markets for labour, capital, raw materials, goods and services. The influence of each specific decision maker varies from country to country depending on the level of development and the social, economic, political and judicial systems in place. There are few female managers of large economic enterprises in the private or public sectors, on the boards of trade unions or in employers and professional organizations. Participation levels are growing, in most cases, at a rate far below trends in education and in the formal employment market. Women are in positions secondary to men, even in traditionally female-dominated professions and sectors.

The set of factors that influence women's access to and ability to perform in decision-making positions—the "potentially restrictive pipeline"—works at all social levels and in all countries, regardless of the level of development. However, it is possible to analyse the main determinants of women's participation in shaping macroeconomic decisions and to identify measures that enhance the participation of women in these processes.

## A.  WOMEN ECONOMIC DECISION MAKERS: WHY, WHERE AND HOW MANY

The main sources of data on women in economic decision-making include International Labour Organization (ILO) data on employment, a survey on the incidence of women among top managers in leading international and United States corporations undertaken by the Division for the Advancement of Women of the United Nations Secretariat, five case studies undertaken for the Division in Morocco, Nigeria, the Philippines, Portugal and the Republic of Korea, data and indicators provided to the Division by national women's organizations, information provided by the African Development Bank, the Inter-American Development Bank and the World Bank, information on women in decision-making posts in economic ministries collected by the Division and non-governmental and academic sources. From these, the following economic actors have been identified as the most important economic decision makers on the basis of the direct and determinative role they play in the economy:

- Top executives of national public bodies dealing with economic matters.

- Senior managers of public and private enterprises at the national and international levels.

- Entrepreneurs at various levels.

- Senior managers of international and regional financial institutions.

- Members of the boards of trade unions, professional and business organizations.

### 1.  The need for more female economic decision makers

There are many reasons women should be fully incorporated in economic decision-making. First, women have equal rights to such participation. The right to non-discrimination in economic activity and public policy-making is set out in the Universal Declaration of Human Rights[1] and codified in the Convention on the Elimination of All Forms of Discrimination against Women.[2] Women should have equal access to obtaining the skills, assets and careers needed to advance to decision-making levels.

Second, impeding women's achievement of their full potential is a waste of human resources. An enabling environment increases women's acquisition of basic skills, as reflected in rates of participation in third-level education and in the labour force. There is a trend in developed countries towards a reduced supply of workers with third-level education because of demographic trends. The number of advanced graduates will drop over the next two decades and skilled employees will become increasingly scarce. In Germany, for example, the federal labour office estimates that there will be a shortage of 500,000 managers by 2000. Women could fill this gap.[3] The same trend is occurring in some Asian countries. In the Republic of Korea, Samsung and Hundai (the largest industrial companies) now recruit female university graduates on a large scale.[4]

Finally, women have skills that are particularly appropriate for modern management. Many of these skills are developed by managing scarce time and resources and multiple care-taking and unpaid work responsibilities in the household. This multi-tasking ability is particularly valuable in industrial enterprises where a premium is placed on efficient time use. Competition between enterprises has led to the development of management styles based on adaptability and the full use of all available resources. There also has been a corresponding change in the preferred management culture. Management experts are beginning to advocate a management style that is more typically feminine, involving such concepts as cooperative leadership, intuitive problem solving and an emphasis on quality.[5]

The increasing feminization of the labour market over the medium and long term, linked to an increase in the level of female employment, should lead to a dynamic sharing of economic power and reproductive roles between men and women at all levels. To help manage this process more female economic decision makers will be needed.

### 2.  Women in national economic decision-making positions

*Administrative and management occupations*

In the classification of the economically active population, the "administrative and management" category describes those whose work involves management. This is an occupational category in which men have historically dominated (see table IV.1). Globally, women hold between 10 and 30 per cent of management positions, and less than 5 per cent of the very highest positions.[6] The gap between women and men has been narrowing, especially over the past decade. Eastern European States, Western European and other States and Latin American and Caribbean States show relatively high shares of women in this occupational category. Africa also has had a rapid rate of increase, though it started from a lower base.

*Table IV.1*

Ratio of women to men in administrative and management occupations by region, 1980 and 1990

Number of women per 100 men

| Region | 1980 | 1990 |
|---|---|---|
| Africa | 10 | 18 |
| Asia and the Pacific | 9 | 10 |
| Eastern Europe | 30 | 66 |
| Latin America and the Caribbean | 24 | 34 |
| Western Europe and other | 23 | 41 |
| World | 19 | 34 |

*Source*: Division for the Advancement of Women of the United Nations Secretariat, from data contained in the Women's Indicators and Statistics Data Base (WISTAT), version 3, 1994.

*Government economic bodies*

The Division for the Advancement of Women has collected information about women in senior executive positions in government since 1987. Data for 1994 indicate that the share of women in top government decision-making positions (ministerial level or higher) is only 6.2 per cent of all ministerial positions.[7] In economic ministries (including finance, trade, economy and planning ministries and central banks) women's participation is even lower, at 3.6 per cent. In 144 countries there are no women at all in these areas and at these levels. However, the participation of women in public economic decision-making has increased since 1987 (see table IV.2). At that time no women held decision-making posts in economic ministries or central banks in 108 of the 162 Governments covered in the study. By 1994 only 90 out of 186 Governments lacked women in these posts.

*Table IV.2*

Female ministers by region, 1987 and 1994

Percentage of total positions

| Region | 1987 All ministries | 1987 Economic ministries | 1994 All ministries | 1994 Economic ministries |
|---|---|---|---|---|
| Africa | 2.9 | 0.9 | 5.4 | 3.0 |
| Asia and the Pacific | 1.8 | 1.7 | 2.9 | 2.0 |
| Eastern Europe | 3.0 | 2.5 | 2.6 | 1.9 |
| Latin America and the Caribbean | 3.1 | 0.9 | 7.5 | 5.1 |
| Western Europe and other | 7.1 | 3.9 | 15.2 | 9.6 |
| World | 3.4 | 1.7 | 6.2 | 4.1 |

The situation is little different if the top four levels of government decision-making—ministerial, vice-ministerial, principal secretary and departmental director levels—are taken into account. The percentage of women in these areas is 6.8 per cent. For economic ministries the share is 5.6 per cent. The participation of women in public economic decision-making at the top four levels has increased since 1987 (see table IV.3).

*Table IV.3*

Female government officials by region, 1987 and 1994

Percentage of total positions

| Region | 1987 All officials | 1987 Officials in economic ministries | 1994 All officials | 1994 Officials in economic ministries |
|---|---|---|---|---|
| Africa | 4.0 | 1.6 | 6.3 | 4.1 |
| Asia and the Pacific | 3.0 | 2.3 | 2.9 | 2.5 |
| Eastern Europe | 3.5 | 5.4 | 5.0 | 4.9 |
| Latin America and the Caribbean | 7.3 | 2.7 | 10.4 | 6.9 |
| Western Europe and other | 9.6 | 3.2 | 13.0 | 10.3 |
| World | 5.4 | 2.4 | 6.8 | 5.1 |

*United States and international corporations*

The low representation of women among public economic decision-making positions is matched by their low representation among the largest private corporations.

The Division for the Advancement of Women examined the incidence of women in top management posts in the 1,000 largest non-United States corporations[8] and the 1,000 largest United States corporations[9] for 1993. The study identified the share of women among three senior levels of management—chief executive, chief operating officer or group managing director and other sectorial managers or corporate members of the board. The study indicates that women's representation among managers in the top corporations is quite low. United States companies have a higher proportion of women managers (8 women for each 100 men) than non-United States companies (mainly from Europe and Asia), which average just one woman executive for every 100 male executives. In both groups there are almost no women at the highest level (chief executive); women hold 1 per cent of chief executive positions. Most female managers were concentrated at lower levels of corporate decision-making, with 97 per cent of women managers in the third tier in United States corporations and 61.5 per cent in non-United States corporations (see table IV.4). The share of women executives is higher in corporations whose main business is wholesale or retail trade or food and lodging.

*Table IV.4*

Female executives in the world's largest corporations, 1993

Percentage

| Sector | Female executives International corporations | Female executives United States corporations |
|---|---|---|
| Mining and quarrying | 0 | 6 |
| Manufacturing | 1 | 7 |
| Electricity, gas and water | 3 | 10 |
| Construction | 2 | 6 |
| Wholesale and retail trade and restaurants and hotels | 0 | 30 |
| Transport, storage and communication | 1 | 8 |
| Financing, insurance, real estate and business services | 1 | 7 |
| Community, social and personal services | 5 | 8 |
| Activities not adequately defined | 2 | 18 |
| All sectors | 1 | 8 |

    a    Excluding United States corporations.

*Trade unions*

An examination of women in union leadership indicates that women's power in trade unions is not relative to their participation in the labour market or their membership in these unions (see chapter III). With few exceptions, such as in teacher and nurse unions, women continue to be underrepresented and, generally, the higher the position, the lower women's participation. Still, women have been the major source of new trade union members in recent years and are the most important factor in strengthening workers' organizations.

While there are no global statistics on the general composition of trade union leadership, the gap between participation as members and on executive boards is illustrated by data from countries in a number of different regions. In the Austrian Confederation of Trade Unions, for example, women represent 31 per cent of total membership, but only 9 per cent of the executive council are women. In the Bangladesh Free Trade Union Congress, 30 per cent of the members are women and 19 per cent are in leadership positions. The figures in the Hind Mazdoor Sabha in India are 25 per cent and 4 per cent; in the Sierra Leone Labour Congress they are 35 per cent and 6 per cent; and in the Swedish Confederation of Professional Employees they are 58 per cent and 2 per cent.[10]

### Professional and employers organizations

Professional and employers organizations have generally been exclusively male in composition and leadership. To compensate for this, women's organizations at the national, regional and international levels have made efforts to facilitate networking among female entrepreneurs and professionals. There are even fewer statistics available about the gender composition of the professional and employers' organizations (apart from government organizations) than for trade unions, and women's entrepreneur organizations have not been systematically documented.

### National case studies

As part of its preparations for this Survey the Division for the Advancement of Women commissioned case studies from Morocco, Nigeria, the Philippines, Portugal and the Republic of Korea. The data for each country indicate that there are few women in top economic decision-making positions, whether in government, labour unions or private enterprises, and little evidence of improvement over time. But the share of women at lower levels of decision-making is increasing. Particularly notable is the increase of women in government and the increase of women entrepreneurs in small- and medium-sized firms.

### Morocco

A 1992 survey on women and enterprises in Morocco found that a historical and sociological turning point occurred during the 1980s as more women entered the labour market and became entrepreneurs. Of women professionals in the public sector, 66.5 per cent assumed their first job after-1980 and 45.5 per cent began their career after 1986. Data show that three quarters of all female-owned enterprises were founded in the 1980s and that 84 per cent of these enterprises had less than 25 employees. These new enterprises were financed mainly from savings and family sources rather than from formal financial institutions. Of the employees earning more than 100,000 dirhams a year, only 8.8 per cent were women.[11]

### Nigeria

*Table IV.5*

Employment distribution by gender, Nigeria, 1993

Percentage

| Level | Male | Female |
|---|---|---|
| Corporate leadership | 90 | 10 |
| Middle management | 65 | 35 |
| Entrepreneurs | 80 | 20 |
| Micro-entrepreneurs | 30 | 70 |
| Civil service leadership | 90 | 10 |
| Trade and labour unions | 95 | 5 |
| Banking and finance leadership | 95 | 5 |

Source: Nigeria, National Commission for Women, "Women's equality in economic decision-making" (unpublished paper, 1994).

### Philippines

Data on employment from 1992 show that just 31 per cent of administrative, executive and managerial workers were women, and the pattern appears not to have changed from 1987 to 1992.[12] The survey also found that 40 per cent of total employees were own-account workers (28 per cent were men and 12 per cent were women). Thus men outnumbered women by more than two to one in these categories, where economic decision-making relies on the individual as either self-employed or as employer. Among employers, there were three times more men than women, and there was little change in the pattern between 1987 and 1992. In the public sector women occupy more second-level career service positions than men, but high-level decision-making positions are occupied mainly by men (see table IV.6).

*Table IV.6*
Gender distribution in government service,
Philippines, 1990

Percentage

| Level | Male | Female |
|---|---|---|
| Third (top) | 71.0 | 29.0 |
| Second | 40.3 | 59.7 |
| First (entry) | 59.5 | 40.5 |
| Total | 47.5 | 52.5 |

## Portugal

An examination of the 1,000 largest corporations in the country revealed changes since 1987.[13] At that time 18 per cent of these enterprises were headed by women executives; by 1992 the proportion had risen to 33.6 per cent. However, if only the 50 most important enterprises are considered, there were no changes at all since 1987,

with no women heads then or in 1992. The share of female entrepreneurs has increased considerably since 1960. From 7 women for each 100 male entrepreneurs in 1960, the ratio reached 19 in 1981 and 20 in 1987.

## Republic of Korea

Of the establishments run by women in 1989, 99.7 per cent were small-sized (having fewer than 20 regular employees). Compared with the distribution of employers in 1980, the number of women running manufacturing firms declined while the number in social and personal services increased. Sixty-four per cent of women employers in 1990 operated wholesale and retail trade firms and 23 per cent ran social and personal services firms. The female share of positions at the assistant manager level and above increased from 2 per cent in 1980 to 12.5 per cent in 1992.[4]

*Table IV.7*
Women by working status, Republic of Korea, 1965-1992

Percentage

| Status | 1965 | 1970 | 1980 | 1990 | 1992 |
|---|---|---|---|---|---|
| Employers | .. | .. | .. | 2.6 | 2.9 |
| Own-account workers | 21.1[a] | 21.0[a] | 23.3[a] | 16.6 | 16.8 |
| Employees | 20.9 | 28.6 | 39.2 | 55.3 | 57.6 |
| Unpaid family workers | 57.9 | 50.4 | 37.4 | 25.5 | 22.8 |
| Total | 100.0 | 100.0 | 100.0 | 100.0 | 100.0 |

*Note*: Two dots (..) indicate that data are not available or are not separately reported.

a   Including employers.

## 3. Women in international economic decision-making positions

The incidence of women in international economic decision-making positions is similar to that at the national level. Again, there are few women at the top, though there has been some improvement. No woman heads a United Nations agency involved with economics, whether in the United Nations Secretariat, the specialized agencies or the Bretton Woods institutions. The same is true of the regional development banks and major transnational public economic bodies like the Commission of the European Union. Moreover, women are not well represented in government delegations to these bodies. There has never been a female chief executive of an international or regional financial institution.

### General Assembly of the United Nations

The Second Committee of the General Assembly deals with economic and financial matters. This Committee

prepares and reviews international development strategies, monitors the implementation of Agenda 21, the action programme adopted by the United Nations Conference on Environment and Development, and deals with economic policy questions. In 1993, 145 governmental delegations did not have any female representatives. Twenty per cent of the delegates to the Second Committee were women, compared with 7 per cent in 1987.[14]

### International Labour Conference of the International Labour Organization

A similar situation is found in the participation of women in delegations to International Labour Conferences during 1975-1993. The composition of delegations shows almost no increase during this period, except in employer delegations, where women's share had historically been very low (see table IV.8).[15]

*Table IV.8*
Women delegates to the International Labour
Conference, 1975-1993
Percentage

| Group | 1975 | 1985 | 1993 |
|---|---|---|---|
| Government delegations | 14.4 | 18.0 | 16.9 |
| Employer delegations | 6.0 | 6.3 | 9.1 |
| Worker delegations | 16.9 | 12.7 | 12.5 |
| All groups | 13.0 | 14.0 | 13.9 |

### *World Bank Group*

A report produced in 1989 indicated that of the nearly 4,000 staff in the World Bank Group at grades 18 and above (high-level staff), 25 per cent were women.[16] More than half of these were concentrated at grades 18 to 21. Women at grades 22 and above represented a small share (15 per cent) of staff at these levels. Male higher-level staff were concentrated at the upper grades, with 59 per cent at grades 24 and above; only 16 per cent of female higher-level staff were at these grades. Women were dramatically underrepresented in management and other senior positions. Of the 498 staff at grades 26 and above, only 3.8 per cent were women. Of the 158 staff at grades 27 and above, only 2.5 per cent were women. In 1994 there was only one woman vice-president and there had only been two in the history of the Bank. The report concluded that the Bank has made limited progress in improving upward mobility for women.

### *African Development Bank/African Development Fund*

Data elaborated by the African Development Bank in 1992 showed that 72 per cent of female Bank staff were concentrated in non-professional categories and that 57 per cent of male Bank staff were concentrated in the professional categories. There were some slight changes between 1989 and 1992.[17] In the professional categories the ratio of women to men increased from 15 women for each 100 men in 1989 to 21 women per 100 men in 1992. Still, in 1992 most female professionals (94 per cent) were concentrated at the lower levels of the professional categories (up to the P5 level); in contrast, 30 per cent of male professionals were found above the P6 level. There were only four women per 100 men at the P6 level or above in 1992.

### *Inter-American Development Bank*

As of 1993, 14 per cent of executive staff, 32 per cent of professional staff and 86 per cent of administrative staff at the Inter-American Development Bank headquarters

were women.[18] There were women at the level of vice-president and above.

### *International Monetary Fund*

A 1994 report revealed that as of May 1993 women made up 45 per cent of the Fund's staff but were heavily concentrated in the lower levels of the Fund's 19-grade structure.[19] Only 7 per cent of Fund managers were women and no woman has ever occupied any of the top management positions—managing director, deputy managing director or department head.

### 4.  *The next generation of economic decision makers*

One reason why there were few women economic decision makers in the past is that there were few to choose from: the pool of potential recruits was almost exclusively male. There is evidence that this is changing. One of the major changes in the enabling environment has been the growth in women's access to third-level education. This growth is particularly marked in regions with significant economic growth (see tables IV.9 and IV.10). Accordingly, the pool of qualified professionals will contain increasingly larger numbers of women.

*Table IV.9*
Ratio of women to men studying science and
technology in third-level education by region, 1970-1990
Number of women for each 100 men

| Region | 1970 | 1980 | 1990 |
|---|---|---|---|
| Africa | 24 | 21 | 24 |
| Asia and the Pacific | 33 | 45 | 70 |
| Eastern Europe | 61 | 81 | 74 |
| Latin America and the Caribbean | 37 | 54 | 80 |
| Western Europe and other | 29 | 49 | 67 |
| World | 32 | 43 | 56 |

*Table IV.10*
Ratio of women to men studying law and business
in third-level education by region, 1970-1990
Number of women for each 100 men

| Region | 1970 | 1980 | 1990 |
|---|---|---|---|
| Africa | 12 | 43 | 36 |
| Asia and the Pacific | 25 | 56 | 70 |
| Eastern Europe | 64 | 134 | 124 |
| Latin America and the Caribbean | 30 | 92 | 115 |
| Western Europe and other | 25 | 54 | 85 |
| World | 25 | 63 | 102 |

## B.   CAREER PATHS FOR WOMEN IN CORPORATE STRUCTURES

Whether in the public or private sector, individuals advance to economic decision-making positions through career paths. The absence of women from top positions suggests that women's career paths are different from men's, or that, in trying to follow the same path, women encounter different or more severe obstacles. Achieving equality in economic decision-making requires understanding and modifying these career paths.

### 1.   *Entry paths*

Few studies have been done on how women who are economic decision makers entered their institutional structures. Evidence from Europe suggests that there are a variety of ways. One way is through family connections—some of Europe's best-known businesswomen run companies that have been family-owned for some time.[20] Another way is through politics, when a prominent female politician moves into private sector management. It has been noted that women are more likely to have gained economic experience in local government, national politics, voluntary organizations and public bodies.[21] Women also have entered decision-making positions through public administration and the service sector more often than through manufacturing because more women are involved in these fields and, in the case of public administration, more objective criteria are applied to fill positions.

### 2.   *Barriers to entry*

Women face several barriers to advancing towards a role in management. These barriers comprise a complex set of factors operating at various stages of career development. Education and training often reproduces the sexual division of labour prevalent in society and places women at an immediate disadvantage. While boys are then trained in technical, commercial and marketable skills that prepare them for management roles, it is more socially acceptable for girls to be trained in fields preparing them for marriage and motherhood. And career guidance and counselling, when available, tend to channel girls into traditional female fields.

The small number of women attaining third-level education in such fields as business, law, economics, finance, technology and science is an important obstacle to women's access to decision-making bodies, though the trend is changing. Still, in Australia, for example,

only 12 per cent of third-level engineering students in 1992 were women.[22]

Women who have attained the requisite education and gained access to entry-level jobs in the formal sector often remain in the lower ranks and concentrated in women-dominated bureaucracies and management organizations. It is at career entry that stereotyped patterns begin to shape women's career prospects and chances for participation in management. Both women and men bear prejudices about women's roles, capabilities and behaviour, and these prejudices become entrenched in recruitment policies, terms and conditions of employment. Women's access to potential career posts also tend to be limited by their gender-ascribed roles.

### 3.   *Obstacles to promotion*

Once in a career, women may encounter structural and behavioural difficulties that restrict their vertical mobility. Structural factors are reflected in employment rules, regulations and performance evaluation norms. These structures are often formulated around the interests of men as employees and employers, and they are often unsympathetic and unsupportive of women's behaviour, roles and styles as employees, mothers and family caretakers. This male corporate culture also perpetrates behaviour patterns that work against women. Such behaviours include sexual harassment, exclusion from formal and informal networks and undervaluation of women's skills.

Taken together these factors form what has been termed a "glass ceiling", an invisible but impassable barrier that prevents women from rising professionally regardless of their education and experience. These barriers are faced by women in civil service and private industry all over the world.[23] Women may be excluded from development opportunities, professional networks, or field work on the basis of gender, depriving them of needed professional experience and almost ensuring marginalization and invisibility.

Because family-care responsibilities are undertaken mainly by women they can be an important obstacle to women's career advancement. Promotion prospects are influenced by the expectation that women will give their family responsibilities first priority. In Singapore, for example, married women, especially those with children, are not as likely to receive training that men are given.[15] In corporations, employers are sometimes reluctant to send women to expensive management training in the belief that investment in men has more secure pay-offs, since women may decide to leave employment after marriage.

Women's responsibilities as mothers, wives and employees are assumed to create role conflicts different from those of men as fathers, husbands and employees. These presumed conflicts can limit career opportunities. Moreover, organizations are generally structured by and for men. Women can find these structures foreign and intimidating because of their different cultural training and life experiences.[10]

Those women who manage to overcome these barriers can have specific problems derived from their minority status in the decision-making group: burdens of coping with the role of "token woman", lack of role models and feelings of isolation, strains of coping with prejudice and sex stereotyping and indirect discrimination from employers, fellow employees and the organizational structure and climate. Combined with family responsibilities, these stresses can create enormous pressures on women in these positions.

## C.  WOMEN ENTREPRENEURS

Although largely absent from decision-making positions in large corporations, women are emerging as major actors in entrepreneurial activities. While large, bureaucratic corporations constitute much of national and global economies, small and medium-sized modern enterprises are beginning to form the basis of growth sectors. The constraints that limit women's access to top positions in large corporations do not exist in these new enterprises, and there is evidence that women are starting to concentrate on working for these enterprises.

### 1.  How many female entrepreneurs are there?

While there are no data on the number of entrepreneurs, the pool of economically active persons from which they are drawn can be estimated from the Women's Indicators and Statistics Data Base (WISTAT). The category "employers and own-account workers" describes those who are economically independent and could be entrepreneurs. Men have historically been more likely to be economically independent than women (see table IV.11). But in the past 20 years the gap between men and women in this category has narrowed, from 26 women for each 100 men in 1970 to 40 women for each 100 men in 1990.

*Table IV.11*

Ratio of women to men among employers and own-account workers by region, 1970-1990

Number of women per 100 men

| Region | 1970 | 1980 | 1990 |
|---|---|---|---|
| Africa | 35 | 50 | 50 |
| Asia and the Pacific | 16 | 9 | 22 |
| Eastern Europe | 67 | 47 | 56 |
| Latin America and the Caribbean | 22 | 33 | 48 |
| Western Europe and other | 22 | 37 | 38 |
| World | 26 | 39 | 40 |

Female entrepreneurs, the exception 20 years ago, are now the new economic actors. National estimates indicate that 10 per cent of the new enterprises in North Africa, 33 per cent in North America and 40 per cent in the states of the former German Democratic Republic were created by women. It has been estimated that 75 to 80 per cent of new enterprises in the United States are created by women.[24] Canadian research shows a 172 per cent increase in the number of self-employed women between 1975 and 1990; the rate of growth for self-employed men during the same period was just 50 per cent.[25]

Women's enterprises are qualitatively different from men's. Studies indicate that there is a specific culture of female entrepreneurs. Women work cooperatively, are fiscally conservative, seem to be aware of their needs and of their environment and their enterprises centre on the delivery of services responding to traditionally unsatisfied needs. The practices followed in these enterprises are beginning to change how business institutions are run. However, though they often form the bulk of micro- and small entrepreneurs, women often have less access than men to support services such as credit, training, technology and information, which would allow them to grow.

### 2.  Facilitating women's entrepreneurial activities

A number of factors have facilitated the increase in female entrepreneurs. Access to education and a growing service sector have both increased opportunities for women. Education enhances self-esteem and provides necessary skills, while the service sector is well-suited to women's management styles, needs and concerns and has low entry barriers. In addition, the increase in female entrepreneurship in many developed countries may also be linked to female long-term unemployment and a perceived lack of prospects for career advancement in large enterprises or in the labour market generally.

### 3.  Obstacles for female entrepreneurs

Enterprises founded by women face obstacles that derive, in large measure, from women's unequal status in society. Although women are entering business rapidly most female-owned businesses are new and unstable. Female entrepreneurs encounter specific constraints when they enter and expand their business, in comparison to men. Discriminatory treatment of female entrepreneurs has been noted in most studies of creditors, suppliers, customers and even employees.

### Restrictions in obtaining financial resources

The first obstacle many female entrepreneurs face is obtaining sufficient capital to launch, maintain or expand an enterprise. While men are not asked for co-signers, many women are asked for a male co-signer on a loan, even when the man has no relationship to the business.[26] While credit is a problem for all small businesses, the problem is worse for women. In some countries banking laws contain discriminatory provisions. Inheritance laws, property rights and matrimonial property rules and laws also can work against women.

Most financial institutions provide non-discriminatory treatment for the credit needs of both women and men. However, women can face considerable problems in obtaining credit because of their lack of collateral, the nature and size of their business and their lack of negotiating experience. Consequently, commercial lenders often discriminate against women. Women often must rely on family members or other personal support systems to capitalize their business. Undercapitalized from the outset, women's businesses tend to start smaller and expand slower. Women in developing countries often must rely on informal financial sources who demand excessive interest.

### Lack of access to management training and technical assistance

Modern business requires management approaches and technical knowledge that can be acquired only through training. The lack of management training and technical assistance is a particularly serious barrier to the success of female-owned businesses and is believed to be a primary cause of business failure.

Women have less access to existing training because they lack their own networks and do not have training courses targeted to them, coupled with lack of time because of domestic responsibilities. Part of the problem is that management training and technical assistance programmes do not take into account the new business areas into which women are moving. There is still a tendency to give higher value to those sectors of the economy where men predominate.

In addition, national development policies in many developing countries are biased towards large public and private enterprises, while the micro- and small enterprises that account for a large number of women are marginalized. Such policies impede the flow of resources and opportunities to women's enterprises. Moreover, the concept of small and medium-sized enterprises needs to be redefined in many of these countries. There is evidence that this is occurring. For example, the African Development Bank's 1989 strategy for promoting the private sector recognizes the importance of the informal sector of African economies as a "major source of entrepreneurial talent for the small business growth that would drive and sustain the growth of a private sector in Africa".[17]

### Lack of networks and informal support

Entrepreneurs also benefit from a variety of informal support networks, ranging from other entrepreneurs to family members. These networks are often more difficult to establish for women entrepreneurs. Business networks help open up the entrepreneurial world, providing informal sources of information on opportunities and developments. However, there are few "old girl" networks to support, encourage and advise female entrepreneurs, and male-dominated associations are not always friendly to them. The influence of role models and mentors in the decision to become an entrepreneur has been widely reported.

A supportive family, including father, mother or husband, is frequently cited in the success of female entrepreneurs. This support can be crucial in helping female entrepreneurs cope with business and domestic responsibilities. In many developing countries, extended families are playing this supportive role. Still, in most countries female entrepreneurs face the same problems as other women working outside the home.

## D.   WOMEN AND TRADE DEVELOPMENT

Growth in many countries has been driven by trade. There is now evidence that there is a gender dimension to the development of trade, a fact that is beginning to be addressed by the United Nations through the International Trade Centre. Three factors have led the International Trade Centre to focus on female entrepreneurship and trade. The first is the expanding private sector, where small and medium-sized enterprises are playing an increasingly large role in developing countries. The second is the increasing visibility of female entrepreneurs. The third is the shift in general economic policy from inward-looking, import-substitution policies to outward-looking, market-oriented strategies.[27]

The literature on entrepreneurship has concentrated on entrepreneurial development at the national level and within the informal sector but has not analysed the crucial role of external marketing systems and outlets. Female entrepreneurs are active at all levels of trade: domestically, regionally and globally.

### 1.   Major constraints

The International Trade Centre has identified a number of constraints on the development of viable strategies for women in trade development at national and regional levels. The constraints include prevailing attitudes, socio-economic conditions and the division of labour; the gap between the objectives and the reality of national legislation on women in development and the inadequacy of policy and institutional frameworks to support women's participation in domestic, intraregional trade; women's inadequate access to the means of production; lack of institutional support for women's cooperative trade organizations; a shortage of women with managerial and technical skills and women's limited access to training facilities; limited access to information on export markets, business opportunities, import sources and import/export facilities; inadequate export credit facilities for female entrepreneurs and limited access to institutional credit markets; and lack of a legal framework to support women's rights in trade and commerce.

### 2.   Actions to be taken

Entrepreneurialism develops within a system that allows entrepreneurial talent to find expression. Explicit market-oriented policies and strategies are required which establish enabling mechanisms for private sector development and facilitate female entrepreneurs' access to basic trade support services. Despite policy and strategy efforts in many developing countries, women's entrepreneurial potential remains untapped. An enabling environment would remove institutional constraints, enhance information flows and improve learning capabilities.

Four major areas for trade development and promotion have been identified:

- Developing awareness of women in trade development issues and the capacity to provide the support services needed to promote trade.
- Optimizing the use of existing information services and sources and creating a mechanism where trade information and market intelligence are channelled to businesswomen.
- Developing managerial and entrepreneurial skills in import/export management, including trade promotion and marketing techniques.
- Providing access to and developing technical know-how, especially in product design, quality and packaging management, market development and trade services, including financial support services.

The Women in Trade Development programme of the International Trade Centre has defined three areas where intervention is needed to achieve these goals. First, at the grass-roots level, where production and marketing should be improved in order to exploit market opportunities through private sector development and rural export enterprises, particularly at the regional and subregional levels. Second, at the operational level of foreign trade, where female entrepreneurs should be given equal access to market information and training in export marketing and management. Finally, at the policy and institutional levels, where measures should be taken to ensure that national policies and strategies give women entrepreneurs and managers equal access to the means of production and trade-related services.

### NOTES

[1]Adopted by the General Assembly in its resolution 217 A (III) of 10 December 1948.

[2]Adopted by the General Assembly in its resolution 34/180 of 18 December 1979.

[3]Ariane Berthoin Antal, "Trapped in the ice", *International Management*, March 1992, and Felice N. Schwartz, "Women as a business imperative", *Harvard Business Review*, March 1992.

[4]Tae-hong Kim, "Equality in economic decision-making: Republic of Korea" (Unpublished paper, 1993).

[5]Berthoin Antal, loc. cit.

[6]"Women reach the top", *World of Work: The Magazine of the ILO*, No. 2, February 1993.

[7]Information provided by Worldwide Government Directories, Inc., 1993.

[8]*Who's Who at the Leading non-U.S. Companies*, International Corporate Yellow Book (New York, Monitor Publishing Company, Fall 1993).

[9]*Who's Who at the Leading U.S. Companies*, Corporate Yellow Book (New York, Monitor Publishing Company, Fall 1993).

[10]International Labour Organization, "Women's participation in trade unions", *Labour Education*, Special Issue, No. 1 (1993).

[11]Morocco, Ministère de l'emploi, de l'artisanat et des affaires sociales: Etudes démographiques, économiques et statistiques appliquées, "Prise de décision économique: cas du Maroc" (Unpublished paper, 1993).

[12]Alejandro N. Herrin and Marina B. Durano, "Filipino women in economic decision-making—What available data so far reveal: Philippines" (Unpublished paper, 1994).

[13]Maria de Lurdes Rodrigues and Eloisa Perista, "A igualdade na tomada de decisáo económica: Portugal" (Unpublished paper, 1993).

[14]"Membership of the Second Committee" (AC.2422 and Corr.1 and 2 and Add.1 and 2 and AC.2488).

[15]Claire Bangasser, "Women's participation in ILO meetings" (Geneva, Office of the Special Adviser on Women Workers' Questions, International Labour Office, 1994).

[16]World Bank Staff Association, "Report on the status of higher level women in the World Bank", Technical Report, November 1989.

[17]African Development BankAfrican Development Fund, "Evolution of Bank staffing position by gender, 1989-1992" (Unpublished paper, 1993) and "Policy paper on women in development" (Unpublished paper, September 1990).

[18]Inter-American Development Bank, "Female staff statistics" (Unpublished paper, August 1993).

[19]International Monetary Fund, "Equity and excellence" (Report by the Working Group on the Status of Women in the Fund, May 1994).

[20]Berthoin Antal, loc. cit.

[21]"Women breach boardroom bar", *Financial Times*, 11 July 1991.

[22]United Nations Industrial Development Organization, "Women's participation in industrial policy and management in selected countries of Asia and the Pacific", background paper, 1993.

[23]Farida Sherrif, "Decision-making: women in management" (paper prepared for the Fourth Meeting of Commonwealth Ministers Responsible for Women's Affairs, 1993); Ferdinand Protzman, "In Germany, the ceiling's not glass, it's concrete", *The New York Times*, 17 October 1993; "Asian women managers", *The Asian Manager*, JanuaryFebruaryMarch 1992; United Nations Industrial Development Organization, "Taller sobre la participación de la mujer en la determinación de políticas industriales y toma de decisiones en el ámbito industrial en América latina" (Final report, May 1991); and Dirasse Laketch, "Reaching the top: women managers in East and Southeast Africa" (Eastern and Southern African Management Institute, 1991).

[24]"L'irrésistible montée des femmes entrepreneurs", *Innovation et emploi* (Organisation for Economic Cooperation and Development and Commission of the European Communities, December 1993).

[25]Canada, Federal Business Development Bank News Release, September 1992.

[26]"L'irrésistible montée des femmes entrepreneurs" ...; Marja Kuiper, *Women Entrepreneurs in Africa* (Geneva, International Labour Office, 1991); Marilyn Carr, "Women in small-scale industries: some lessons from Africa", *Small Enterprise Development*, vol. 1, No. 1 (March 1990); Instituto Centroamericano de Administración de Empresas, "Diagnóstico sobre la situación de la mujer de la pequeña y microempresa en Costa Rica, Nicaragua, Guatemala, Honduras, El Salvador" (Unpublished paper, 1991); United States Department of Labor, Women's Bureau, *Women Business Owners*, Facts on Working Women (Washington, D.C., 1989); and United Nations Industrial Development Organization, "Women's participation ..." and "Taller sobre la participación de la mujer ...".

[27]This section is based on information provided by the International Trade Centre.

# V

## Increasing women's effective participation in development: Some conclusions

The global economic restructuring process, coupled with improvements in women's legal status and their access to education, has made women a decisive part of the global economy. Although women have always been an important component of the economy, their contributions have not always been visible. Women are still not represented in economic decision-making, though the growing number of female entrepreneurs indicates that this could change. Global development depends on the implementation of policies and programmes that address the remaining barriers to women's effective participation in development and accelerate existing trends. Policies should take gender into account in economic policy-making, use a gender focus in poverty eradication programmes, restructure the working world to make it more gender-friendly and take rapid and affirmative steps to increase women's participation in economic decision-making.

### A. TAKING GENDER INTO ACCOUNT IN GLOBAL AND NATIONAL POLICY-MAKING

Economic restructuring assumed global proportions in the past decade. Countries had to adjust to internal changes in their economies and to external changes in the economic environment. Restructuring policy emphasized efficiency, outward orientation, getting prices right and the role of markets in resource allocation. The move towards greater economic freedom was accompanied by the spread of democracy and broadened civil and political freedoms. Global competition intensified, and the complexity, interdependency and vulnerability of the world economy increased.

Economic restructuring affected women everywhere, often to a greater extent than men. There appears to be a correlation between economic performance and changes in the socio-economic status of women. Countries that were able to stabilize their economies and achieve greater openness in their development efforts also experienced significant improvement in employment prospects for women. But the link between outward openness and the increase in jobs for women is based on a segment of the labour market that ensures low female wages. Increased industrial employment for women under export-promotion trade regimes has rested on the treatment of female labour as inferior to male labour. As export-promotion policies lowered the average wage in manufacturing and removed factor-price distortions, women were able to gain more jobs than men while losing in terms of equal pay and quality of employment. Women's economic position did not improve relative to men's and probably deteriorated.

The success of the export-promotion development strategy in improving female labour force participation creates a dilemma for policy makers. Export promotion policies imply deregulation of the labour market to ensure wage flexibility. When the market is left to determine the optimal wage, the social value of the female reproductive role is not adequately accounted for. This market failure may necessitate policy intervention. But government failure to choose a proper blend of pro-market regulatory policies could price female labour out of the labour market.

Global polarization in terms of economic growth produced a similar polarization in terms of the economic situation of women. Women shared the fortunes of their respective countries. In Asia women experienced significant improvement in their economic situation, as measured by the availability of paid employment in sectors with high productivity and better pay. In Africa women's participation in the labour force declined.

It is clear that the outcomes of economic policies and development strategies are not gender-neutral—

women are more susceptible than men to the failures and successes of economic restructuring. But what is good for growth is also good for advancing women's economic position. While economic growth is not a sufficient condition for women's advancement, it is surely a necessary one.

## B.   ADDRESSING GENDER DIMENSIONS OF POVERTY

Economic development does not automatically lead to equitable distribution or redistribution of resources, especially to the poor. Neither are egalitarian processes sufficient to raise living standards. Global problems of critical importance, including poverty, must be considered in terms of their interdependence.

Women and men experience poverty differently and unequally and become impoverished through different processes. Women are disproportionately represented among the poor, and they do not automatically benefit from development to the same extent as men. If ignored, gender inequality could prevent the successful implementation of poverty elimination strategies.

Women are disadvantaged by their need to earn a living and provide care for family members, tasks that are not shared equally. Despite their constrained circumstances women have proved themselves capable of managing extremely scarce resources to ensure the survival and well-being of their families. However, there is a significant gap between women's activities and the assessment of their contribution. The contributions made by women aimed at meeting the basic needs of family members—their reproductive role—are, to a large extent, not taken into account.

The assumption that all members of a household enjoy uniform living standards is false. Men often exercise substantial control over women's income, property, jobs, how they care for themselves and their families and so on. And women's refusal to submit to men's claims often leads to intrahousehold conflict which typically victimizes women. Women are also disadvantaged when it comes to acquiring formal education and specialized skills that would improve their productivity in both household- and market-based production.

Another crucial issue is access to productive resources such as capital, technology and land. Women are seldom direct beneficiaries of these resources, and administrative, economic and cultural constraints often deny women ownership and effective control. Such factors limit, for example, women's ability to take advantage of the commercialization of agriculture in rural areas or to start their own enterprises in urban areas. These circumstances are aggravated when women become the sole income-earners in the household; female-headed households are likely to be among the poorest in most countries.

The link between gender and poverty is also revealed in the intergenerational transmission of poverty. Women's roles as mothers and their ability to manage resources within poor households have important consequences for their children's ability to escape poverty. The advancement of women should start from infancy.

Taken in a social context, poverty includes not only the condition of economic insufficiency, but also social and political exclusion. Women are systematically excluded from participating in the formulation of social, economic and political decisions, and their influence on policy designs (such as for poverty eradication) has been minimal. Policies are elaborated mostly by men and reflect the values, perspectives and life experience of only half the population. Development depends on recognizing women as economic actors and enabling them to realize their untapped potential. This approach challenges the assumption that equity and efficiency are mutually exclusive outcomes that have to be traded off against one other. But meeting both equity and efficiency goals requires significant changes in the social structure, and these changes are a major challenge to society.

Structural change—building new institutions and establishing new rules of the game—is the process through which society both responds to the changing needs of its members and accommodates new constraints and possibilities emerging from technical and economic change. Technical and economic changes impact on cultural values, which also undergo change, though much more slowly. Social change ensures that old institutions and outdated rules do not become major obstacles to development.

Structural change depends on all individuals, both women and men, playing an active role in shaping society. Women's opportunities to influence the adjustment process have been minimal and their share of the benefits resulting from change limited. Empowering women to become active agents in shaping adjustment requires redefining the relationships between the social, economic and political factors that currently inhibit women's participation and life choices. It means applying a new perspective to the causes of inequality, which implies changes in men's life patterns. The rewards of change will not accrue exclusively to women—men's lives will also be enhanced. For example, men miss the emotional awards of child care because they are constrained by the gender-based division of productive and reproductive responsibilities. Society as a whole will benefit from an integrated policy strategy.

While there is significant diversity among countries in terms of both the economic integration of women and social, political and cultural structures, the common feature is that three actors must be involved in structural change: the State, the market and the household. The State can discourage or enhance quality by adopting appropriate legislation and monitoring its implementation. However, the State has limited financial resources. The market provides employment opportunities and freedom of choice, but creates or perpetuates inequality by supporting the traditional division of labour. The household is where the efforts of structural changes are felt. The challenge is finding the proper combination of each of the agents, introducing gender awareness and achieving social innovation.

The education of women is a societal responsibility. All available resources should be harnessed to meet this challenge, from governmental and non-governmental organizations to the private sector. To provide opportunities for poor women, attention must be given to day-care services for children. Additional incentives and inducements may be necessary to enrol girls from disadvantaged families. It is not only monetary costs, but also—often mainly—opportunity costs that keep women and girls from pursuing education. Yet without improved access to education, the advancement of women will be stymied. Improved knowledge and skills enable women and their families to escape from poverty. Education is a prerequisite for most forms of remunerative employment, including self-employment. Hence, while education is not a sufficient condition for promoting the progress and well-being of women, it is an essential part of the process.

There is also a need for more training programmes for women to enable them to take part in social and economic development. Programmes designed to help women as wives and mothers should be expanded to help them develop small businesses, engage in income-earning activities and bring a knowledge of science and technology to bear on their daily lives. Management training programmes are necessary for women to enable them to become candidates for executive positions. Governments, agencies and businesses should also consider employing women in executive positions and involving them in decision-making activities.

## C. REMAKING THE WORKING WORLD: POLICIES AND ACTORS

Technological transformation, economic restructuring, the transition to market economies, the increasing globalization of markets, production and finance and changes in work organization, production processes and demographic trends will continue to create risks and opportunities for female workers. New challenges to the promotion of gender equality are therefore posed for working women's social protection, working conditions, legislative frameworks and enforcement, labour market policies and the roles of Government, employers, trade unions and other relevant institutions and actors at national, regional and international levels. A multidisciplinary approach that integrates coherent strategies is required at the global, regional, national and sectoral levels. This approach should involve the active participation of all the relevant actors and institutions—including women—to effectively tackle the multiple dimensions of gender equality in the working world.

### 1. *Integrated policies and strategies*

Coherent, integrated policies and strategies involve a range of actions. If any one is slighted, the others are weakened. There is, however, evidence that workable policies can be developed and implemented for each approach.

*A supportive legislative framework and enforcement mechanisms*

As noted in the introduction a vast majority of States have pursued, over the course of the past two decades, constitutional and other legal instruments to prohibit discrimination on the basis of sex or to proclaim equality between men and women as a fundamental right. Equality provisions have been included in labour codes and in legislation dealing with gender equality. While this trend has stimulated public sensitivity to the issue, there remain many shortcomings both with the adequacy of the legislation itself and with its implementation.

Despite national legislation, the principle of equality is often not applied to particular groups of workers, such as public servants, domestic workers, agricultural workers and those engaged in small enterprises or family undertakings. This exclusion constitutes a serious impediment to gender equity, since these categories—which generally comprise considerable number of women—make up the majority of wage earners in some countries. Beyond this question of coverage is the adequacy of the legal provisions themselves. Equality provisions should be broad enough to encompass every aspect of work. They should include provisions for vocational guidance and training, recruitment, working conditions, remuneration, dismissal, retirement and social security. Again, legislation is often too restrictive and usually only deals with certain aspects of employment.

The pursuit of equal opportunity and treatment in employment requires that attention be paid to eliminating direct and indirect discrimination in other areas. These areas include, for example, family law, customary and legal prescriptions concerning inheritance and access to land, credit and other resources. Such areas may appear to be distinct from the world of work, but they have an intimate and complementary relationship to women's right to employment equity and productive resources.

The effective enforcement of policies and legal principles remains problematic. The implementation of policies and legislation has generally been uneven and, for the most part, inadequate. Indeed, considerable progress would be made towards equality if existing legislation were implemented fully and if Governments accorded high priority to the issue. Gains would also be realized if the necessary measures were undertaken with the agreement and support of national employers and workers organizations.

International Labour Organization (ILO) standards promote equality for women. Although most international labour standards apply without distinction to male and female workers, a number of conventions and recommendations refer specifically to women. The ILO's work in this area is based on two concerns. The first is guaranteeing equality of opportunity and treatment in education, training, employment, promotion, organization and decision-making, as well as securing equal conditions of remuneration, benefits, social security and welfare services provided in connection with employment. The second is protecting female workers, especially in working conditions that pose a threat to pregnant women.

Until the 1950s labour standards emphasized the protection of female workers, mainly because women were perceived as being both physically and socially fragile. It was felt that women should not engage in certain work at certain times. The primary objective of such standards was safeguarding the health of women, particularly pregnant women. The 1919 Maternity Protection Convention, one of the first instruments adopted by the International Labour Conference, set minimum standards regarding maternity leave, rights and benefits. Other conventions and recommendations were adopted in areas not directly concerned with the function of women as mothers. These instruments prohibited women in certain sectors or restricted their employment during specific periods.

In 1951 the Equal Remuneration Convention and Recommendation were adopted to promote the principle of equal pay for male and female workers for work of equal value, a concept that is still not fully applied in most countries. In 1958 the Discrimination (Employment and Occupation) Convention and Recommendation established the principle of non-discrimination on a number of grounds, including sex, with regard to vocational training, hiring policies and particular occupations and terms of employment. Both Conventions have been widely ratified: as of January 1994 the Equal Remuneration Convention had been ratified by 120 member States and the Discrimination Convention by 118.

Recognizing that gender inequalities are linked closely to women's traditional role in the family—and that changes in the roles of both men and women are necessary to achieve gender equality—the International Labour Conference adopted the 1981 Convention and Recommendation concerning workers with family responsibilities. These instruments promote the principle of equal opportunity and treatment for all workers with family responsibilities through measures that harmonize work and family obligations (community planning, child-care and family services and facilities, reorganizing working time and conditions, assisting the entry and re-entry into employment of workers with family responsibilities and so on) and through educational programmes that promote public understanding of this principle. A significant number of Governments, employers and workers organizations do not appear to understand the purpose and requirements of these instruments. ILO is trying to sensitize national decision makers and the international community to the need to apply these instruments within the overall framework of equality measures.

### Gender-sensitive labour market, macroeconomic and micro-economic policies

An approach to labour policy is needed that does not separate equality issues from more general labour-market and macroeconomic and micro-economic policies. Gender sensitivity is essential to labour market policies as women's labour-market participation increasing becomes the norm. Policies for equality in the working world represent both common sense and economic rationality in this context. In discussions at the ILO's 1994 International Forum on Equality for Women in the World of Work, it was stressed that the ILO should demonstrate the economic disadvantage in neglecting half the world's human resources. The Secretary-General's report on preparations for the Fourth World Conference on Women maintains that the advancement of women is the necessary condition to achieve the goals of development and that rather than being a consequence of development, gender equality itself can make profound changes in the socio-economic organization of societies.

Macroeconomic and micro-economic policies must give consideration to employment promotion. Such policies have to be formulated through continuous tripartite dialogue and consultations and the effects of the policies on women's work situations, job segregation and gender pay differentials should be monitored regularly.

### Education and training

Education and training are fundamental to improving the status of women. Such activities should be encouraged, of only because policies that make the most of women's skills and potential benefit both employees and employers. Rapid transformations in technology and work patterns have generated demand for a well-educated labour force with flexible skills. The labour market has much to gain by validating the skills women acquire through domestic, family and voluntary activities.[1] Work-related training can help match skills with the expectations of employers. Training programmes in the newly industrializing countries of Asia, for example, have increased and diversified women's employment, including access to non-traditional jobs.

Work-related training programmes in countries provide a comprehensive assistance package to facilitate the integration of persons into the work force who would otherwise find such participation difficult. In many cases policies have not been formulated to increase women's participation in training and retraining programmes or promote vocational and technical education for girls and young women. And while child care is integral to such programmes,[2] legislation providing child-care facilities is often non-existent.

Programmes to improve women's access to education have had a positive effect, especially for younger women. Nevertheless, literacy rates are still low among women in many developing countries. Nevertheless, literacy rates are still low among women in many developing countries. For example, about 91 per cent of adult women in the Sudano-Sahelian region of Africa are illiterate.[3] And the ratio of girls to boys in first-level education has improved little since the 1970s (see table 3).[4] Literacy is critical to facilitating women's access to training and to the formal institutions essential to economic activity.

Society and parents still tend to direct girls towards "women's occupations". The imbalance between young women and men in craft and technician training is large in developed and developing countries. Some countries have extended affirmative action programmes in educational, vocational, technical and scientific fields to influence the career choice of young women. The attitudes and behaviour of teachers is also important and the low numbers of female teachers and administrators in technical institutions and polytechnics affects their ability to influence policy and provide role models.

### Equal pay for equal work

The issue of equal pay for work of equal value represents an ongoing struggle even in those countries where relevant legislation exists. Despite the high ratification rate of the ILO's 1951 Equal Remuneration Convention, wage differentials are one of the most persistent forms of discrimination against women.

While pay differentials do narrow after the adoption of legislation promoting equal pay for equal work, a number of factors subject women to less direct forms of discrimination. These include occupational segregation, shorter work hours, forced career breaks, women's limited availability for overtime, night work and shift work and differences in the value assigned to "male" and "female" skills and occupations. Opinions differ on the appropriate criteria for judging the comparable worth of different activities. These difficulties are compounded by new forms of work organization and by the growth of the informal sector, which increase the number of women excluded from equal pay legislation. Where provision is made for the implementation of the principle of equal pay through collective agreements, the greater flexibility provided by bargaining could be an advantage in responding to such innovative work practices.[5]

### Family-friendly societies

A recent ILO report suggests that the double burden of family responsibilities and productive employment may be the cause of women's low working status.[6] Even where women have access to higher-level jobs, their careers may flounder if they cannot combine their professional duties with their domestic responsibilities.[7] Family-friendly societies recognize and accept that child care is not solely the mother's or even the family's responsibility, but that children represent future human capital and their care should therefore be shared by the society. The trend towards labour market equality will continue to increase the number of dual-earner and single-adult households, exacerbating the need for societal provision of the caring functions traditionally provided by women as unpaid labour.[8]

The ILO has adopted standards to help women overcome the handicap that family responsibilities place on them as workers and to encourage the idea that child care is as much the responsibility of men as it is of women. The 1981 Workers with Family Responsibilities Convention and Recommendation called for the development of support services for both women and men to relieve tensions between family and work. Few countries have ratified this Convention.

While few countries have national policies that support workers with family responsibilities, a number of Governments and enterprises are realizing that it makes economic sense to do so. Far-sighted employers have discovered that helping employees meet their family obligations can enhance corporate reputation, lower absenteeism and staff turnover and provide access to the full potential available in a given society.[9]

Child care at the societal level varies enormously but is almost always inadequate. A few countries (among them the Nordic countries) have comprehensive national systems which provide day-care services for children. In Central and Eastern Europe child-care facilities have suffered as state-sponsored social support measures disintegrate. The ILO recommends that these Governments reopen these facilities or create new ones to encourage women's continued strong involvement in the labour force. Many developing countries are also addressing this issue, mainly for the poorest members of the population.[6] In the absence of government-sponsored measures, many such facilities are provided commercially or through informal community-based arrangements.

### Social protection and security

Any social protection policy or programme should consider women's needs as integral to a well-functioning society. Social protection in maternal and paternal leave provisions should be treated as a fundamental right that is the responsibility of the entire society. Provision could be shared by a new collective of cooperatives, government and employers. The diversity of women and their families makes it difficult to create appropriate social security schemes. Studies are needed to evaluate the needs of various women and the impact that social security arrangements have on them. Equal treatment must be taken into account in any reform of the redistribution made by social schemes.

Providing for the needs of poor women requires developing non-contributory equalization systems. Non-conventional measures based on community organizations and social and economic groups should be encouraged as useful vehicles of social protection.[10] In many developing countries there is a growing number of non-conventional forms of social protection organized by non-governmental organizations (NGOs) and women's self-help groups, such as the maternity benefit scheme and private group comprehensive coverage scheme of the 30,000-member Self-Employed Women's Association in India.[11] These systems have to be designed as supplements—not substitutes—to conventional social security systems if women's rights in the intermediate categories and their progress towards equality are to be preserved.

### Occupational safety and sexual harassment

Women are often exposed to occupational and safety hazards in the workplace. These dangers range from unhygienic work environments and dangerous pesticides to sexual harassment. Sexual harassment for example, can generate emotional and physical stress including anxiety, depression and ulcers, reducing worker efficiency and imposing costs for the employer. While some countries have adopted legal and institutional protection for workplace safety others have not. Relevant positions and guidelines can be adopted not only by governments, but also by employers, workers and women's organizations. In addition, awareness-raising programmes, training and advisory services should be undertaken to combat sexual harassment at work.[12]

### Self-employment and entrepreneurship

Self-employment is being pursued by increasing numbers of women in the developing economies, especially in Latin America, as well as in developed economies and the economies in transition. While there is a need for business management training for women, this form of labour market participation can provide a solution only for a minority of women.

Still, the contraction of formal sector employment in most regions and rapid technological change are encouraging self-employment and small businesses as viable alternatives to wage employment. It has been argued that it is the successful promotion of self- employment and micro-enterprises that will determine whether the informal sector in a country is the sector of last resort or a potentially productive and viable form of employment for women.[13] If women acquire the necessary entrepreneurial and technical skills, self-employment and entrepreneurship could work to their advantage. However, the long hours necessary to ensure the success of small businesses may be incompatible with family responsibilities, particularly for female-headed households[14]

Industrial districts based on cooperatives and shared resources (such as marketing services) might be a viable alternative for women wishing to move into self-employment as entrepreneurs rather than as home-based workers. Child care and other social support mechanisms could be written into the shared services that underpin the most successful industrial districts. Women's self-employment in the informal and rural sectors of developing countries has often been predicted on community-based formulas.

### Organization and empowerment

Mobilizing female workers in groups such as trade unions and workers and employers organizations empowers their productive and income-generating activities, enhances their access to productive resources and helps address their problems in the working world. Women's participation in trade unions is linked to achieving equality in employment. Women's empowerment in the unions will not occur unless women, unions, employers and Governments deliberate on policies and practical measures to promote it.

Given the challenges posed by casualization of work and the growth of the informal sector and atypical career patterns, expanding unions will require innovative strategies for mobilizing workers particularly where workplaces are scattered and when workers are isolated and not easily identifiable. Women have not benefited much from trade unions in countries where women are concentrated in informal sector or agricultural activities. Since traditional recruitment practices have failed to advance women's role in unions, unions are increasingly using group activities planned around leisure, education, training and income-generating projects. Traditional recruitment practices have proved equally irrelevant for mobilizing the self-employed, whose collective action is not likely to be directed towards an employer. Here the unions have encouraged activities, cooperative or pre-cooperative again with a view to mobilizing and empowering women around income-generating projects. A number of alliances have been established between unions and women's self-help groups in recent years improve women's groups access to formal government and economic institutions.

The most relevant—and therefore sustainable—strategies for assisting women working in the informal sector address the totality of needs of specific groups of women. Training is just one element in the self-improvement and development process, which includes credit schemes, maternity benefits, child care, legal assistance and social security.[15] While the Self-Employed Women's Association of India is considered a classic example of a broad-based approach to the economic empowerment of women, similar approaches are being undertaken elsewhere.

It is also important to increase the visibility of homeworkers, both by including them in labour force statistics and by promoting tripartite debate and national advisory bodies. A two-pronged strategy combining employment promotion with the extension of social protection to homeworkers is vital; ILO has had a programme for homeworkers since 1978.[16] Finally, homeworkers need to organize themselves in networks and cooperatives.

### Affirmative action

Affirmative action—including quotas to ensure women's representation in decision-making bodies—is increasingly seen as crucial to fostering women's access to a wider range of employment opportunities. While the concept of affirmative action originated in the United States, its wider acceptance in relation to women's equality in employment stems from its inclusion in the Convention on the Elimination of All Forms of Discrimination

Against Women. The Convention enjoined States to accelerate gender equality by adopting temporary provisions that would redress previous discrimination and put women on an equal footing with men.[17]

Affirmative action has been used in some countries alongside legislative provisions prohibiting discrimination to address persistent inequalities in employment. While affirmative action programmes are no longer confined to developed market economies and have been adopted by some countries in Africa and Asia, they are by no means widespread and have been challenged as being discriminatory to men. Given the opportunities being created by changes at the macroeconomic level, particularly in relation to technological developments, the changing nature of the labour force and new managerial and entrepreneurial skills, affirmative action programmes in labour, education and training could be crucial to fostering women's access to a wider range of employment opportunities.

While most enterprises adopt such programmes in response to legal requirements or financial incentives, one of the largest voluntary affirmative action schemes is Opportunity 2000 in the United Kingdom. Opportunity 2000's members include banks, building societies, government departments, the police, educational establishments, and most of the United Kingdom's recently privatized large employers. Members agree to increase the number of women in key business areas through affirmative action and statistical targets. Unions also are writing affirmative action programmes into their own structures to ensure female unionists participate in the upper echelons of union structures and in all major decision-making bodies.

Affirmative action has been criticized as affecting a small and unrepresentative part of both organizational structures and the labour market, but an evaluation of companies with affirmative action programmes indicates that these companies are in fact held to higher standards. It has been suggested that affirmative action will succeed only if it tackles discrimination on as many fronts as it exists.

### The importance of regular data collection

The working world is dynamic. Socio-economic developments continually bring about changes that impact male and female workers differently. Regular data collection and updating of the analytical and conceptual base and measurement instruments relating to gender equality are essential to providing a relevant basis for effective action and appropriate policies.

The recent ILO International Forum on Equality for Women in the World of Work stressed the need for more data collection and analytical work. Such research should recognize women's active role in economic development rather than regarding women as victims of policies over which they have no control. Since women now account for almost half the workforce in many countries, seeing women as actors in the labour market rather than as passive objects of economic and social policies will promote recognition of the way that women's economic participation influences and is influenced by the directions in which the labour market develops.

There is also recognition that making women's achievements in the labour market more visible requires marketing their skills and talents. Much creative work needs to be done in this area. Exchanging information and networking are vital to bridging differences and validating women's strengths and achievements. Information exchanges and networking also empower women to speak and act on their own behalf.

### 2.  Actors and alliances

The actors involved in these policies and strategies go beyond Governments and the social partners of the formal sector to include a number of non-governmental organizations and self-help groups working in informal and rural sectors. Alliances are emerging between the formal sector and those outside it to empower women who are being marginalized by economic problems, technological innovation and changing patterns of trade and investment.

### Government as an actor

Government departments in many countries have a better record than the private sector in employing women and providing equal pay and safe working conditions. Governments should continue to play this role. They should also enforce equality legislation and implement standards to integrate women and improve their conditions in the labour market. Public expenditure cuts in some countries, such as child-care facilities, have impeded women's ability to harmonize labour and family commitments. This is wrong—the State should facilitate women's entry into the labour force, or at least remove barriers to their integration. In view of the globalization of capital and international trade, however, there is concern over the degree to which Governments and other national organizations (including trade unions) can effectively promote the equality of women.

Various strategies are available to Governments. The State can intervene directly in the economy, create jobs for women, providing social protection and alleviating poverty, for example by providing food security. Alternatively, the Government can act as a facilitator, creating an environment conducive to job creation. Increasingly, it is the facilitation role that Governments are taking.

Achieving gender equality requires extra effort in the context of globalization, economic restructuring and reform, which in some countries have had a devastating impact not only on women's employment opportunities but also on the educational and social support structures which underpin and could improve their labour market access. Governments should provide adequate resources to strengthen national women's organizations. One useful example is an initiative in Jamaica in 1989 that established working groups within all ministries whose function is ensuring that women are not overlooked in policy formulation and implementation.[18] Such programmes could go a long way towards developing a systemic approach to the issue of equality for women in the working world, cutting across a wide range of concerns that affect their economic activity, provided the groups have sufficient political power and resources and are able to work together across ministries to plan common strategy.

Governments should collect and compile gender disaggregated statistics, especially on the labour force. The Government should link its funding of institutions to their efforts to improve women's work situation within their structures.

### Social partners and equality

Employers can promote or impede gender equality. They can, for example, have equal opportunity programmes that are properly implemented and closely monitored. Such policies, which should be adopted in consultation with trade unions, should be clearly expressed in personnel policies, and all employees and job applicants should be informed of them. Adopting equal opportunity policies is not just ethically and morally right, it is good business. Discriminatory practices can lower morale and productivity and tarnish a company's image.

Employers need to adopt policies and programmes that:

• Accommodate family issues and encourage equal family responsibility by both parents.

• Provide child-care arrangements at or near the workplace.

• Respond to union demands on behalf of women workers, such as on equal pay and family policies that support single parents and dual-job households.

• End gender-based job segregation.

• Enforce affirmative action programmes to move women into skilled and non-traditional jobs and managerial and decision-making positions.

• Establish on-the-job training programmes, especially for female workers, and sponsor women for skills training outside the enterprise.

• Encourage equality provisions in collective agreements with unions.

• Eliminate sexual harassment and discrimination.

• Create family-friendly work places, including support for family, maternal and paternal leave.

Employers are beginning to respond to the need to create a better-educated, more flexible and highly skilled workforce able to respond to rapid technological innovation. More women should be represented in the decision-making bodies of employers associations to promote education and training for labour market equality. Together with Governments and trade unions, employers need to revitalize and assume responsibility for tripartism.

For employers organizations whose structures have been based on centralized negotiation, the decentralization of bargaining on wages and working conditions may lessen their influence on questions of equality in these areas. The internationalization of business and increasing competitiveness are likely to reinforce this trend. But regardless of the level at which decisions are taken, changing labour market trends will require employers organizations, as important social actors, to bring the probable consequences of these developments to the attention of their members.

The growth of the informal sector in developing countries and the blurring of the lines between it and the formal sector are one of the major challenges of the 1990s. Employers organizations in Latin America that have recognized that small and microenterprises are likely to be the main growth area are encouraging these associations to become involved in their activities.[6] The same is true of employers organizations in Africa and Asia; one of the favoured means of outreach in these regions is through training in entrepreneurial and business skills. Female microentrepreneurs in some South Asian countries have benefited from ILO-supported training.[19] An emphasis on human resources development is encouraging closer links between employers organizations and the educational system, a move as likely to influence the career choices of girls as of boys.

Trade unions need to implement innovative strategies to deal with the growth of the informal sector, casualization of the workplace and the growing atypical work patterns. Union membership must be extended to all workers, including those in the informal sector and the unemployed. Some unions have begun to campaign for equal rights for part-time workers and to find ways of organizing the unorganized. However, much needs to be done since the record of union efforts on behalf of female workers is not positive in many countries. Unions need to ensure that women are represented in their organizational structures and leadership positions and accord greater priority to women in their policies and programmes.

Within the formal sector, collective bargaining complements legislation and is potentially one of the most effective ways of challenging inequality in the workplace. But a 1991 International Confederation of Free Trade Unions (ICFTU) survey of its membership noted that while almost all organizations accorded equality issues high priority in theory no more than half have policy documents or action programmes, and even fewer are active in this area. These results suggest that there are still too few women in the negotiating and decision-making bodies of unions, and male negotiators are not sufficiently well-informed on issues of specific concern to female workers. ICFTU also noted that women were frequently absent from the employers' side of the bargaining table and suggests that female interlocutors tend to be more sympathetic to women's issues. Equality issues are more likely to be taken up where women constitute a large majority of union membership or where women's committees and conferences provide forums for mobilizing women.

Unions have generally adopted one of two strategies regarding part-time, temporary and casual workers: supporting legislation that would reduce the incidence of atypical work or extending legislation and collective agreements to include these peripheral workers. Some trade unions are also incorporating the entire range of family-related questions in their bargaining agendas—from child-care facilities and non-statutory parental leave to flexible work schedules. While collective bargaining on issues of specific concern to women is less widespread than might be hoped, there appears to be a correlation between unions that have undergone internal restructuring and those that have been most active in bringing equality issues to the bargaining table.

## Non-governmental organizations and grass-roots associations

Non-governmental organizations (NGOs) have long played a vital role in the mobilization of poor women in both urban informal and rural areas and are worth considering as actors in many alliances. NGOs cover a wide spectrum of activities ranging from the provision of credit through training, employment creation and marketing services to legal assistance and social welfare programmes. While some of these organizations specialize in one particular activity (the Grameen Bank, for example, restricts its assistance to providing credit), many provide a package of services that addresses the needs of women at the grass-roots level. Alliances between NGOs and Governments and trade unions are increasingly common, as are alliances between NGOs and international organizations and funding agencies working in the same field. International organizations and funding agencies use NGOs to channel resources to target groups and to serve as intermediary agencies, not only between themselves and the target populations, but also between target populations and local government structures.

Since NGOs encourage solidarity and collective action between the groups they help set up, the increasing contact between NGOs and formal sector institutions could build a web of alliances dedicated to the empowerment of women. The role of the partners in these new social pacts should build on the survival strategies devised by poor women in cooperatives and associated movements. Unions and women's groups should also organize on an international basis to meet the challenges of global capital mobility.

## National women's organizations

To be effective in promoting gender equality, national women's organizations should be located at the highest level of government, with sufficient resources and authority to ensure that women's concerns are integrated into policy and programmes in all sectors. Involving the tripartite bodies—the government and workers and employers organizations—in such organizations is necessary for promoting equality for female workers.

Women's organizations should be involved in advocacy, decision-making, resource allocation, implementation and monitoring processes, as well as be able to influence other decision makers and articulate and prioritize issues of concern to working women. These organizations can play a major role in raising awareness about the rights of female workers. Furthermore, the organizations should link up with other actors at the national level to coordinate their efforts. National women's groups and other specialized bodies bridge the gap between normative prescriptions and their practical application. Unfortunately, shortcomings in some of these organizations have limited their visibility and placed them at the periphery of economic policy-making.

Government women's networks should be decentralized to the local level, where they would be more receptive to the needs of local women. In addition to providing a support system to local women and serving as a contact for NGOs working at this level, the networks could be an effective channel between women at the grass-roots level and formal government institutions. By default, this role is often undertaken by NGOs. Decentralization would also reflect current trends towards the decentralization of work and labour relations and would facilitate the monitoring of women's equality of opportunity and treatment at the local level.

*Other alliances*

A number of other alliances should be considered as actors in promoting equality for women working outside the formal sector. Alliances between professional women and those at the grass-roots level are becoming more common, with the professionals using their skills, knowledge of and access to the judiciary and formal government institutions to help the grass-roots women set up self-help groups.[20] Trade unions have also joined forces with national women's groups to lobby Governments on equality opportunity issues such as wages, employment and measures to facilitate women's participation in the labour market.

*International Labour Organization*

The ILO's tripartite structure of Governments, employers and workers organizations allow it to actively involve the relevant social partners in promoting gender equality in the working world. Since ILO's international labour standards cover a wide range of social and labour issues, they provide an appropriate framework for formulating integrated strategies and a comprehensive reform agenda. Member States should ratify and implement these standards as the basis for a gender-sensitive legislative and policy framework for promoting equal opportunity in employment.

ILO should continue to monitor member States' ratification and implementation of these standards. It should also focus on employment and the social impacts of economic restructuring, globalization, regionalization and technological transformation. Finally, ILO should intensify its technical advisory services and assist member States and social partners in formulating integrated strategies to promote gender equality in the working world.

### 3. *Trends and challenges*

One of the most striking features of women's economic activity in the changing global environment is the astonishing similarity of its evolution across countries, though its level and degree differs with the level of national (or local) development and with the institutional systems that govern women's entry into and participation in the labour market. These commonalities allow national agendas, which share a common base of legislation, policies, culture, practices and situations, to be guided by a global agenda. Both agendas should be committed to a policy of full and equitable employment. Several trends pose new challenges (or revive old ones) for women's equality in the world of work. These trends are the changing nature of the formal sector, the emergence of an intermediate sector, the growth of the informal sector, flexibility and deregulation and the impact of macroeconomic changes on rural women.

The first trend is the changing nature of the formal sector in response to the global recession, international competition, trade liberalization and, in the more developed parts of the world, advanced technology. The economies in transition and the developing countries must restructure industry, phasing out uncompetitive heavy industry and rebuilding or reorienting light industry in an international market even more competitive than was faced by developed economies and the newly industrializing economies of Asia in the 1970s. Female industrial workers are among the growing unemployed in both country groups and both are looking to foreign investment to revitalize their industrial sectors.

Women may hope to access the jobs created as developing countries attract foreign direct investment (FDI) through export-processing zones and special economic zones, but since they presuppose investment in female human resources, the quality and long-term economic and social viability of these jobs are questionable. Cheap female labour has a limited time span for foreign investors since technological change and product development eventually demand a highly skilled workforce. Until new opportunities develop, women in developing countries must drop out of the formal sector and turn to the overcrowded and precarious informal sector.

Computer-facilitated rationalization and restructuring are starting to affect the service sector. Low-level jobs in developed economies are expected to be absorbed by computers or exported to on- and off-shore data processing centres. Occupational profiles are emerging that combine generic skills already held by many women with technical skills which they may have to acquire if they are to hold their own in this sector and aspire to its upper ranks. The education levels of women in these countries put this goal within reach.

In Central and Eastern Europe, where career choice is less gender-dictated, the privatization of this sector should create jobs for women whose education and work experience gives them, in theory, the same advantages as the men with whom they will compete. Still, current training is not gender-neutral and women risk being segregated (or segregating themselves) into the lower-level clerical and service jobs that are disappearing in Western economies. Central and Eastern European women face a triple challenge: acquiring the skills that would afford them the same opportunities as men in the market-oriented occupations that are emerging, using the opportunity afforded them by the transition to acquire labour equality and safeguarding the social support systems that underpin their economic activity.

Although women in developing countries have long been present in the legal, teaching and medical professions, little is known about the changes that are taking place in the private sector services. It has been suggested that better-educated women are breaking into the middle ranks of financial and retail sectors and that more female entrepreneurs are emerging.[14] But most women work in the clerical and secretarial ranks of the service sector and are likely to remain there for some time. The possible exceptions are the growing numbers of keyboard operators at on- and off-shore data-processing centres and the small share of female software programmers. As with women in developed market economies and the economies in transition, education and training are the key to upward mobility and greater equality.

Cutbacks in public spending and the consequent retrenchment or privatization of public services affect women both as consumers and as workers. As consumers, especially in developing countries, more women are working and women are working more to pay for previously subsidized services such as education and health care. As noted earlier, the most devastating impact of spending cutbacks in Central and Eastern Europe has been the disintegration of child-care facilities and maternity provisions that had supported working women. Cuts in health care and other welfare provisions also have had a negative impact on vulnerable population groups, women high among them.

The effects of public-sector retrenchment on women as workers vary. In the developing countries the informal sector is the "employer of last resort" for low-ranking female workers laid off as a result of structural adjustment programmes. In Central and Eastern Europe female unemployment has been rising in the administrative, clerical and secretarial ranks of public sector enterprises and services. In the developed market economies privatization and management reforms have more serious impacts than retrenchment. Affirmative action programmes in the public sector may suffer, thereby distorting its "good employer" signals to the private sector.

The second major trend is the emergence of an intermediate sector between the declining formal sector and the increasingly crowded informal sector.[21] Identified as a high-growth area, this sector comprises dynamic, modern industrial enterprises based on high technology and served by small and highly skilled service providers such as accountants, insurance agents, legal and financial consultants, marketing firms and computer analysts and consultants. Jobs also will be emerging in corporate catering, cleaning and janitorial services.

The intermediate sector holds many opportunities for women in the industrial and service sectors, especially, but not exclusively, in the developed market economies and in Central and Eastern Europe. Women in these regions have high education levels and many of the professional and technical skills required by this new market, as is evidenced by the rising numbers of women starting their own businesses. The greatest challenge to women may lie not in acquiring technical skills but in acquiring entrepreneurial skills. Employers organizations could play an important role in this regard.

The third major trend is the growth of the informal sector and the blurring of the lines between it and the formal sector with deregulation, casualization and the increase in atypical work patterns (subcontracting, outsourcing, home-based work and self-employment). The informal sector has become a vital part of survival strategies in developing countries undergoing structural adjustment, absorbing labour shed by the formal sector (especially the public sector) and migrants displaced by technology from rural, export-oriented commercial farming.

One of the major challenges for the informal sector will be building informal cooperative relations (such as in garments, food processing, handicrafts and petty trading) to form cooperative microenterprises that can provide women with entrepreneurial skills (such as accountancy and marketing) and access to credit and markets. The second, longer-term challenge for the informal sector is extending legislative and social protection to this area that guarantees workers a minimum standard of living.

The fourth trend in the labour market is that of flexibility and deregulation. Such developments have powerful implications in an interdependent world, where decisions in one country can affect jobs in another. Making labour markets more flexible to changes in international markets requires workforce preparedness—education and training—which will benefit women and men. In an international labour market created assets, including human resources, are crucial determinants of investment flows and the location of transnational corporations.[22]

Labour market flexibility also has negative aspects. Its emphasis on loosening legally and administratively established frameworks of rules and collective agreements has eroded employment and income protection and increased precarious and non-standard employment. Most workers with non-standard employment contracts (part-time workers, temporary and casual workers, home workers and the self-employed) are women and, while such forms of work may facilitate their family responsibilities, they do not carry the same benefits, legal protection, career prospects or training opportunities as full-time jobs.[23]

Other problems resulting from labour flexibility and deregulation include the question of workers with family responsibilities, the segregation of women into certain sectors and jobs, the continuing hindrance of the "glass-ceiling" and the persistence of wage differentials, even where they cannot be justified by educational levels or work experience. The main challenges for the 1990s will be extending legal and social protection to atypical workers, enforcing the principle of equal pay, encouraging a closer link between education, training and the workplace, creating "family-friendly" societies and workplaces and, in the loner term, encouraging functional flexibility as the key to investment and job creation.

The fifth trend is the impact of macroeconomic changes on rural women, which is of particular relevance to developing countries. However, with land privatization, the break-up of rural cooperatives and the uncertain future of rural industry, such changes also are a potential problem area for Central and Eastern Europe and the former Soviet Union.

Structural adjustment programmes and technological advances in the agricultural sector have tended to benefit large and medium-sized farms in the cash-crop sector. Such benefits accrue to the detriment of female farmers either because of their concentration in subsistence farming or because of the small size of their farms and limited access to extension services and credit facilities. Uncertain land rights and tight time budgets compound their problems. In addition, the commercialization of agriculture and the disruption of long-standing tenancy rights have increased landlessness and poverty in female-headed households as males migrate in search of wage employment. Women also are migrating into the overcrowded informal sector and into domestic services as casual and seasonal labour on large landholdings.

The challenges in this area have to be addressed at various levels. The land tenure issue will remain unresolved so long as the "head of household" criterion used in the allocation of land rights and in resettlement schemes is assumed to be male, despite the growth in female-headed households. Access to credit is another issue that must be addressed. Government programmes should be established on women's savings and credit strategies. NGOs can extend credit to rural women for activities considered too small-scale and non-viable by normal lending institutions.

Equal opportunity policies and strategies are evolving to meet these trends and challenges. These responses include equal remuneration legislation, affirmative action programmes, community-based approaches to training and employment, extensions of social protection and social security schemes and state support for family responsibilities such as child care and maternity protection. These measures need to be coherently integrated to provide greater operational reinforcement within specific national situations. The policies will fail without active involvement of the actors in civil society, particularly trade unions, enterprises, employers organizations, cooperatives and women's groups. These actors prompt legislation, ensure its implementation, mobilize opinion, forge alliances, articulate dissent and provide delivery systems for policies and programmes.

While some women will inevitably find themselves the victims of change, others are using the new opportunities to become agents of change by positioning themselves in political structures, trade unions, employers organizations, NGOs, as heads of enterprises and as role models to other women.

## D. POLICIES AND PROGRAMMES TO INCREASE WOMEN'S PARTICIPATION IN ECONOMIC DECISION-MAKING

Increasing women's participation in the top levels of administration and management is important for both the public and private sectors. It requires public policy and private support at the microeconomic and macroeconomic levels. Obstacles to participation must be removed from patterns of socialization that create gender stereotypes through discriminatory laws and organizational procedures.

The responsibility for creating opportunities rests more heavily on the public sector, and some actions should be undertaken regardless of the types or level of economic decision-making. These actions should create an enabling environment that facilitates changing the attitudes and behaviour of both women and men. The educational system has a particularly important role in this process. Actions in this area should:

- Promote gender equality.
- Improve women's access to training and third-level education. In some cases special measures may be needed to bypass discrimination. In the Republic of Korea, for example, a special engineering college has been opened for women.[24]
- Monitor curriculum and teaching materials.
- Create gender sensitization programmes for parents, educators and the media.
- Supply adequate child care and parental leave.

### 1. Increasing the number of female managers

Increasing the share of women managers at all levels requires a commitment from all the actors concerned. Change in this area is like any cultural change: obtaining commitment from leaders, creating popular support and implementing the change.

*Implementing and enforcing legislation on equal employment opportunities and preventing sexual harassment*

Equality legislation is the first step most ILO member States have taken to create the legal framework needed for women's advancement in decision-making. Several countries have also established gender-based affirmative action strategies. In some countries, such as Canada and Zimbabwe, affirmative action strategies have been applied only at the governmental or federal levels. In other cases, as in Australia, affirmative action has been more far-reaching and innovative. Australia applies affirmative action principles to both public and private activities (privately, to companies with 100 or more employees bidding on government contracts).[25]

The private sector can also accelerate the move of women to executive positions. European companies have been engaged in such efforts. According to a report from the Brussels-based Conference Board Europe, one in every three companies in the European Union is discriminating in favour of female employees and recruiting female candidates for top jobs. More than two fifths of companies is providing management training specifically for women to improve their promotion prospects.[26] The European Union adopted a code of measures to combat sexual harassment in 1992. The motivation for these efforts may be somewhat mixed. A study in Spain revealed that companies carried out equal opportunities schemes only because they wanted to maintain their image or because it was imposed by multinational companies or perceived market needs. Companies were not motivated by a sense that they were improving human resources management.[27]

*Developing information on women managers and supporting networking*

Stereotypes wither when they are proved unreliable. Discriminatory practices are easier to change if they are publicized. Several steps can be taken to improve information about the role and contribution of women managers, including publicizing their existence. Governments and interest associations can document and publicize cases of flagrant discrimination against women. Recognizing businesses that have made strides in promoting equal opportunities and career development for women provides positive reinforcement.

Networking facilitates the creation of role models and mentoring systems among women. It also facilitates access to information and lobbying mechanisms. National women's organizations and non-governmental organizations can encourage networking by giving it value and by providing opportunities for it.

### Developing corporate recruitment and promotion policies

Changing recruitment policies and employment regulations is necessary to facilitate equality at the entry level. Areas of particular concern involve parenting, posting, compensation, training, evaluation systems and career planning and guidance. Procedures should be transparent and merit-oriented with careful application of affirmative action to ensure equal opportunities. In the public sector this can be done through civil service rules. In the private sector agreed norms and standards are appropriate. The rules should establish a gender-equal corporate culture and can include mentoring, orienting managers of both sexes to the role of gender in the workplace and sanctions for improper behaviour.

### Accommodating the needs of dual-career managerial couples and families

Ensuring that women are as effective as men requires recognizing the fact of maternity. There should be no illusion that biological differences between the sexes do not exist. At the same time, maternity—or parenthood generally—should not be an obstacle to long-term advancement. This requires carefully elaborated policies and programmes.

First, maternity-leave policies need to be developed separately from parental-leave policies. This implies providing short-term flexibility to women in exchange for the long-term gain to the institution, the economy and society. A second element is child care. Working parents, especially mothers, require affordable child care, to function effectively and without interruption. Now that women make up almost half the workforce and a growing share of managers, corporate and public policies on child care are practical responses to economic and social priorities. While the issue requires exploration to identify the best approaches, both the public and private sectors should provide the quantity and variety of child care that their employees need.

The sharing of parenting between parents is becoming a global norm as changes in the economic environment require both parents to work. Appropriate policies are needed to encourage this. Such policies should include measures that allow parents to cut back to part-time work and then re-enter the competition for senior management jobs. Since most management careers are not compatible with part-time work, these policies involve rethinking the time dimensions of management. Policies also should permit fathers to take paternity leave in sequence with their wives, encouraging men to take an active role in parenting.

### 2  Actions to support female entrepreneurs

Given the opportunities, female entrepreneurs will perform as well as, or better than, men in the economy. However, macroeconomic policies, investment codes and incentive systems must take into account the role that female entrepreneurs play. Successful programmes to support female entrepreneurs include financing, technical assistance, information, training and counselling.

### Access to credit

Many countries are creating specific financial institutions to serve as guaranty funds for the creation and growth of female-owned enterprises. Such funds provide the guaranties required by formal financial institutions, which consider small enterprises too risky and costly. In France, for example, Le Fonds de garantie pour la création, la reprise et le développement d'entreprises à l'initiative des femmes has been created and financed by the Government. A national credit fund for women was set up in India in 1993.[28] Women's World Banking (WWB), an independent international financial institution created in 1979, provides financing for women's activities. To ensure women's ventures are viable, WWB combines financial and technical assistance for the beneficiaries.

Other organizations mainstream the needs of women through existing institutions. For example, the African Development Bank has a women in development division which advises the Bank on facilitating women's access to the bank's financial facilities. In the United Republic of Tanzania the Small Industries Development Organization has established a women's desk that surveys the needs of female entrepreneurs and designs programmes to assist them. The number of loans approved for women clients has increased from 35 to 129 in two years. Another example, the secretariat of the Preferential Trade Area (PTA) of Eastern and Southern African States organized roundtable discussions for female-headed businesses in Zambia in 1992. These discussions recommended creating a revolving loan fund accessible to all businesswomen to be managed by the PTA Bank.[29]

*Collecting information on and for women entrepreneurs*

Women business owners are, to a certain extent, invisible. Lack of data on women's businesses is a barrier not only because women are undercounted but also because they are not taken into account when public policies are formulated. One action that has proven useful is compiling national and local directories on women entrepreneurs at all levels and all sectors. For example, a directory of the African Association of Women Entrepreneurs has been created by the Economic Commission for Africa containing information on 25 associations. Another action is making information on markets available to women. For example, a number of Governments have invited female exporters from Asia to acquire first-hand experience of their potential market's preferences. Involving female entrepreneurs in trade fairs and exhibitions has likewise been encouraged.

*Providing management and marketing training and technical assistance*

Training opportunities should be developed in management and marketing, either through existing programmes (public and private) or by creating new facilities. The European Commission has developed a programme called New Opportunities for Women, which promotes enterprise creation and female entrepreneurship, strengthens existing enterprises, establishes centres for counselling and assistance and obtains financial resources for women's enterprises.[30] The United Nations Industrial Development Organization, in partnership with several organizations of female entrepreneurs, has organized training workshops on issues of concern to female managers. An innovative programme providing consulting services to align women's products with market needs has been tried by a development bank in India. Payment for services was in the form of a percentage of eventual profits.[24] In 1987 the European Commission created the Réseau d'initiatives locales pour l'emploi to develop female entrepreneurship and reduce female unemployment. Awards are given to women who create enterprises and employ other women, and technical support is provided by female experts.

## NOTES

[1]Organisation for Economic Cooperation and Development, *Report on the Helsinki Conference on Women and Structural Change: A Mirror on the Future* (Paris, 1993).

[2]M. Fromont, "Employment: one controllable factor", *World of Work: The Magazine of the ILO (Geneva, International Labour Office, 1994)*.

[3]A. Ouédraogo, "Women's employment in Africa: obstacles and challenges" (Regional report prepared for the ILO International Forum on Equality for Women in the World of Work: Challenges for the Future, Geneva, 1-3 June 1994).

[4]*The World's Women, 1970-1990: Trends and Statistics*, Social Statistics and Indicators, Series K, No. 8 (United Nations publication, Sales No. E.90.XVII.3).

[5]C. Eyraud and others, *Equal Pay Protection in Industrialised Market Economies: In Search of Greater Effectiveness* (Geneva, International Labour Office, 1993).

[6]*World Labour Report, 1994* (Geneva, International Labour Office, 1994).

[7]For examples, see "Women in science: comparisons across cultures", *Science*, vol. 129, 1994 (American Association for the Advancement of Science, New York).

[8]G. Schmid, "Women and structural change in the 90s" (Report on a meeting of trade union experts held under the OECD Labour/ Management Programme, Paris, 1993).

[9]"Reforming labour markets in Central and Eastern Europe and the rise of unemployment", *Employment Outlook* (Paris, Organisation for Economic Cooperation and Development, 1992).

[10]See the report of the Director-General of the International

Labour Organization on social protection and social insurance (Geneva, 1993).

[11]L. L. Lim, "Social protection for women workers" (unpublished paper).

[12]*A Conditions of Work Digest: Combating Sexual Harassment at Work* (Geneva, International Labour Office, 1992).

[13]L. L. Lim, "Women at work in Asia and the Pacific: recent trends and future challenges" (Regional report prepared for the ILO International Forum on Equality for Women in the World of Work: Challenges for the Future (Geneva, 1-3 June 1994)).

[14]S. Mitter, "Innovations in work organization at the enterprise level: changes in technology and women's employment", BRIDGE Paper (Brighton, England, Institute for Development Studies, 1993).

[15]R. Jhabvala, "Self-Employed Women's Association: organising women by struggle and development", in *Dignity and Daily Bread*, S. Rowbotham and S. Mitter (eds.) (London, Routledge, 1994).

[16]For further details of ILO strategies to assist homeworkers, see "Silent no more" (Bangkok, ILO Regional Office for Asia and the Pacific, 1993).

[17]Unless otherwise stated, information for this section was drawn from C. Thomas, ed., *Towards Equality: Positive Action for Women* (Geneva, International Labour Office, 1994).

[18]*The Report on Rural Women Living in Poverty* (Rome, International Fund for Agricultural Development, 1993).

[19]V. Pandit, *Integrating Women in Economic and Social Development* (Geneva, International Labour Office, 1993).

[20]J. Donaldson, "Finding common ground: redefining women's work in Colombia", *Grassroots Development*, vol. 16, No. 1 (1992).

[21]The intermediate sector is defined as lying between the modern formal sector and the flexible informal sector and comprising modern small-scale enterprises employing between 10 and 50 workers and reputedly included in official statistics; given that modern small-scale enterprises are increasingly considered as the growth area of the future, the intermediate sector is likely to assume considerable importance in the medium term (see I. Palmer, *Gender and Population in the Adjustment of African Economies: Planning for Change* (Geneva, International Labour Office, 1991)).

[22]D. Campbell, "Integrated international production and labour market interdependence" (Unpublished paper, 1994).

[23]*World Labour Report, 1992* (Geneva, International Labour Office, 1992).

[24]United Nations Industrial Development Organization, "Women's participation in industrial policy and management in selected countries of Asia and the Pacific" (Vienna, unpublished paper, 1993).

[25]Farida Sherrif, "Decision-making: women in management" (Paper prepared for the Fourth Meeting of Commonwealth Ministers Responsible for Women's Affairs, 1993).

[26]Ariane Berthoin Antal, "Trapped in the ice", *International Management*, March 1992.

[27]Matilde Fernandez Vazquez, "Women in management and women employers in Spain" (Madrid, Instituto de la Mujer, 1991).

[28]Economic and Social Commission for Asia and the Pacific, "Review and appraisal of the implementation of the Nairobi Forward-looking Strategies for the Advancement of Women—Regional priority issues and proposals for action: women and empowerment" (Paper prepared for the Second Asian and Pacific Conference on Women in Development, Bangkok, May 1994).

[29]Economic Commission for Africa, "Advancement of women in Africa: progress report on the establishment of the federation of African women entrepreneurs, the African bank for women and preparations for the Fourth World Conference on Women" (E/ECA/CM.19/16, 9 February 1993).

[30]"L'irrésistible montée des femmes entrepreneurs", *Innovation et emploi* (Organisation for Economic Cooperation and Development and Commission of the European Communities, December 1993).

كيفية الحصول على منشورات الأمم المتحدة

يمكن الحصول على منشورات الأمم المتحدة من المكتبات ودور التوزيع في جميع أنحاء العالم . استعلم عنها من المكتبة التي تتعامل معها أو اكتب إلى : الأمم المتحدة ، قسم البيع في نيويورك أو في جنيف .

如何购取联合国出版物

联合国出版物在全世界各地的书店和经售处均有发售。请向书店询问或写信到纽约或日内瓦的
联合国销售组。

## HOW TO OBTAIN UNITED NATIONS PUBLICATIONS

United Nations publications may be obtained from bookstores and distributors throughout the world. Consult your bookstore or write to: United Nations, Sales Section, New York or Geneva.

## COMMENT SE PROCURER LES PUBLICATIONS DES NATIONS UNIES

Les publications des Nations Unies sont en vente dans les librairies et les agences dépositaires du monde entier. Informez-vous auprès de votre libraire ou adressez-vous à : Nations Unies, Section des ventes, New York ou Genève.

## КАК ПОЛУЧИТЬ ИЗДАНИЯ ОРГАНИЗАЦИИ ОБЪЕДИНЕННЫХ НАЦИЙ

Издания Организации Объединенных Наций можно купить в книжных магазинах и агентствах во всех районах мира. Наводите справки об изданиях в вашем книжном магазине или пишите по адресу: Организация Объединенных Наций, Секция по продаже изданий, Нью-Йорк или Женева.

## COMO CONSEGUIR PUBLICACIONES DE LAS NACIONES UNIDAS

Las publicaciones de las Naciones Unidas están en venta en librerías y casas distribuidoras en todas partes del mundo. Consulte a su librero o diríjase a: Naciones Unidas, Sección de Ventas, Nueva York o Ginebra.

Litho in United Nations, New York
00190—February 1995—5,000
93655—August 1995—1,500

United Nations publication
Sales No. E.95.IV.1
ST/ESA/241
ISBN 92-1-130163-7